W9-BRO-722

Further Praise for Michael Palma's *Inferno*

"I think highly of Michael Palma's *Inferno*. It is accurate as to sense, fully rhymed, and easy, as a rule, in its movement through the tercets. Readers will find it admirably clear and readable." —Richard Wilbur

"Without ever betraying the literal sense of every line, Palma renders the music of Dante's thinking in a remarkable way. This is a grand accomplishment and a genuine surprise." —Guiseppe Mazzotta

"As a translation into triple rhyme I believe that Palma's work will become the translation of choice for most readers. Despite the strictures of rhyme, it contains so many strong passages which capture the economy and speed of Dante's original that it stands in a class apart." —John Ahern

"Palma's apparently effortless mastery of rhyme; his control of syntax; and his skill at pacing and variety are all crucial components of this translation's weight, its authority, and at the same time its deceptive simplicity." —Rachel Hadas

"By retaining the exact metrical pattern of the original, Michael Palma has restored to Dante's *Inferno* the rhythmic grace that it has lacked in recent English renderings. I consider this translation a singular poetic achievement." —William Jay Smith

"Michael Palma's *Inferno* is not only a superb translation, but a true poem. It is a gift for all of us, scholars and students, poets and the general intelligent reader." —Felix Stefanile

"Dante's visual precision and depth of feeling are unmistakable. This version by a skilled poet and distinguished translator should become the authoritative *Inferno* for our time." —Daniel Hoffman

"[R]emains marvelously faithful to the wording and rhythms of the original. . . . The English-language reader looking for an accessible Dante text is spoiled for choice; but he should find this edition with the Palma translation wholly satisfactory."   —*The Spectator*

DANTE ALIGHIERI

INFERNO

A New Verse Translation by Michael Palma

W. W. NORTON & COMPANY / NEW YORK / LONDON

Copyright © 2002 by Michael Palma

All rights reserved
Printed in the United States of America
First published as a Norton paperback 2003

For information about permission to reproduce selections from this
book, write to Permissions, W. W. Norton & Company, Inc.,
500 Fifth Avenue, New York, NY 10110

The text of this book is composed in Centaur, with the display set in Centaur
Composition by Sue Carlson
Book design by Chris Welch
Production manager: Julia Druskin

Library of Congress Cataloging-in-Publication Data

Dante Alighieri, 1265–1321
[Inferno. English]
Inferno / Dante Alighieri ; a new verse translation by Michael Palma.
p. cm.
ISBN 0-393-04341-X
I. Palma, Michael, 1945–
PQ4315.2.P27 2002
851'.1—dc21   2001004318

ISBN 0-393-32387-0 pbk.

W. W. Norton & Company, Inc.
500 Fifth Avenue, New York, N.Y. 10110
www.wwnorton.com

W. W. Norton & Company Ltd., Castle House
75/76 Wells Street, London W1T 3QT

2 3 4 5 6 7 8 9 0

Contents

FOR VICTORIA,

who should have a Paradise instead.

INTRODUCTION

As new translations of Dante's *Inferno* continue to appear, it has become the fashion for each new perpetrator to apologize for inflicting yet another version on the public. But we are dealing, after all, with the author that most people regard as the greatest European poet of all time, with the work universally acknowledged to be his masterpiece, and with the part of that work generally considered to be its most vivid component. The *Inferno* is a poem of stunning originality, complexity, subtlety, and power. It speaks to many different audiences on many different levels. Dante himself, in the dedicatory letter to Can Grande that forms the preface to the *Paradiso*, identifies several levels of meaning in the *Comedy*, the literal, allegorical, moral, and anagogical, to which we might add the autobiographical, historical, political, mythical, philosophical, psychological, and so on. And all of these levels interact to generate further dimensions and possibilities in our reading of the poem. Given the inexhaustible richness of Dante's achievement, perhaps we should wonder not why there are so many versions available, but why there are not even more.

The *Inferno* is one of those books, like *Don Quixote* and *Moby-Dick*, whose broad outlines are known to everyone: Dante strays into a dark wood where he is rescued by the shade of the Roman poet Virgil, who takes him on a guided tour of hell, which consists of many levels filled with many damned souls undergoing many gruesome and hellishly apt punishments. This physical journey is paralleled by the spiritual one that is its ultimate purpose, as the pilgrim gradually learns, with a fair amount of very human recidivism along the way, that hating the sin but loving the sinner ceases to apply to those who have died unreconciled to God's mercy and grace. The poem and its themes are universal in scope: as the very first line tells us, it is "the journey of our life," not just his own, that the pilgrim is embarked upon. But this detour on that journey is uniquely his own, and the fictional character who undertakes this obviously fictional journey shares his name and a great deal of his personal history with his creator.

Readers who come to the text for the first time may be surprised to discover the extent of its autobiographical dimension. Like John Milton, the author of the other great Christian epic, Dante weaves a surprising amount of personal information into ostensibly objective and universal works. But while Milton tends to confine himself to occasional asides or, as in *Samson Agonistes,* to situations that parallel his own circumstances, Dante, in making himself the central character of his own poem, assigns equally essential roles to his time and place—Florence and, more broadly, Tuscany, in the second half of the thirteenth century. There are constant references to events and persons that were fresh then but are now remote. Much of this material would have been familiar to his original readers (and some of it would not: extensive commentaries upon the *Comedy* began to be written within decades of its completion). But, like the frequent mythological and biblical allusions, these historical references mean little or nothing to contemporary audiences. I have sought to provide this necessary background in my notes, but it would be helpful also to present a brief overview of the autobiographical and historical context of the *Inferno.*

Dante Alighieri was born in Florence in 1265, sometime between mid-May and mid-June (he tells us in Canto XXII of the *Paradiso* that he was born under the sign of Gemini). While of modest financial circumstances, his family was of notable lineage; his ancestor Cacciaguida degli Elisei had been a cavalier and a crusader. While Dante was still young, both of his parents died—his mother, Donna Bella, when he was still under ten years of age; his father, Alighiero di Bellincione degli Alighieri, a moneychanger who married again and had three more children, when Dante was about eighteen. In 1277, Dante was betrothed to Gemma di Manetto Donati. Their marriage, which took place around 1285, produced three sons and a daughter who later became a nun under the name of Beatrice. Dante never mentions Gemma in his writings, and it has been traditionally, but not necessarily reliably, assumed that their relationship was an unhappy one.

Nonetheless, according to Dante's own testimony in the *Vita nuova*, a gathering of thirty-one poems set within the framework of a narrative and a commentary upon them, the most important relationship of his life began when, at the age of nearly nine, he first beheld an eight-year-old girl named Beatrice. Beginning with the first biography of Dante, that of Giovanni Boccaccio in 1348, she has been identified with Beatrice Portinari, who married a wealthy banker named Simone de' Bardi, had several children, and died in 1290 at the age of twenty-four. But even if we had much more factual information than we do, it would of course be impossible to determine the precise relation between autobiography and mythmaking in the presentation of the protagonist of the *Vita nuova*—or, for that matter, in the *Comedy* itself. In the *Vita nuova*, which dates in all likelihood from his late twenties and is his first major work, Dante describes an intense love that sustained itself upon the slightest and most occasional of contacts, that gradually deepened and transformed itself as the lover came to terms with defects in his own nature, and that led to a resolve, after the death of the beloved, not to write of her again until he could do so in a way that would be worthy of her. It has been observed, with justice, that even if he had written nothing else, the *Vita nuova* would have been enough to ensure Dante's literary immortality.

But beyond its own merits, we can see in it several elements that prefigure the much greater masterpiece that was to come. In both works we find the autobiographical protagonist, and in both there is the figure of

Beatrice as moral inspiration and spiritual guide. Both derive from literary sources—the *Vita nuova* from the "sweet new style" of Dante's friend Guido Cavalcanti, whose lyric verse drew upon Sicilian court poetry and Provençal troubadour songs; the *Comedy*, and especially the *Inferno*, from Book VI of Virgil's *Aeneid*, in which the protagonist leaves his present-day reality to make a ritual journey through the underworld, a journey that combines past and future as the shades of the dead tell their own histories and prophesy what is to come—and both build on those sources to create something new and original.

The very title of the *Comedy* (Dante called it simply *La commedia*; the adjective was applied long after his death) signifies, in classical terms, that it is a work written in the low style (as opposed to the "lofty verses" of Virgil's *Aeneid*, as Dante describes them several times), which tends toward a happy ending (in this case, the availability of salvation to the protagonist, and to all who truly desire it); yet, following its model, it is a work of epic length, scope, and depth. And like the *Vita nuova*, which combines a group of poems, detailed analyses of those poems, and a narrative of artistic and moral development, the *Comedy* draws together some extremely disparate elements and forges them into a coherent whole.

One of those elements, and one of the most significant, is the political. In his twenties and thirties, Dante took an increasingly active part in the public affairs of his city. In June 1289, he was a cavalryman at the battle of Campaldino, and in August of that year he witnessed the surrender of the Pisan fortress of Caprona. Both of these events, and other elements of his military experience, are reflected in the *Inferno*. But these engagements are only two incidents in a century's worth of political and military strife that is thoroughly ingrained in the text and texture of the poem. Many of the dead souls encountered by Dante had taken part in the seemingly endless power struggles between the Guelphs, who were, broadly speaking, supporters of the increasing temporal power of the papacy, and the Ghibellines, supporters of the empire as the legitimate secular authority. (The names of the parties derived from the German factions of Welf and Waiblinger, whose struggle had begun in 1125, when the archbishops of Mainz and Cologne prevented the accession of Frederick of Swabia, the hereditary heir to the throne of the Holy Roman Empire.)

In 1266, the year after Dante's birth, Charles of Anjou, acting on behalf of the pope, engaged Manfred, illegitimate son of Emperor Frederick II, at the battle of Benevento. With Manfred's defeat and death, the Ghibellines were effectively destroyed as a political force in Florence, and the city thereafter enjoyed a quarter century of relative stability. But in the 1290s, factionalism revived and the Guelphs were split into opposing groups: the Blacks, led by the wealthy and powerful Donati family, to whom Dante was related by marriage, and the Whites, who evolved into Ghibellinism as Pope Boniface VIII sided with the Blacks in an effort to consolidate power.

Dante, who saw the empire as the divine instrument of temporal authority and fiercely decried the corruption wrought within the Church by its pursuit and exercise of secular power, allied himself with the Whites. In the late spring of 1300, he served a two-month term as one of the six priors of the city, as that ruling council struggled to stem the steady degeneration of the political situation. Late the following year, he was a member of a delegation to Pope Boniface that sought to persuade him to cease his interference in the city's affairs. While Dante was still away from Florence, Charles of Valois, brother of the king of France, marched into the city; his occupation established the Blacks in total control and led to the expulsion of the leading White families. On January 27, 1302, Dante was convicted in absentia of trumped-up charges of barratry and defiance of the pope, stripped of all his property, and banished from Florence. He refused to stoop to answering the charges against him, and, despite his sporadic hopes of negotiating an end to his exile, the banishment was later intensified to include a sentence of death should he be found inside the city. He never saw Florence again. After years of wandering through Italy, he died in Ravenna, probably of malarial fever, on September 13, 1321.

Awareness of these facts not only provides us with a context in which to comprehend the historical references, but also deepens our understanding of other aspects of the *Inferno*. April 1300, when the poem is set, is not only the eve of Dante's thirty-fifth birthday, when he was, in biblical terms, exactly "midway through the journey" of his own life; it is also the eve of the commencement of his public service to Florence, which would culminate so soon in such disastrous consequences for him. His sojourn through the afterlife—especially hell, the one land that is emphatically not his own—parallels the rootless travels of the last two decades of his earthly existence (as with James Joyce, who never lived in Dublin after the age of twenty-two, absence from his native city only intensified his preoccupation with it).

Pier delle Vigne's sudden passionate outburst, in Canto XIII, about the false accusations that have ruined his good name clearly echoes Dante's own feelings. And might not the uproarious farce of Cantos XXI and XXII, which is otherwise so uncharacteristic of the *Comedy*, have at least one of its roots in an attempt by Dante to distance himself from the painfulness of the situation, since the sin punished in that particular ditch is barratry, the very crime of which he himself was falsely convicted? (It will no doubt surprise most readers to discover that barrators, along with thieves and even flatterers, are punished much more severely in Dante's hell than murderers and tyrants. But, as Virgil explains in Canto XI, violence is a trait we share with the animals, while crimes that require a perversion of reason, the faculty that God gives to us alone, are more heinous in nature.)

I have emphasized the *Inferno's* integration of many disparate elements. In addition to those already mentioned, we might briefly note the frequent and famous similes that appear throughout the text—comparisons drawn from topography, history, myth, and even domestic life, which serve, among other functions, to let some light and air into the claustrophobic chambers of hell—and even such extraneous-seeming set pieces as Virgil's long speech about Manto in Canto XX, passages which remind us that one of the components of much of the greatest art is an irreducible strangeness. All these, and more, Dante seeks to integrate into a comprehensive whole, so comprehensive that mythological figures are invested with a reality equal to that of historical ones.

One of the essential components of that integration is the form of the poem, the *terza rima* (triple rhyme) structure that Dante invented for the writing of his *Comedy*, in which the tercet (three-line unit) functions as the basic unit of the narrative, and these units are fused into the larger unit of the canto through the pattern of linking rhyme, in which the middle line of each tercet rhymes with the two outer lines of the next one. American translators of the *Inferno* in the last half century have employed a wide range of formal options, from a modified formalism that relies upon off-rhymes or the abandonment of the linking rhyme, to blank verse, to a free verse that is essentially lineated prose, to undisguised prose. Whatever the individual approach, all these translations share the assumption that the form of the original cannot be fully replicated without doing unacceptable damage to other, more important elements of the work.

There seems to be an underlying assumption in some contemporary approaches to translation that a poem's paraphrasable content *is* the poem, and must be preserved absolutely unharmed. In its more extreme manifestations—which are usually found in the writings of critics, not translators—the text is regarded as, if not quite sacred, then certainly inerrant, and we are treated to grimly and inadvertently entertaining explanations of the appropriateness, even the necessity, of some odd usage, explanations that take no account of the fact that the word in question comes at the end of a line. In 1927, in his little book on Dante, John Jay Chapman very neatly addressed this subject and its practical applications:

> The reason that translators are slashed, maimed, and borne bleeding from the field after a duel with Dante, is that they accept the conditions which the judges lay down. . . . Dante is permitted to write as obscurely as he pleases. . . . Dante is given the privilege of inventing his own language as he proceeds, freely changing his vowels, genders,

and participles to eke out his rhymes, and throwing in words of his own manufacture according to inner sentiment and personal fancy. . . . The translator, however, must use his own idiom in a conventional, flat-footed way. He must punctuate in such a manner as to show which of the possible interpretations he adopts; he must avoid solecisms and, of course, must never be obscure or hieratic.

From there, Chapman goes on to argue for greater latitude in translating—for a much greater latitude, in fact, than I would ever wish to adopt. I reject the premise of some mid-twentieth-century British translators that, as a medieval poet, Dante may be properly rendered into English through the constant use of archaic diction and inversion of word order, just as I reject the practice of certain translators who sought to enliven Dante's plainspokenness with rhetorical flourishes that are antithetical to his own practice and sensibility. I have tried to make poetry in the way that Dante does, which is, for the most part, through rhythm and sound, not through extravagant figures of speech. Rhythmically, I have employed a somewhat flexible pentameter that will in places be more reminiscent of Robert Frost or late Shakespeare than of Alexander Pope. Needless to say, I have found it necessary in places to use imperfect rhymes and to run over at either end of tercets that are self-contained in the original. But by making small, local compromises as needed in the rhyme, or the structure, or the precise literal statement, I have tried to remain as faithful as I could to Dante's general practice. The ideal of such an approach is the preservation and communication of as much as possible of all the elements of the original.

As I suggested at the outset, there are many different constituencies for Dante in English and many different ways of serving them. As I write, a book called *The Poets' Dante*, edited by Peter S. Hawkins and Rachel Jacoff, has just been published. It gathers responses to Dante by twentieth-century English-language poets, its contents divided equally between standard texts by such masters as Pound, Yeats, Eliot, and Auden and newly commissioned essays by contemporary poets. The appearance of this volume is a welcome reminder that in the *Inferno* Dante is first and foremost a poet, and one of the very greatest that Western culture has produced. Almost no one in the last seven hundred years has written better poetry than Dante's; and with all the constraints upon translation, no practitioner of that maligned art can hope to equal or even approximate his achievement. But, like those essays, this translation is a poet's response to the poetry of the *Inferno,* and an attempt to convey to readers of English, as far as it is in my power to do so, some sense of the integrity and the artistry of that extraordinary and inimitable work.

ACKNOWLEDGMENTS

An earlier version of Canto XIII appeared in *Chelsea* 62 (1997). I wish to thank Richard Foerster and Alfredo De Palchi of that journal for their solicitation and acceptance of my work. While the translation was in progress, especially in its initial stages, several friends read individual cantos. Their comments and responses were both helpful and sustaining, and it is a pleasure to record their names here: Luigi Bonaffini, John and Ellen Mahon, Robert McPhillips, Harvey Minkoff, Suzanne Noguere, Thomas Pendleton, Leonard Poggiali, John Paul Russo, and Paul Violi. I am grateful to William H. Johnston for his careful recension of the Giorgio Petrocchi text of the *Inferno*, and to Terry Smith for allowing me to devote working hours to Dante, thus making herself a true patron of the arts.

My work on the *Inferno* had its origin in the annual Dante reading at the Cathedral of St. John the Divine in New York. Two successive poets in residence at the cathedral, Daniel Hoffman and Molly Peacock, were most generous in the prominence they afforded me in the readings and in their own responses to my work. Pivotal roles were played by Dana Gioia, who suggested my inclusion in the first reading in 1994 and provided advice and encouragement as the translation proceeded, and by Charles Martin, who—along with Johanna Keller—used my version in his own readings at the cathedral and who first brought my translation to the attention of W. W. Norton & Company.

With Norton I have been twice lucky, first by having the book accepted by my publisher of choice and then by receiving as much welcome and support as any author could hope for. I wish to acknowledge Peter Simon, my first contact at Norton, for his enthusiastic response; Marian Johnson, for her scrupulous and thoughtful copy-editing; Brian Baker, for his unfailing helpfulness and expertise; and Eleen Cheung, for her striking design of the jacket. I am grateful to the advisory readers, Professor Giuseppe Mazzotta of Yale University, whose own thoughtful and elegant writings on Dante also deepened my understanding of my author, and Professor John Ahern of Vassar College, whose detailed and incisive comments were of invaluable assistance in the final revision. I am especially indebted to Carol Bemis, for her belief in the project, from which all else flowed; for her ready and right solutions to all the little problems that inevitably came up; and for her zealous efforts to assure that the book would receive the finest possible presentation.

My son, Brian, provided inestimable assistance in several ways, through his reading of the translation as it evolved, through his own enthusiasm for the *Comedy*, and especially through his familiarity with the historical context and background of the work, which made for some very pleasant conversations that helped to clarify many a passage for me along the way.

As always, my greatest debt is to my wife, Victoria, to whom this book is dedicated. She eagerly awaited the completion of each canto, and responded to each with enthusiastic support and insightful suggestions. As I overburdened myself with projects, she kept me focused on the centrality of this one. She provided the circumstances, emotional and otherwise, that made it possible for me to continue with an enterprise that so frequently felt overwhelming. And, since it was her idea originally that I should translate the entirety of the *Inferno*, I can truly say that without her this book would not exist.

The Plan of Dante's Hell

INFERNO

Canto I

Nel mezzo del cammin di nostra vita
    mi ritrovai per una selva oscura,
    ché la diritta via era smarrita.   3
Ahi quanto a dir qual era è cosa dura
    esta selva selvaggia e aspra e forte
    che nel pensier rinova la paura!   6
Tant' è amara che poco è più morte;
    ma per trattar del ben ch'i' vi trovai,
    dirò de l'altre cose ch'i' v'ho scorte.   9
Io non so ben ridir com' i' v'intrai,
    tant' era pien di sonno a quel punto
    che la verace via abbandonai.   12
Ma poi ch'i' fui al piè d'un colle giunto,
    là dove terminava quella valle
    che m'avea di paura il cor compunto,   15
guardai in alto e vidi le sue spalle
    vestite già de' raggi del pianeta
    che mena dritto altrui per ogne calle.   18
Allor fu la paura un poco queta,
    che nel lago del cor m'era durata
    la notte ch'i' passai con tanta pieta.   21
E come quei che con lena affannata,
    uscito fuor del pelago a la riva,
    si volge a l'acqua perigliosa e guata,   24
così l'animo mio, ch'ancor fuggiva,
    si volse a retro a rimirar lo passo
    che non lasciò già mai persona viva.   27

CANTO I

Midway through the journey of our life, I found
    myself in a dark wood, for I had strayed
    from the straight pathway to this tangled ground.   3
How hard it is to tell of, overlaid
    with harsh and savage growth, so wild and raw
    the thought of it still makes me feel afraid.   6
Death scarce could be more bitter. But to draw
    the lessons of the good that came my way,
    I will describe the other things I saw.   9
Just how I entered there I cannot say,
    so full of sleep when I began to veer
    that I did not see that I had gone astray   12
from the one true path. But once I had drawn near
    the bottom of a hill at the far remove
    of the valley that had pierced my heart with fear,   15
I saw its shoulders mantled from above
    by the warm rays of the planet that gives light
    to guide our steps, wherever we may rove.   18
At last I felt some calming of the fright
    that had allowed the lake of my heart no rest
    while I endured the long and piteous night.   21
And as a drowning man with heaving chest
    escapes the current and, once safe on shore,
    turns back to see the dangers he has passed,   24
so too my mind, still lost in flight, once more
    turned back to see the passage that had never
    let anyone escape alive before.   27

Poi ch'èi posato un poco il corpo lasso,
    ripresi via per la piaggia diserta,
    sì che 'l piè fermo sempre era 'l più basso.   30
Ed ecco, quasi al cominciar de l'erta,
    una lonza leggera e presta molto,
    che di pel macolato era coverta;   33
e non mi si partia dinanzi al volto,
    anzi 'mpediva tanto il mio cammino,
    ch'i' fui per ritornar più volte vòlto.   36
Temp' era dal principio del mattino,
    e 'l sol montava 'n sù con quelle stelle
    ch'eran con lui quando l'amor divino   39
mosse di prima quelle cose belle;
    sì ch'a bene sperar m'era cagione
    di quella fiera a la gaetta pelle   42
l'ora del tempo e la dolce stagione;
    ma non sì che paura non mi desse
    la vista che m'apparve d'un leone.   45
Questi parea che contra me venisse
    con la test' alta e con rabbiosa fame,
    sì che parea che l'aere ne tremesse.   48
Ed una lupa, che di tutte brame
    sembiava carca ne la sua magrezza,
    e molte genti fé già viver grame,   51
questa mi porse tanto di gravezza
    con la paura ch'uscia di sua vista,
    ch'io perdei la speranza de l'altezza.   54
E qual è quei che volontieri acquista,
    e giugne 'l tempo che perder lo face,
    che 'n tutti suoi pensier piange e s'attrista;   57
tal mi fece la bestia sanza pace,
    che, venendomi 'ncontro, a poco a poco
    mi ripigneva là dove 'l sol tace.   60

I paused to let my weary limbs recover,
    and then began to climb the lone hillside,
    my fixed foot always lower than the other.   30
But I had hardly started when I spied
    a leopard in my pathway, lithe and fleet,
    all covered with a sleek and spotted hide.   33
And as I faced it, it would not retreat,
    but paced before me and so blocked my way
    that more than once I had to turn my feet   36
to retrace my steps. It was the break of day,
    the sun was mounting in the morning sky
    with the same stars as when that whole array   39
of lovely things was first given movement by
    divine love. The sweet season of the year
    and the hour made me think that I might try   42
to evade that bright-skinned beast as it came near,
    but then I felt my good hopes quickly fade
    and in an instant I was numbed with fear   45
to see a lion in my path that made
    straight for me, head held high and ravenous,
    and seemed to make the very air afraid.   48
And a she-wolf too, that in its leanness was
    laden with every craving. Those who seek
    fulfillment there find only wretchedness.   51
The sight of this one made me feel so weak,
    so overcome with dread, that instantly
    I lost all hope of climbing to the peak.   54
As a man is eager in prosperity
    but when time brings him losses can be found
    giving way to weeping and to misery,   57
so did I feel as the she-wolf pressed me round
    so relentlessly that bit by bit I stepped
    back where the sun is mute on the low ground.   60

Mentre ch'i' rovinava in basso loco,
dinanzi a li occhi mi si fu offerto
chi per lungo silenzio parea fioco.   63
Quando vidi costui nel gran diserto,
«*Miserere* di me», gridai a lui,
«qual che tu sii, od ombra od omo certo!».   66
Rispuosemi: «Non omo, omo già fui,
e li parenti miei furon lombardi,
mantoani per patrïa ambedui.   69
Nacqui *sub Iulio*, ancor che fosse tardi,
e vissi a Roma sotto 'l buono Augusto
nel tempo de li dèi falsi e bugiardi.   72
Poeta fui, e cantai di quel giusto
figliuol d'Anchise che venne di Troia,
poi che 'l superbo Ilïón fu combusto.   75
Ma tu perché ritorni a tanta noia?
perché non sali il dilettoso monte
ch'è principio e cagion di tutta gioia?».   78
«Or se' tu quel Virgilio e quella fonte
che spandi di parlar sì largo fiume?»,
rispuos' io lui con vergognosa fronte.   81
«O de li altri poeti onore e lume,
vagliami 'l lungo studio e 'l grande amore
che m'ha fatto cercar lo tuo volume.   84
Tu se' lo mio maestro e 'l mio autore,
tu se' solo colui da cu' io tolsi
lo bello stilo che m'ha fatto onore.   87
Vedi la bestia per cu' io mi volsi;
aiutami da lei, famoso saggio,
ch'ella mi fa tremar le vene e i polsi».   90
«A te convien tenere altro vïaggio»,
rispuose, poi che lagrimar mi vide,
«se vuo' campar d'esto loco selvaggio;   93

And as I drove myself into the depth,

　　a shape was offered to my vision, wan

　　　　as if from a long silence it had kept.　　　　　　63

Seeing him in that great desert, I began

　　to call out. "*Miserere*—on me," I cried,

　　　　"whatever you are, a shade or a solid man!"　　　66

"Not man, although I was a man," he replied.

　　"My parents were both Mantuans. I descend

　　　　from those of Lombardy on either side.　　　　69

I was born *sub Julio,* at the latter end.

　　Under the good Augustus I lived in Rome

　　　　in the days when false and lying gods still reigned.　　72

I was a poet, and I sang of him,

　　Anchises' righteous son, who sailed from Troy

　　　　after the burning of proud Ilium.　　　　　　75

But why do you turn back toward trouble? Why

　　do you not ascend the delectable mount instead,

　　　　the origin and cause of every joy?"　　　　　78

"Are you that Virgil then, that fountainhead

　　that spills such a mighty stream of eloquence?"

　　　　I said this with a shame-filled brow, and said:　　81

"Light and glory of all poets, may my intense

　　love and long study of your poetry

　　　　avail me now for my deliverance.　　　　　84

You are my master, my authority,

　　for it is from you alone that I learned to write

　　　　in the noble style that has so honored me.　　87

You see why I have turned back from the height.

　　Illustrious sage, please help me to confound

　　　　this beast that makes my pulses shake with fright."　　90

"It were best to go another way around,"

　　he answered, seeing tears start from my eyes,

　　　　"if your hope is to escape this savage ground,　　93

ché questa bestia, per la qual tu gride,

> non lascia altrui passar per la sua via,
>
> ma tanto lo 'mpedisce che l'uccide;   96

e ha natura sì malvagia e ria,

> che mai non empie la bramosa voglia,
>
> e dopo 'l pasto ha più fame che pria.   99

Molti son li animali a cui s'ammoglia,

> e più saranno ancora, infin che 'l veltro
>
> verrà, che la farà morir con doglia.   102

Questi non ciberà terra né peltro,

> ma sapïenza, amore e virtute,
>
> e sua nazion sarà tra feltro e feltro.   105

Di quella umile Italia fia salute

> per cui morì la vergine Cammilla,
>
> Eurialo e Turno e Niso di ferute.   108

Questi la caccerà per ogne villa,

> fin che l'avrà rimessa ne lo 'nferno,
>
> là onde 'nvidia prima dipartilla.   111

Ond' io per lo tuo me' penso e discerno

> che tu mi segui, e io sarò tua guida,
>
> e trarrotti di qui per loco etterno;   114

ove udirai le disperate strida,

> vedrai li antichi spiriti dolenti,
>
> ch'a la seconda morte ciascun grida;   117

e vederai color che son contenti

> nel foco, perché speran di venire
>
> quando che sia a le beate genti.   120

A le quai poi se tu vorrai salire,

> anima fia a ciò più di me degna:
>
> con lei ti lascerò nel mio partire;   123

ché quello imperador che là sù regna,

> perch' i' fu' ribellante a la sua legge,
>
> non vuol che 'n sua città per me si vegna.   126

because this creature that provokes your cries
    allows no man to get the best of her,
    but blocks each one, attacking till he dies.   96
Of such a vile and vicious character
    and greedy appetite, she is never sated,
    and when she has fed is even hungrier.   99
Many the animals with whom she has mated.
    Her couplings—till her painful deathblow is dealt
    by the greyhound—will continue unabated.   102
This greyhound will not feed on land or wealth,
    but on virtue, love, and wisdom. He will be
    born in the region between felt and felt.   105
He will restore low-lying Italy,
    for which Euryalus, Turnus, the maid Camilla,
    and Nisus gave their life's blood. Tirelessly   108
he will track the beast through every town until
    he comes at last to drive her back into
    that hell from which she sprang at Envy's will.   111
Therefore I think it would be best for you
    to follow me. I will be your guide, and I
    will lead you out of here and take you through   114
an eternal place where you will be greeted by
    the shriekings of despair and you will see
    ancient tormented spirits as they cry   117
aloud at the second death. Then you will be
    with those who are content within the fire,
    for they hope to join the blest eventually.   120
You will see those blest, if that is your desire,
    with a worthier soul than I. Into her hands
    I will entrust you when I can go no higher.   123
That emperor who presides above commands,
    since I did not heed his law, that none may gain
    entrance through me to where his city stands.   126

In tutte parti impera e quivi regge;
  quivi è la sua città e l'alto seggio:
  oh felice colui cu' ivi elegge!».   129
E io a lui: «Poeta, io ti richeggio
  per quello Dio che tu non conoscesti,
  acciò ch'io fugga questo male e peggio,   132
che tu mi meni là dov' or dicesti,
  sì ch'io veggia la porta di san Pietro
  e color cui tu fai cotanto mesti».   135
Allor si mosse, e io li tenni dietro.

His rule is everywhere. There is his reign,
   his city, and his throne! Happy are they
   whom he chooses to inhabit that domain!"   129
"Poet," I said to him, "so that I may
   escape this harm and worse that may await,
   in the name of that God you never knew, I pray   132
you lead me out to see Saint Peter's gate
   and all those souls that you have told me of,
   who must endure their miserable state."   135
I followed him as he began to move.

Notes

line 1   The poem is set in 1300, when Dante was thirty-five, halfway through his biblically allotted threescore years and ten.

line 17   The planet is the sun, which in Ptolemaic, pre-Copernican cosmology was believed to revolve around the earth, the fixed center of the universe.

line 30   This line is commonly given an allegorical as well as a physical interpretation. The feet are understood to be the limbs of the soul. The fixed foot is the left, representing will, which lags behind the right one, intellect. The fullest discussion of the line is John Freccero's "The Firm Foot on a Journey Without a Guide," in his *Dante: The Poetics of Conversion* (Harvard, 1986).

lines 31–60   The encounter with the three beasts is one of the most frequently and variously interpreted passages of the poem. Traditionally, the leopard, the lion, and the she-wolf have been understood to represent lust, pride, and avarice, respectively—or, in some interpretations, envy, pride, and avarice, the qualities ascribed to the Florentines by Ciacco in Canto VI (line 75) and Brunetto Latini in Canto XV (line 67). They have also been associated with incontinence, violence, and fraud, the three categories of sin described by Virgil in Canto XI. Some feel that the leopard must represent fraud, given Dante's reference to the belt with which he had hoped to snare that beast (Canto XVI, lines 106–8); there Geryon, who also has a spotted hide, is clearly linked to fraud. If this view is accepted, then the she-wolf represents lust or, more broadly, incontinence. Thus, the she-wolf gives Dante the most trouble because, while incontinence is the least grievous category of sin, it is the one to which he is most susceptible.

line 37 It is the morning of Good Friday. The sun is in Aries, as it was believed to have been at the time of creation.

line 70 Virgil (Publius Vergilius Maro, 70–19 B.C.E.) was born before the reign of Julius Caesar. He was in his mid-twenties when Caesar was assassinated.

lines 73–75 The Trojan prince Aeneas, son of Anchises and the goddess Venus, sailed to Italy after the fall of Troy (Ilium) and became the legendary founder of Rome.

lines 100–105 This is one of the most obscure and hotly debated passages in the poem. The greyhound has been identified with various historical and religious figures, and has even been taken to signify the second coming of Christ. The most frequently proposed candidate is Can Grande della Scalla, who ruled Verona from 1308 to 1329; his name suggests "great dog," and his native city, Verona, lies between the towns of Feltre and Montefeltro. The "felt" reference has also been interpreted astrologically (the Gemini, Castor and Pollux, were commonly depicted as wearing felt caps), spiritually (an allusion to the Franciscan and Dominican orders), and sociologically (suggestive of humble birth).

lines 106–8 Nisus and Euralyus were young Trojan soldiers. Turnus, king of the Rutulians, and Camilla, daughter of the king of the Volscians, were leaders of the indigenous Italian peoples who resisted the Trojan invasion. Enemies in life, they are joined here as patriots and as participants in the events that would lead to the founding of Rome.

line 122 The worthier spirit is Beatrice, whose name signifies "one who makes blessed." Associated with Dante's neighbor Beatrice Portinari (1266–1290), she appears as a living person in his *La Vita Nuova*, where she is celebrated for both her beauty and her spiritual example.

lines 124–26 As one who lived before Christ, Virgil did not accept Christ as his savior and consequently cannot enter heaven (see Canto IV, lines 31–42). This change of guides midway through the journey suggests that salvation can be achieved only through divine grace, not by reason and virtue alone.

line 133 Like other details in this canto, St. Peter's gate has inspired controversy, some maintaining that it alludes to the traditional gate of heaven, which does not appear in *The Divine Comedy*, others that it refers to the gate of purgatory, which does.

Canto II

Lo giorno se n'andava, e l'aere bruno
    toglieva li animai che sono in terra
    da le fatiche loro; e io sol uno 3
m'apparecchiava a sostener la guerra
    sì del cammino e sì de la pietate,
    che ritrarrà la mente che non erra. 6
O muse, o alto ingegno, or m'aiutate;
    o mente che scrivesti ciò ch'io vidi,
    qui si parrà la tua nobilitate. 9
Io cominciai: «Poeta che mi guidi,
    guarda la mia virtù s'ell' è possente,
    prima ch'a l'alto passo tu mi fidi. 12
Tu dici che di Silvïo il parente,
    corruttibile ancora, ad immortale
    secolo andò, e fu sensibilmente. 15
Però, se l'avversario d'ogne male
    cortese i fu, pensando l'alto effetto
    ch'uscir dovea di lui, e 'l chi e 'l quale 18
non pare indegno ad omo d'intelletto;
    ch'e' fu de l'alma Roma e di suo impero
    ne l'empireo ciel per padre eletto: 21
la quale e 'l quale, a voler dir lo vero,
    fu stabilita per lo loco santo
    u' siede il successor del maggior Piero. 24
Per quest' andata onde li dai tu vanto,
    intese cose che furon cagione
    di sua vittoria e del papale ammanto. 27

Canto II

The day was waning, and the darkening sky
    called all the creatures of the earth to rest
    after the long day's labors. Only I   3
was preparing all alone to endure the test
    of the journey and the pity of what I would see,
    as unerring memory will now attest.   6
Muses, high genius, aid me! Memory,
    that recorded what I saw among the dead,
    here you will show your true integrity.   9
"O poet, you who are my guide," I said,
    "weigh whether I am fit for what lies in wait
    before you entrust me to the path ahead.   12
Of Silvius's father you narrate
    how he saw the immortal world with his mortal sense
    while still immured in our corrupted state.   15
That evil's foe showed him such preference,
    aware of the result that it would bring,
    of who and what would come as consequence—   18
to a thoughtful mind this seems a proper thing.
    Empyrean heaven in her high decrees
    chose him to be the father of fostering   21
Rome and her empire. Truly, both of these
    were founded to be the holy ground whereon
    the successor to great Peter keeps the keys.   24
On his journey which you celebrate, he was shown
    and told of things that served as the foundation
    of his victory and of the papal throne.   27

Andovvi poi lo Vas d'elezïone,

    per recarne conforto a quella fede

    ch'è principio a la via di salvazione.   30

Ma io, perché venirvi? o chi 'l concede?

    Io non Enëa, io non Paulo sono;

    me degno a ciò né io né altri 'l crede.   33

Per che, se del venire io m'abbandono,

    temo che la venuta non sia folle.

    Se' savio; intendi me' ch'i' non ragiono».   36

E qual è quei che disvuol ciò che volle

    e per novi pensier cangia proposta,

    sì che dal cominciar tutto si tolle,   39

tal mi fec' ïo 'n quella oscura costa,

    perché, pensando, consumai la 'mpresa

    che fu nel cominciar cotanto tosta.   42

«S'i' ho ben la parola tua intesa»,

    rispuose del magnanimo quell' ombra,

    «l'anima tua è da viltade offesa;   45

la qual molte fïate l'omo ingombra

    sì che d'onrata impresa lo rivolve,

    come falso veder bestia quand' ombra.   48

Da questa tema acciò che tu ti solve,

    dirotti perch' io venni e quel ch'io 'ntesi

    nel primo punto che di te mi dolve.   51

Io era tra color che son sospesi,

    e donna mi chiamò beata e bella,

    tal che di comandare io la richiesi.   54

Lucevan li occhi suoi più che la stella;

    e cominciommi a dir soave e piana,

    con angelica voce, in sua favella: 57

"O anima cortese mantoana,

    di cui la fama ancor nel mondo dura,

    e durerà quanto 'l mondo lontana,   60

The Chosen Vessel then brought confirmation,
 by journeying there, of the true faith that must be
 the beginning of the path to our salvation.   30
But why must I? On whose authority?
 I am not Aeneas, not Paul. Why should I seek
 what neither I nor anyone thinks me   33
worthy to do? Why start upon a bleak
 and, I fear, foolish journey? You are filled
 with wisdom, and hear more clearly than I speak."   36
Like someone who unwills what he has willed,
 and with new thoughts sees his resolve go by,
 letting what was begun go unfulfilled,   39
so, standing on that shadowy slope, was I.
 Rethinking what with such impulsiveness
 I had begun, I let my impulse die.   42
"If I have rightly comprehended this,"
 the shade of that magnanimous soul replied,
 "your spirit has been seized by cowardice,   45
which has often harried men and nullified
 many a worthy enterprise, as when
 a beast will see a shadow and turn aside.   48
To free you from this fear, let me explain
 why I have come, and tell you of the request
 that first made me take pity on your pain.   51
I was among the suspended ones when a blest
 and lovely lady called me. So fair was she,
 I begged that I might serve at her behest.   54
Brighter than stars, her eyes shone brilliantly,
 and in a tone so sweet and soft and pure,
 with an angel's voice, I heard her say to me: 57
'O gentle Mantuan soul, with fame secure
 in the world above, whose name will still resound
 as long as the world continues to endure,   60

l'amico mio, e non de la ventura,
    ne la diserta piaggia è impedito
    sì nel cammin, che vòlt' è per paura;   63
e temo che non sia già sì smarrito,
    ch'io mi sia tardi al soccorso levata,
    per quel ch'i' ho di lui nel cielo udito.   66
Or movi, e con la tua parola ornata
    e con ciò c'ha mestieri al suo campare,
    l'aiuta sì ch'i' ne sia consolata.   69
I' son Beatrice che ti faccio andare;
    vegno del loco ove tornar disio;
    amor mi mosse, che mi fa parlare.   72
Quando sarò dinanzi al segnor mio,
    di te mi loderò sovente a lui".
    Tacette allora, e poi comincia' io: 75
"O donna di virtù sola per cui
    l'umana spezie eccede ogne contento
    di quel ciel c'ha minor li cerchi sui,   78
tanto m'aggrada il tuo comandamento,
    che l'ubidir, se già fosse, m'è tardi;
    più non t'è uo' ch'aprirmi il tuo talento.   81
Ma dimmi la cagion che non ti guardi
    de lo scender qua giuso in questo centro
    de l'ampio loco ove tornar tu ardi".   84
"Da che tu vuo' saver cotanto a dentro,
    dirotti brievemente", mi rispuose,
    "perch' i' non temo di venir qua entro.   87
Temer si dee di sole quelle cose
    c'hanno potenza di fare altrui male;
    de l'altre no, ché non son paurose.   90
I' son fatta da Dio, sua mercé, tale,
    che la vostra miseria non mi tange,
    né fiamma d'esto 'ncendio non m'assale.   93

my friend, who is not fortune's friend, has found
    so many obstacles upon his way
    up the desert slope that fear has turned him round.   63

I fear, from all that I have heard them say
    in heaven, that I have made too late a start,
    that already he has gone too far astray.   66

Go now and, with the words of your high art
    and the skill to rescue him from this distress,
    assist him and bring solace to my heart.   69

I who now send you forth am Beatrice.
    I have come from a place I long to see again.
    Love prompted me. Love makes me ask you this.   72

How often I will speak to praise you when
    I stand before my Lord upon his throne.'
    She said no more, and I responded then: 75

'O lady of virtue, through whose power alone
    humanity is able to rise higher
    than all within the least-circling heaven's zone,   78

I am so pleased to do what you desire
    that were it already done, it would be late.
    All you need do is say what you require.   81

But how is it that you did not hesitate
    to leave that longed-for spacious place on high
    and descend into this center where we wait?'   84

'Since you have such deep desire to know why
    I am not at all afraid to venture here,'
    she told me, 'I will briefly clarify.   87

The only things that should inspire fear
    are those that can inflict an injury.
    The rest need not oppress us, it is clear.   90

God's grace has made me so I cannot be
    moved in my heart by all your suffering
    or touched by all the flames surrounding me.   93

Donna è gentil nel ciel che si compiange
  di questo 'mpedimento ov' io ti mando,
  sì che duro giudicio là sù frange.   96
Questa chiese Lucia in suo dimando
  e disse:—Or ha bisogno il tuo fedele
  di te, e io a te lo raccomando—.   99
Lucia, nimica di ciascun crudele,
  si mosse, e venne al loco dov' i' era,
  che mi sedea con l'antica Rachele.   102
Disse:—Beatrice, loda di Dio vera,
  ché non soccorri quei che t'amò tanto,
  ch'uscì per te de la volgare schiera?   105
Non odi tu la pieta del suo pianto,
  non vedi tu la morte che 'l combatte
  su la fiumana ove 'l mar non ha vanto?—.   108
Al mondo non fur mai persone ratte
  a far lor pro o a fuggir lor danno,
  com' io, dopo cotai parole fatte,   111
venni qua giù del mio beato scanno,
  fidandomi del tuo parlare onesto,
  ch'onora te e quei ch'udito l'hanno".   114
Poscia che m'ebbe ragionato questo,
  li occhi lucenti lagrimando volse,
  per che mi fece del venir più presto.   117
E venni a te così com' ella volse:
  d'inanzi a quella fiera ti levai
  che del bel monte il corto andar ti tolse.   120
Dunque: che è? perché, perché restai,
  perché tanta viltà nel core allette,
  perché ardire e franchezza non hai,   123
poscia che tai tre donne benedette
  curan di te ne la corte del cielo,
  e 'l mio parlar tanto ben ti promette?».   126

In heaven a noble lady, pitying
    that great distress I send you to repair,
    has made a breech in the strict reckoning   96
that rules above. She summoned Lucia there,
    and said: —Your follower, who is faithful still,
    needs you, and I commend him to your care.—   99
Lucia, who is the enemy of all
    cruelty, came immediately to the place
    where I was sitting with the venerable   102
Rachel, and said: —Beatrice, God's true praise,
    why do you not help him who loved you so
    that he forsook the crowd and its crass ways?   105
Do you not hear him crying out below?
    Do you not see Death battle him by that flood
    the mighty ocean cannot overthrow?—   108
Never on earth did any seize his good
    or flee his harm as quickly as I flew,
    once I had heard such words and understood,   111
leaving my heavenly seat to come to you,
    trusting your words of such nobility
    that they honor you and all who hear them too.' 114
She turned when she had spoken. I could see
    tears shining in her eyes, making me still
    more eager to fulfill her charge to me.   117
So I have come to you, as was her will,
    saving you from the beast that blocked your way
    along the short path up the lovely hill.   120
What is this, then? Why, why do you delay,
    why does your heart make room for cowardice,
    why not be bold and resolute, when they,   123
those three great ladies of high blessedness
    in heaven's court, are keeping you in sight,
    when I promise you great good to come of this?" 126

Quali fioretti dal notturno gelo
    chinati e chiusi, poi che 'l sol li 'mbianca,
    si drizzan tutti aperti in loro stelo,   129
tal mi fec' io di mia virtude stanca,
    e tanto buono ardire al cor mi corse,
    ch'i' cominciai come persona franca: 132
«Oh pietosa colei che mi soccorse!
    e te cortese ch'ubidisti tosto
    a le vere parole che ti porse!   135
Tu m'hai con disiderio il cor disposto
    sì al venir con le parole tue,
    ch'i' son tornato nel primo proposto.   138
Or va, ch'un sol volere è d'ambedue:
    tu duca, tu segnore e tu maestro».
    Così li dissi; e poi che mosso fue,   141
intrai per lo cammino alto e silvestro.

As flowers droop and close in the chill of night,

> then stand and open out upon the stem

> when the sun returns and touches them with light,   129

so my exhausted strength revived like them

> and, feeling courage rush into my heart,

> like one who has been set free I said to him: 132

"How compassionate she was, who took my part!

> How courteous you were, who quickly went

> in response to her true plea. Now let us start,   135

for the forcefulness of what you say has sent

> my heart new eagerness to go with you,

> reawakening my original intent.   138

Lead on. There is one will between us two.

> You are my guide, my lord and master." Thus

> I spoke. And when he moved, I entered too   141

the pathway through the savage wilderness.

Notes

lines 7–9   The invocation of the muse, a traditional component of epic poetry. Canto I may be regarded as a proem to the entire *Comedy*, leaving 33 cantos for the journey through hell. Both the *Purgatorio* and the *Paradiso*, which also begin with such invocations, contain 33 cantos, making the complete work exactly 100 cantos long.

line 13   In the *Aeneid*, Silvius is the son of Aeneas and his second wife, Lavinia, daughter of King Latinus of Latium. In Book VI, Aeneas makes the epic hero's ritual journey to the underworld, where his father's shade reveals to him the coming glories of Rome.

lines 28–30   The Chosen Vessel, so described in Acts 9.15, is Saint Paul. In 2 Corinthians 12.1–7, Paul speaks of having been raised to the "third heaven" and alludes to its secret messages. In the *Visio Sancti Pauli*, an early medieval text, there is a description of his journey to hell.

lines 76–78   In Ptolemaic cosmology, the "heaven," or planet, with the "least-circling zone," or smallest orbit, is the moon. Within that zone—the center of the physical universe—is the earth.

line 94   The "noble lady" is the Virgin Mary. Her name, like that of Jesus
                Christ, is never spoken aloud in hell.

line 97   Lucia is Saint Lucy of Syracuse, a third-century virgin martyr,
                patroness of those with vision problems and a symbol of illuminating
                grace.

lines 102–3   Rachel, in Genesis the wife of Jacob, is usually taken to be a symbol of
                the contemplative life. She is mentioned again in Canto IV, line 60.

Canto III

'Per me si va ne la città dolente,
    per me si va ne l'etterno dolore,
    per me si va tra la perduta gente.   3
Giustizia mosse il mio alto fattore;
    fecemi la divina podestate,
    la somma sapïenza e 'l primo amore.   6
Dinanzi a me non fuor cose create
    se non etterne, e io etterno duro.
    Lasciate ogne speranza, voi ch'intrate'.   9
Queste parole di colore oscuro
    vid' ïo scritte al sommo d'una porta;
    per ch'io: «Maestro, il senso lor m'è duro».   12
Ed elli a me, come persona accorta:
    «Qui si convien lasciare ogne sospetto;
    ogne viltà convien che qui sia morta.   15
Noi siam venuti al loco ov' i' t'ho detto
    che tu vedrai le genti dolorose
    c'hanno perduto il ben de l'intelletto».   18
E poi che la sua mano a la mia puose
    con lieto volto, ond' io mi confortai,
    mi mise dentro a le segrete cose.   21
Quivi sospiri, pianti e alti guai
    risonavan per l'aere sanza stelle,
    per ch'io al cominciar ne lagrimai.   24
Diverse lingue, orribili favelle,
    parole di dolore, accenti d'ira,
    voci alte e fioche, e suon di man con elle   27

Canto III

THROUGH ME THE WAY TO THE CITY OF DESOLATION,
 THROUGH ME THE WAY TO EVERLASTING PAIN,
 THROUGH ME THE WAY TO SOULS IN ABOMINATION.   3
JUSTICE MOVED MY GREAT MAKER IN MY DESIGN.
 I WAS CREATED BY THE PRIMAL LOVE,
 WISDOM SUPREME AND POTENCY DIVINE.   6
BEFORE ME NOTHING WAS CREATED SAVE
 THE ETERNAL, AND I ENDURE ETERNALLY.
 ALL YOU WHO ENTER, LET NO HOPE SURVIVE.   9
In darkly colored letters I could see
 these words inscribed on a portal overhead.
 "Master," I said, "this saying is hard for me."   12
Like one who knows and understands, he said:
 "Here all your doubt is to be left behind,
 here all your cowardice is to fall dead.   15
Now we are in the place where you will find
 the ones I told you of, the wretched race
 of those who have lost the good use of the mind."   18
And then, with his hand on mine, and on his face
 a cheerful look that helped to calm my fears,
 he led me down into that secret place.   21
Sighs and laments and loud wails filled my ears.
 Those cries resounding through the starless air
 so moved me at first that I burst into tears.   24
A babble of tongues, harsh outcries of despair,
 noises of rage and grief, the beating of hands,
 and shrill and raucous voices everywhere   27

facevano un tumulto, il qual s'aggira
     sempre in quell' aura sanza tempo tinta,
     come la rena quando turbo spira.   30

E io ch'avea d'error la testa cinta,
     dissi: «Maestro, che è quel ch'i' odo?
     e che gent' è che par nel duol sì vinta?».   33

Ed elli a me: «Questo misero modo
     tegnon l'anime triste di coloro
     che visser sanza 'nfamia e sanza lodo.   36

Mischiate sono a quel cattivo coro
     de li angeli che non furon ribelli
     né fur fedeli a Dio, ma per sé fuoro.   39

Caccianli i ciel per non esser men belli,
     né lo profondo inferno li riceve,
     ch'alcuna gloria i rei avrebber d'elli».   42

E io: «Maestro, che è tanto greve
     a lor che lamentar li fa sì forte?».
     Rispuose: «Dicerolti molto breve.   45

Questi non hanno speranza di morte,
     e la lor cieca vita è tanto bassa,
     che 'nvidïosi son d'ogne altra sorte.   48

Fama di loro il mondo esser non lassa;
     misericordia e giustizia li sdegna:
     non ragioniam di lor, ma guarda e passa».   51

E io, che riguardai, vidi una 'nsegna
     che girando correva tanto ratta,
     che d'ogne posa mi parea indegna;   54

e dietro le venìa sì lunga tratta
     di gente, ch'i' non averei creduto
     che morte tanta n'avesse disfatta.   57

Poscia ch'io v'ebbi alcun riconosciuto,
     vidi e conobbi l'ombra di colui
     che fece per viltade il gran rifiuto.   60

all made a mad uproar that never ends,

    revolving in that timeless darkened breeze

    the way a whirlwind whips the desert sands.   30

"Master, what do I hear? And who are these,"

    I cried, as the horror swirled around my head,

    "who seem so shattered by their agonies?"   33

"This is the miserable estate," he said,

    "of the sorry souls of those who lived and died

    winning neither praise nor blame for the lives they'd led.   36

They are mixed with the base angels who stood aside,

    who neither hastened to their Lord's defense

    nor rose against him in rebellious pride.   39

Heaven repels them lest its magnificence

    be tarnished, and they are turned away by hell

    lest sinners exalt themselves at their expense."   42

"Master," I said, "why do they thrash and yell?

    What is the fate that makes them carry on?"

    He answered: "I will very briefly tell.   45

They have no hope of death's oblivion.

    Because theirs is a life so blind and low,

    they are envious of every other one.   48

Mercy and justice scorn them. The world lets no

    report of them remain, not even a trace.

    Let us not speak of them, but look and go."   51

Looking again, I saw a banner race,

    whirling about so madly that it seemed

    unfit to make a stand in one fixed place.   54

Following it a line of people streamed,

    an endless line as far as I could see.

    That death had undone so many, I had not dreamed.   57

There were some among them who were known to me,

    and I saw the shade of him whose cowardice

    made him make the great refusal. Instantly   60

Incontanente intesi e certo fui
    che questa era la setta d'i cattivi,
    a Dio spiacenti e a' nemici sui.   63

Questi sciaurati, che mai non fur vivi,
    erano ignudi e stimolati molto
    da mosconi e da vespe ch'eran ivi.   66

Elle rigavan lor di sangue il volto,
    che, mischiato di lagrime, a' lor piedi
    da fastidiosi vermi era ricolto.   69

E poi ch'a riguardar oltre mi diedi,
    vidi genti a la riva d'un gran fiume;
    per ch'io dissi: «Maestro, or mi concedi   72

ch'i' sappia quali sono, e qual costume
    le fa di trapassar parer sì pronte,
    com' i' discerno per lo fioco lume».   75

Ed elli a me: «Le cose ti fier conte
    quando noi fermerem li nostri passi
    su la trista riviera d'Acheronte».   78

Allor con li occhi vergognosi e bassi,
    temendo no 'l mio dir li fosse grave,
    infino al fiume del parlar mi trassi.   81

Ed ecco verso noi venir per nave
    un vecchio, bianco per antico pelo,
    gridando: «Guai a voi, anime prave!   84

Non isperate mai veder lo cielo:
    i' vegno per menarvi a l'altra riva
    ne le tenebre etterne, in caldo e 'n gelo.   87

E tu che se' costì, anima viva,
    pàrtiti da cotesti che son morti».
    Ma poi che vide ch'io non mi partiva,   90

disse: «Per altra via, per altri porti
    verrai a piaggia, non qui, per passare:
    più lieve legno convien che ti porti».   93

I understood beyond a doubt that this
    was that craven company whom all despise,
    that God and his enemies find odious.   63
Those souls who had never lived, whose lives were lies,
    were naked, and were harried through their paces
    by swarms of stinging wasps and biting flies.   66
Blood mingling with their tears ran down their faces
    and splashed the earth around them, where it fed
    disgusting worms that wriggled in their traces.   69
Then I saw a crowd of people up ahead
    on the bank of a broad river. "What do I see,
    Master, who are those people there," I said,   72
"what compulsion makes them wait so eagerly
    for the chance to cross the river and be gone—
    or so in this dim light it seems to me."   75
And he replied: "These things will be made known
    when we must still our steps a while before
    we go across the somber Acheron."   78
Afraid I might offend, I said no more,
    but walked with eyes downcast, and shame-filled too,
    until we found ourselves upon the shore.   81
An old man white with age in a boat that drew
    toward where we all were gathered gave a cry:
    "Woe unto you, you miserable crew   84
of sinners! Put all hope of heaven by!
    I take you to the other shore, to the land
    of heat and cold, where darkness cannot die.   87
And you there, you who are still living, stand
    aside from all those others who are dead."
    But when I did not follow his command,   90
"By another way, by other ports," he said,
    "not here, you will be brought across to shore.
    A lighter craft will carry you instead."   93

E 'l duca lui: «Caron, non ti crucciare:
    vuolsi così colà dove si puote
    ciò che si vuole, e più non dimandare».   96

Quinci fuor quete le lanose gote
    al nocchier de la livida palude,
    che 'ntorno a li occhi avea di fiamme rote.   99

Ma quell' anime, ch'eran lasse e nude,
    cangiar colore e dibattero i denti,
    ratto che 'nteser le parole crude.   102

Bestemmiavano Dio e lor parenti,
    l'umana spezie e 'l loco e 'l tempo e 'l seme
    di lor semenza e di lor nascimenti.   105

Poi si ritrasser tutte quante insieme,
    forte piangendo, a la riva malvagia
    ch'attende ciascun uom che Dio non teme.   108

Caron dimonio, con occhi di bragia
    loro accennando, tutte le raccoglie;
    batte col remo qualunque s'adagia.   111

Come d'autunno si levan le foglie
    l'una appresso de l'altra, fin che 'l ramo
    vede a la terra tutte le sue spoglie,   114

similemente il mal seme d'Adamo
    gittansi di quel lito ad una ad una,
    per cenni come augel per suo richiamo.   117

Così sen vanno su per l'onda bruna,
    e avanti che sien di là discese,
    anche di qua nuova schiera s'auna.   120

«Figliuol mio», disse 'l maestro cortese,
    «quelli che muoion ne l'ira di Dio
    tutti convegnon qui d'ogne paese;   123

e pronti sono a trapassar lo rio,
    ché la divina giustizia li sprona,
    sì che la tema si volve in disio.   126

My leader told him, "Charon, no need to roar.
    Thus it is willed where there is power to do
    what has been willed, so question it no more."   96
This stopped the grizzled chops of the boatman who
    ferried the dead across the marshy river.
    Around his eyes two flaming circles flew.   99
But those weary, naked souls began to shiver,
    teeth gnashing, color gone from every face,
    at the harsh tirade that they'd heard him deliver.   102
They blasphemed God, they cursed the human race,
    their parents, the father's seed, the mother's womb,
    their birth, and even its very time and place.   105
Then they all drew together in the gloom,
    and weeping loudly they began to go
    to the evil shore that waits for all to whom   108
the fear of God means nothing. Eyes aglow
    like live coals, demon Charon herds them now
    and with his oar beats those who are too slow.   111
As one by one the leaves drop from the bough
    when autumn comes, and branches watch them fall
    till the earth has all their treasures, that is how   114
it was with Adam's evil seed. They all,
    one at a time, when signaled, left the shore,
    just as a bird will answer to its call.   117
So they cross the murky water, and before
    they have even landed on the other side,
    a new crowd gathers on this bank once more.   120
"My son," said my courteous master, "those who have died
    in the wrath of God all come together here
    from every country, eager now to ride   123
across the river as their time draws near.
    As God's own justice works upon them, they
    begin to feel desire in place of fear.   126

Quinci non passa mai anima buona;

 e però, se Caron di te si lagna,

 ben puoi sapere omai che 'l suo dir suona».   129

Finito questo, la buia campagna

 tremò sì forte, che de lo spavento

 la mente di sudore ancor mi bagna.   132

La terra lagrimosa diede vento,

 che balenò una luce vermiglia

 la qual mi vinse ciascun sentimento;   135

e caddi come l'uom cui sonno piglia.

No worthy spirit ever comes this way,
     so if Charon complained about you, it should be
     clear to you now just what his words convey."   129
And then the dark plain shook so violently
     that I start to bathe in sweat all over again
     reliving the terror in my memory.   132
Up from the tear-soaked ground a great wind ran,
     flashing a bright red light out of its swell
     that blasted all my senses, and like a man   135
that sleep has overtaken, down I fell.

Notes

line 32   Here I have departed from Petrocchi's edition of the text, which gives *error* for the more frequently preferred *orror*. Those who accept the latter reading often cite the *Aeneid*, Book II, line 559: "At me tum primum saevus circumstetit horror" ("For the first time a savage horror surrounded me").

lines 34–36   These souls chose neither good nor evil, the lukewarm scorned by Christ. Rudyard Kipling treats this theme delightfully in his poem "Tomlinson."

lines 59–60   This passage has been taken to refer to Esau, to Pontius Pilate, and to several others. One of the earliest identifications, and certainly the most common, is that of Celestine V, whose abdication of the papacy in 1294 led to the ascension of the corrupt Boniface VIII (Boniface, who was still pope in 1300, when the *Inferno* is set, is the object of Dante's scorn at several places in the poem; see note to Canto XIX, lines 52–57). Opposition to this assumption is founded in part on Celestine's canonization in 1313, while Dante was still alive.

line 94   Among the rivers of the underworld, Charon is traditionally represented as the ferryman of the Styx, not the Acheron. He appears in Aristophanes' *The Clouds* and in Book VI of the *Aeneid*, where Virgil's physical description of him furnishes Dante with several details.

Canto IV

Ruppemi l'alto sonno ne la testa
    un greve truono, sì ch'io mi riscossi
    come persona ch'è per forza desta;   3
e l'occhio riposato intorno mossi,
    dritto levato, e fiso riguardai
    per conoscer lo loco dov' io fossi.   6
Vero è che 'n su la proda mi trovai
    de la valle d'abisso dolorosa
    che 'ntrono accoglie d'infiniti guai.   9
Oscura e profonda era e nebulosa
    tanto che, per ficcar lo viso a fondo,
    io non vi discernea alcuna cosa.   12
«Or discendiam qua giù nel cieco mondo»,
    cominciò il poeta tutto smorto.
    «Io sarò primo, e tu sarai secondo».   15
E io, che del color mi fui accorto,
    dissi: «Come verrò, se tu paventi
    che suoli al mio dubbiare esser conforto?».   18
Ed elli a me: «L'angoscia de le genti
    che son qua giù, nel viso mi dipigne
    quella pietà che tu per tema senti.   21
Andiam, ché la via lunga ne sospigne».
    Così si mise e così mi fé intrare
    nel primo cerchio che l'abisso cigne.   24
Quivi, secondo che per ascoltare,
    non avea pianto mai che di sospiri
    che l'aura etterna facevan tremare;   27

CANTO IV

A crashing thunderclap made me awaken,
    putting the thick sleep in my head to rout.
    I started up like someone roughly shaken   3
out of a slumber. Standing, I looked about,
    gazing and turning my rested eyes around
    in every direction, trying to make out   6
just where I was. The truth is, I soon found
    I was standing on the edge of the abyss
    of pain, where roars of endless woe resound.   9
It was so dark and deep, so nebulous,
    I could see nothing in the depths although
    I stared intently from the precipice.   12
"Now let us descend into the blind world below,"
    the poet said, appearing pale and drawn.
    "I will be first, you second, as we go."   15
Seeing his pallor, I said: "I lean upon
    your strength when I falter, when I am afraid.
    If you are frightened, how shall I go on?"   18
"The anguish of the people here," he said,
    "colors my face in ways you read amiss,
    thinking the pity that I feel is dread.   21
But let us go. The long road beckons us."
    And so he went, and had me follow, where
    the first circle runs, surrounding the abyss.   24
I heard no wails of lamentation there,
    no loud complaints, only the sound of sighs
    that agitated the eternal air.   27

ciò avvenia di duol sanza martìri,

  ch'avean le turbe, ch'eran molte e grandi,

  d'infanti e di femmine e di viri.   30

Lo buon maestro a me: «Tu non dimandi

  che spiriti son questi che tu vedi?

  Or vo' che sappi, innanzi che più andi,   33

ch'ei non peccaro; e s'elli hanno mercedi,

  non basta, perché non ebber battesmo,

  ch'è porta de la fede che tu credi;   36

e s'e' furon dinanzi al cristianesmo,

  non adorar debitamente a Dio:

  e di questi cotai son io medesmo.   39

Per tai difetti, non per altro rio,

  semo perduti, e sol di tanto offesi

  che sanza speme vivemo in disio».   42

Gran duol mi prese al cor quando lo 'ntesi,

  però che gente di molto valore

  conobbi che 'n quel limbo eran sospesi.   45

«Dimmi, maestro mio, dimmi, segnore»,

  comincia' io per volere esser certo

  di quella fede che vince ogne errore: 48

«uscicci mai alcuno, o per suo merto

  o per altrui, che poi fosse beato?».

  E quei che 'ntese il mio parlar coverto,   51

rispuose: «Io era nuovo in questo stato,

  quando ci vidi venire un possente,

  con segno di vittoria coronato.   54

Trasseci l'ombra del primo parente,

  d'Abèl suo figlio e quella di Noè,

  di Moïsè legista e ubidente;   57

Abraàm patrïarca e Davìd re,

  Israèl con lo padre e co' suoi nati

  e con Rachele, per cui tanto fé,   60

From a sadness without torments rose the cries
    of children and of women and of men.
    Many and vast were the crowds before my eyes.   30
"Do you not ask," said my good master then,
    "what spirits these may be that fill this place?
    I will have you know, before we walk again,   33
they did not sin. But their merit won no grace
    because they lacked baptism, which must be
    the gateway to the faith that you embrace.   36
Those who preceded Christianity
    did not worship God according to his law,
    and I myself am of this company.   39
For this defect, and for no other flaw,
    we are lost, with this one punishment laid on,
    that without hope we feel desire gnaw."   42
Great sadness gripped my heart when he had done.
    Among those suspended in that limbo were
    many a worthy, honorable one.   45
"Tell me, my master," I said then, "tell me, sir,"
    feeling a need to be assured anew
    of the faith that conquers all ideas that err,   48
"did any ever leave here for heaven, through
    their own or another's merit?" And he said,
    seeing what my covert words were leading to: 51
"When I was newly placed among these dead,
    a mighty one came among us, whom I saw
    wearing the sign of victory on his head.   54
He took the shade of our first progenitor,
    Abel his son, and Noah, and God-honoring
    Moses who was the giver of the law,   57
patriarch Abraham and David the king,
    Israel with his father and his sons
    and Rachel, for whom he did much laboring.   60

e altri molti, e feceli beati.

    E vo' che sappi che, dinanzi ad essi,

      spiriti umani non eran salvati».   63

Non lasciavam l'andar perch' ei dicessi,

    ma passavam la selva tuttavia,

      la selva, dico, di spiriti spessi.   66

Non era lunga ancor la nostra via

    di qua dal sonno, quand' io vidi un foco

      ch'emisperio di tenebre vincia.   69

Di lungi n'eravamo ancora un poco,

    ma non sì ch'io non discernessi in parte

      ch'orrevol gente possedea quel loco.   72

«O tu ch'onori scïenzïa e arte,

    questi chi son c'hanno cotanta onranza,

      che dal modo de li altri li diparte?».   75

E quelli a me: «L'onrata nominanza

    che di lor suona sù ne la tua vita,

      grazïa acquista in ciel che sì li avanza».   78

Intanto voce fu per me udita:

    «Onorate l'altissimo poeta;

      l'ombra sua torna, ch'era dipartita».   81

Poi che la voce fu restata e queta,

    vidi quattro grand' ombre a noi venire:

      sembianz' avevan né trista né lieta.   84

Lo buon maestro cominciò a dire:

    «Mira colui con quella spada in mano,

      che vien dinanzi ai tre sì come sire: 87

quelli è Omero poeta sovrano;

    l'altro è Orazio satiro che vene;

      Ovidio è 'l terzo, e l'ultimo Lucano.   90

Però che ciascun meco si convene

    nel nome che sonò la voce sola,

      fannomi onore, e di ciò fanno bene».   93

He blessed all these and other paragons.
>   And I would have you know that till that day
>   no souls were saved. They were the earliest ones."   63

We did not stop, but went along our way
>   while he was speaking, passing now through some
>   thick woods—not woods made out of trees, I say,   66

but of crowding spirits. We were not far from
>   the place where I had slept so deeply, when
>   I saw a dark hemisphere that was overcome   69

by a fiery light. Though still a bit distant then,
>   we were close enough that I could see in part
>   that the ground was held by honorable men.   72

I said: "O you who honor science and art,
>   who are those men who even in this place
>   possess such honor that sets them apart?"   75

And he: "Their fame, which time does not erase,
>   still resounding in your world this very day,
>   allows them to advance through heaven's grace."   78

Meanwhile I heard a voice before me say:
>   "Hail to the highest poet! His honorable
>   shade has returned to us, which had gone away."   81

Then when the voice had finished and was still,
>   I saw four noble shades all moving forward,
>   their faces neither glad nor sorrowful.   84

Said my master: "See the one who bears the sword,
>   the one who walks before the other three
>   acknowledged as their leader and their lord.   87

Homer the sovereign of all bards is he.
>   Horace the satirist is the second one.
>   Ovid comes third, and Lucan finally.   90

Because, along with me, they all have won
>   the name by which I was just now addressed,
>   they do me honor, and it is well done."   93

Così vid' i' adunar la bella scola
    di quel segnor de l'altissimo canto
    che sovra li altri com' aquila vola.   96
Da ch'ebber ragionato insieme alquanto,
    volsersi a me con salutevol cenno,
    e 'l mio maestro sorrise di tanto;   99
e più d'onore ancora assai mi fenno,
    ch'e' sì mi fecer de la loro schiera,
    sì ch'io fui sesto tra cotanto senno.   102
Così andammo infino a la lumera,
    parlando cose che 'l tacere è bello,
    sì com' era 'l parlar colà dov' era.   105
Venimmo al piè d'un nobile castello,
    sette volte cerchiato d'alte mura,
    difeso intorno d'un bel fiumicello.   108
Questo passammo come terra dura;
    per sette porte intrai con questi savi:
    giugnemmo in prato di fresca verdura.   111
Genti v'eran con occhi tardi e gravi,
    di grande autorità ne' lor sembianti:
    parlavan rado, con voci soavi.   114
Traemmoci così da l'un de' canti,
    in loco aperto, luminoso e alto,
    sì che veder si potien tutti quanti.   117
Colà diritto, sovra 'l verde smalto,
    mi fuor mostrati li spiriti magni,
    che del vedere in me stesso m'essalto.   120
I' vidi Eletra con molti compagni,
    tra ' quai conobbi Ettòr ed Enea,
    Cesare armato con li occhi grifagni.   123
Vidi Cammilla e la Pantasilea;
    da l'altra parte vidi 'l re Latino
    che con Lavina sua figlia sedea.   126

Assembled there before me were the best
>   of poets, the school of that sweet lord of style
>   who like an eagle soars above the rest. 96
When they had talked together for a while,
>   they turned to me with a nod of salutation,
>   at which I saw my master broadly smile. 99
And then they made far greater demonstration
>   of honor, bringing me up to their height,
>   making me sixth in their wisdom's congregation. 102
So we walked onward, moving toward the light,
>   and the things that were said among us it is good
>   not to say here, as to say them there was right. 105
We came to where a noble castle stood
>   circled by seven high walls. All around
>   that citadel a lovely streamlet flowed. 108
We crossed the stream as though on solid ground.
>   Through seven gates those sages passed with me.
>   We came to a fresh green meadow, where we found 111
people with looks of great authority,
>   whose eyes moved slowly and were serious,
>   who spoke in quiet tones, infrequently. 114
Then we moved off to one side, where there was
>   a luminous broad hillside that would yield
>   a view of the whole gathering to us. 117
Before me on that green enameled field
>   such glorious spirits appeared that I still prize
>   within my soul the sights that were revealed. 120
I saw Electra, and could recognize
>   Aeneas and Hector among those with her,
>   and armored Caesar with his hawklike eyes. 123
I saw Camilla and Penthesilea there,
>   and I saw King Latinus sitting in
>   another place, with his daughter Lavinia near. 126

Vidi quel Bruto che cacciò Tarquino,
    Lucrezia, Iulia, Marzïa e Corniglia;
    e solo, in parte, vidi 'l Saladino.   129
Poi ch'innalzai un poco più le ciglia,
    vidi 'l maestro di color che sanno
    seder tra filosofica famiglia.   132
Tutti lo miran, tutti onor li fanno:
    quivi vid' ïo Socrate e Platone,
    che 'nnanzi a li altri più presso li stanno;   135
Democrito che 'l mondo a caso pone,
    Dïogenès, Anassagora e Tale,
    Empedoclès, Eraclito e Zenone;   138
e vidi il buono accoglitor del quale,
    Dïascoride dico; e vidi Orfeo,
    Tulïo e Lino e Seneca morale;   141
Euclide geomètra e Tolomeo,
    Ipocràte, Avicenna e Galïeno,
    Averoìs, che 'l gran comento feo.   144
Io non posso ritrar di tutti a pieno,
    però che sì mi caccia il lungo tema,
    che molte volte al fatto il dir vien meno.   147
La sesta compagnia in due si scema:
    per altra via mi mena il savio duca,
    fuor de la queta, ne l'aura che trema.   150
E vegno in parte ove non è che luca.

I saw that Brutus who overthrew Tarquin.
    Lucretia, Cornelia, Julia, and with these three
      was Marcia. Alone, apart, was Saladin.   129
And lifting my eyes higher, I could see,
    seated, the master of all those who know,
      amid his philosophic family.   132
All of them gaze upon him, all of them show
    all honor to him. Plato and Socrates
      stand closest to him. I saw row on row,   135
Anaxagoras, Thales, and Diogenes,
    Heraclitus, Zeno, and Democritus
      who imputes the world to chance, Empedocles,   138
Dioscorides who collected things' essences,
    Hippocrates, Galen, the moral philosopher
      Seneca, Cicero, Linus, and Orpheus,   141
Ptolemy, Euclid the geometer,
    Avicenna, and Averroës whose monument
      is the great commentary. So many of them there were,   144
I cannot describe them to the full extent,
    for often, with my long theme to set the pace,
      the telling must fall short of the event.   147
We six become two. Out of the quiet space,
    through another route into the trembling air,
      now my wise guide has led me to a place   150
where there is nothing shining anywhere.

Notes

lines 52–63   These lines refer to the legendary harrowing of hell. The "mighty one"
    of line 53 is Christ. Salvation was impossible until he had redeemed by
    his crucifixion the taint of original sin. At his death, which occurred
    roughly fifty years after Virgil's, Christ descended to the underworld to
    effect the salvation of many worthies who had believed in the prophe-
    cies of his coming.

lines 59–60   Israel, meaning "soldier of God," was a name given to Jacob after he wrestled with the angel. His father was Isaac, son of Abraham. Rachel was Jacob's wife. His twelve sons were the founders of the twelve tribes of Israel.

line 88   Virgil's description of Homer as "the sovereign of all bards" acknowledges the *Aeneid*'s heavy borrowings from the *Iliad* and *Odyssey* (Dante, who did not read Greek, knew Homer only indirectly).

line 89   Horace (Quintus Horatius Flaccus, 65–8 B.C.E.), who was known in the Middle Ages more for his satires than for his odes, describes himself as a satirist in the *Ars poetica.*

line 90   The *Metamorphoses* of Ovid (Publius Ovidius Naso, 43 B.C.E.–c. 17 C.E.) provided Dante with his chief source for classical myth. Lucan (Marcus Annaeus Lucanus, 39–65 C.E.) is the author of *Pharsalia*, an epic concerning the conflict between Caesar and Pompey.

lines 100–102   This apparent nomination of himself as one of the six greatest poets of all time seems at first to be an act of breathtaking hubris on Dante's part. But Dante would have regarded his poetic talent as a God-given attribute, not a personal attainment worthy of boast, and in a poem describing the horrific fates of those who misused their God-given gifts, he can legitimately claim to be employing his, like the poets named here, for the highest ends—a claim that Milton would more overtly make for his own intentions at the beginning of *Paradise Lost* (see also Canto XXVI, lines 19–24).

lines 121–22   The Electra named here is not the daughter of Agamemnon and Clytemnestra about whom Sophocles and Euripides wrote tragedies, but the daughter of Atlas and mother of Dardanus, the founder of Troy. Aeneas and Hector, leader of the Trojan forces in the *Iliad*, are her descendants.

line 124   For Camilla, see note to Canto I, lines 106–8. Penthesilea, the queen of the Amazons, fought for Troy and was killed by Achilles.

lines 125–26   For Latinus and Lavinia, see note to Canto II, line 13.

lines 127–29   Tarquin was the last of the legendary Roman kings; the rape of Lucretia by his son led to his expulsion by Lucius Junius Brutus, brother of Lucretia and nephew of Tarquin, and thus the establishment of the republic. Brutus is not to be confused with Caesar's assassin Marcus Junius Brutus. Julia was the daughter of Caesar and wife of Pompey. Cornelia was the daughter of Scipio Africanus and mother of the Gracchi, the tribunes Caius and Tiberius. Marcia was the wife of Cato the Younger.

line 129   Saladin, who became sultan of Egypt in 1174, won some victories against the Crusaders before his defeat by Richard Coeur de Lion.

Despite his resistance to the Christian invaders of the Holy Land, Saladin was highly regarded in medieval Europe for his piety, justice, and nobility of spirit.

lines 130–38   Aristotle (line 131) was translated into Latin in the twelfth and thirteenth centuries and was quickly established as the principal classical philosopher, in large part through Thomas Aquinas's incorporation of his work into a Christian context. The others named here were predecessors or contemporaries of Socrates and Plato; they are all presented as stages along the way to the culmination of thought in "the master of those who know."

line 139   Pedanius Dioscorides, a first-century Greek physician and author of *De materia medica*, catalogued the properties of plants.

line 140   Hippocrates (fifth century B.C.E.) and Galen (second century C.E.) were Greek physicians.

lines 140–41   The mythical Greek poets Linus and Orpheus are grouped with the Roman moralists Cicero (Marcus Tullius Cicero, 106–43 B.C.E.) and Seneca (Lucius Annaeus Seneca, 4 B.C.E.–65 C.E.), suggesting an association of poetry with wisdom and moral values.

line 142   Ptolemy (Claudius Ptolemaeus, c. 90–168) was the Egyptian astronomer whose *Almagest* outlines his system. Euclid (third century B.C.E.) wrote the *Elements* of geometry.

line 143   The Arabic philosopher Avicenna (ibn Sina, 980–1037) was the author of a standard medical textbook. Ibn Rushd Averroës (1126–1198), Spanish Islamic philosopher, wrote the most important medieval commentary on Aristotle. Their inclusion, with that of Saladin, might be seen as a partial mitigation of Dante's hostility to Islam as a schism, as shown by the mosques of the city of Dis (Canto VIII, lines 70–72) and the damnation of Mohammed (Canto XXVIII, line 22ff.).

Canto V

Così discesi del cerchio primaio
    giù nel secondo, che men loco cinghia
    e tanto più dolor, che punge a guaio.   3
Stavvi Minòs orribilmente, e ringhia:
    essamina le colpe ne l'intrata;
    giudica e manda secondo ch'avvinghia.   6
Dico che quando l'anima mal nata
    li vien dinanzi, tutta si confessa;
    e quel conoscitor de le peccata   9
vede qual loco d'inferno è da essa;
    cignesi con la coda tante volte
    quantunque gradi vuol che giù sia messa.   12
Sempre dinanzi a lui ne stanno molte:
    vanno a vicenda ciascuna al giudizio,
    dicono e odono e poi son giù volte.   15
«O tu che vieni al doloroso ospizio»,
    disse Minòs a me quando mi vide,
    lasciando l'atto di cotanto offizio,   18
«guarda com' entri e di cui tu ti fide;
    non t'inganni l'ampiezza de l'intrare!».
    E 'l duca mio a lui: «Perché pur gride?   21
Non impedir lo suo fatale andare:
    vuolsi così colà dove si puote
    ciò che si vuole, e più non dimandare».   24
Or incomincian le dolenti note
    a farmisi sentire; or son venuto
    là dove molto pianto mi percuote.   27

Canto V

Thus I went down from where the first circle lies
    into the second, which surrounds less space
    but much more pain, provoking wails and cries.   3
There Minos stands with his horrid snarling face.
    He examines the sinners at the entranceway.
    Entwining, he assigns each one its place.   6
Each misbegotten soul, that is to say,
    confesses all as it faces him, and so
    that connoisseur of sinfulness can weigh   9
how far each spirit will be sent below.
    Each time his tail coils round him indicates
    another level that the soul must go.   12
Always a swarming multitude awaits.
    They tell, they hear, they are hurled into the air,
    flung one by one to their eternal fates.   15
Minos addressed me when he saw me there,
    halting the meting out of punishments:
    "O you who come to this house of pain, beware   18
how you enter and where you place your confidence.
    Do not let yourself be fooled by the wide door!"
    And my leader: "Why do you too take offense?   21
Do not obstruct the path he is fated for.
    Thus it is willed where there is power to do
    what has been willed, so question it no more."   24
Now all the mournful sounds are starting to
    surround and overwhelm me. Now I arrive
    where the roar of lamentation runs me through.   27

Io venni in loco d'ogne luce muto,
    che mugghia come fa mar per tempesta,
    se da contrari venti è combattuto.   30
La bufera infernal, che mai non resta,
    mena li spirti con la sua rapina;
    voltando e percotendo li molesta.   33
Quando giungon davanti a la ruina,
    quivi le strida, il compianto, il lamento;
    bestemmian quivi la virtù divina.   36
Intesi ch'a così fatto tormento
    enno dannati i peccator carnali,
    che la ragion sommettono al talento.   39
E come li stornei ne portan l'ali
    nel freddo tempo, a schiera larga e piena,
    così quel fiato li spiriti mali   42
di qua, di là, di giù, di sù li mena;
    nulla speranza li conforta mai,
    non che di posa, ma di minor pena.   45
E come i gru van cantando lor lai,
    faccendo in aere di sé lunga riga,
    così vid' io venir, traendo guai,   48
ombre portate da la detta briga;
    per ch'i' dissi: «Maestro, chi son quelle
    genti che l'aura nera sì gastiga?».   51
«La prima di color di cui novelle
    tu vuo' saper», mi disse quelli allotta,
    «fu imperadrice di molte favelle.   54
A vizio di lussuria fu sì rotta,
    che libito fé licito in sua legge,
    per tòrre il biasmo in che era condotta.   57
Ell' è Semiramìs, di cui si legge
    che succedette a Nino e fu sua sposa:
    tenne la terra che 'l Soldan corregge.   60

Here the light is mute and the atmosphere alive
    with the noise of constant howling, like the sea
    under assault by violent gusts that strive   30
with one another. The hellish wind blows free,
    sweeping the spirits headlong through the air.
    It whirls and pounds and mauls them endlessly.   33
It carries them back before the ruin, where
    they shriek and moan and utter their laments
    and curse the almighty power that sent them there.   36
The souls condemned to bear these punishments,
    I learned, are the carnal sinners, of lust so strong
    that they let it master reason and good sense.   39
As large, dense flocks of starlings are borne along
    by their wings in the cold season of the year,
    just so that blast propels the sinful throng,   42
drives them now up, now down, now there, now here.
    No hope consoles them, whether for repose
    or even for their pain to be less severe.   45
As it may happen that we see long rows
    of cranes above us as they chant their lay,
    so I saw spirits crying out their woes   48
as the wild windstorm carried them our way,
    till I said: "Master, all these souls I see
    lashed onward by the black air, who are they?"   51
"The first of those," my master said to me,
    "of whom you wish to hear was an empress
    over many languages in antiquity.   54
She was so enslaved by lust, so lecherous,
    that to keep the blame for her misdeeds at bay
    her laws gave license to licentiousness.   57
She is Semíramis, who, as histories say,
    succeeded her husband Ninus as ruler of
    all of the lands where the sultan reigns today.   60

L'altra è colei che s'ancise amorosa,

   e ruppe fede al cener di Sicheo;

   poi è Cleopatràs lussurïosa.   63

Elena vedi, per cui tanto reo

   tempo si volse, e vedi 'l grande Achille,

   che con amore al fine combatteo.   66

Vedi Parìs, Tristano»; e più di mille

   ombre mostrommi e nominommi a dito,

   ch'amor di nostra vita dipartille.   69

Poscia ch'io ebbi 'l mio dottore udito

   nomar le donne antiche e ' cavalieri,

   pietà mi giunse, e fui quasi smarrito.   72

I' cominciai: «Poeta, volontieri

   parlerei a quei due che 'nsieme vanno,

   e paion sì al vento esser leggeri».   75

Ed elli a me: «Vedrai quando saranno

   più presso a noi; e tu allor li priega

   per quello amor che i mena, ed ei verranno». 78

Sì tosto come il vento a noi li piega,

   mossi la voce: «O anime affannate,

   venite a noi parlar, s'altri nol niega!».   81

Quali colombe dal disio chiamate

   con l'ali alzate e ferme al dolce nido

   vegnon per l'aere, dal voler portate;   84

cotali uscir de la schiera ov' è Dido,

   a noi venendo per l'aere maligno,

   sì forte fu l'affettüoso grido.   87

«O animal grazïoso e benigno

   che visitando vai per l'aere perso

   noi che tignemmo il mondo di sanguigno, 90

se fosse amico il re de l'universo,

   noi pregheremmo lui de la tua pace,

   poi c'hai pietà del nostro mal perverso.   93

Next is the one who killed herself for love
      and betrayed Sichaeus's ashes. Here the bold
      Cleopatra comes, whom wanton passions drove.   63
See Helen, for whom such dreadful years unrolled.
      See the great Achilles. In the end he came
      to battle love. Behold Paris, and behold   66
Tristan—" More than a thousand, and all the same—
      love took them from our life. And one and all
      he showed to me and told me each one's name.   69
And as I listened to my teacher call
      the list of each high lady and grand knight,
      I was overwhelmed, and I felt my senses fall   72
to pity. "Poet," I told him, "if I might,
      I willingly would speak now to those two
      who are paired. Upon the wind they seem so light."   75
"The wind will bring them into closer view,"
      he said, "and you must call them, when it does,
      by the love that leads them. They will come to you."   78
When the wind had turned them near to where I was,
      "O weary spirits," I began to cry,
      "if another does not forbid, come speak with us!"   81
As doves with wings held steady and raised high
      are called by desire back to the sweet nest
      and carried by their will across the sky,   84
so from the flock of Dido and the rest
      they came through the evil air to where we stood,
      through the power of my compassionate request.   87
"O living creature, gracious and so good
      that through this black air you have dared to go
      to visit us who stained the world with blood,   90
if the king of the universe were not our foe,
      then we would surely pray to him to fill
      your heart with peace for pitying our woe.   93

Di quel che udire e che parlar vi piace,
    noi udiremo e parleremo a voi,
    mentre che 'l vento, come fa, ci tace.   96
Siede la terra dove nata fui
    su la marina dove 'l Po discende
    per aver pace co' seguaci sui.   99
Amor, ch'al cor gentil ratto s'apprende,
    prese costui de la bella persona
    che mi fu tolta; e 'l modo ancor m'offende.   102
Amor, ch'a nullo amato amar perdona,
    mi prese del costui piacer sì forte,
    che, come vedi, ancor non m'abbandona.   105
Amor condusse noi ad una morte.
    Caina attende chi a vita ci spense».
    Queste parole da lor ci fuor porte.   108
Quand' io intesi quell' anime offense,
    china' il viso, e tanto il tenni basso,
    fin che 'l poeta mi disse: «Che pense?».   111
Quando rispuosi, cominciai: «Oh lasso,
    quanti dolci pensier, quanto disio
    menò costoro al doloroso passo!».   114
Poi mi rivolsi a loro e parla' io,
    e cominciai: «Francesca, i tuoi martìri
    a lagrimar mi fanno tristo e pio.   117
Ma dimmi: al tempo d'i dolci sospiri,
    a che e come concedette amore
    che conosceste i dubbiosi disiri?».   120
E quella a me: «Nessun maggior dolore
    che ricordarsi del tempo felice
    ne la miseria; e ciò sa 'l tuo dottore.   123
Ma s'a conoscer la prima radice
    del nostro amor tu hai cotanto affetto,
    dirò come colui che piange e dice.   126

We will speak and hear of whatever it is your will
  to speak and hear of, while the wind will permit,
  as it is doing now, by keeping still.   96
The place where I was born is the city set
  along the shore where the Po descends to be
  at peace at last with those that follow it.   99
Love, which in gentle hearts flares rapidly,
  seized this one for my lovely body—how
  it was violently stripped away still injures me.   102
Love, which, when one is loved, does not allow
  that it be refused, seized me with joy in him,
  which, as you see, is with me even now.   105
Love led us to a single death. The grim
  Caïna waits to claim our murderer."
  These words were borne across to us from them.   108
When I had heard those afflicted souls, there were
  long minutes while I stood and bowed my head,
  until the poet's question made me stir: 111
"What are you thinking?" When I spoke, I said:
  "How strong desires and thoughts of sweet allure
  have brought them to this grievous pass instead!"   114
And then I turned to face those souls once more:
  "Stinging tears of pain and pity fill my eyes,
  Francesca, for the torments you endure.   117
But tell me how you came to recognize
  those dubious desires. How did love show
  its purpose in the hour of sweet sighs?"   120
And she replied: "There is no greater woe
  than looking back on happiness in days
  of misery. Your guide can tell you so.   123
But if you are so eager to retrace
  our love's first root, then I will make it known
  as one who speaks with tears upon her face.   126

Noi leggiavamo un giorno per diletto
    di Lancialotto come amor lo strinse;
    soli eravamo e sanza alcun sospetto.   129
Per più fïate li occhi ci sospinse
    quella lettura, e scolorocci il viso;
    ma solo un punto fu quel che ci vinse.   132
Quando leggemmo il disïato riso
    esser basciato da cotanto amante,
    questi, che mai da me non fia diviso,   135
la bocca mi basciò tutto tremante.
    Galeotto fu 'l libro e chi lo scrisse:
    quel giorno più non vi leggemmo avante».   138
Mentre che l'uno spirto questo disse,
    l'altro piangëa; sì che di pietade
    io venni men così com' io morisse.   141
E caddi come corpo morto cade.

In reading how Lancelot had been overthrown
>   by love, we chanced to pass the time one day.
>   We sat, suspecting nothing, all alone.   129
Some of the things we read made our eyes stray
>   to one another's and the color flee
>   our faces, but one point swept us away.   132
We read how that smile desired so ardently
>   was kissed by such a lover, one so fine,
>   and this one, who will never part from me,   135
trembling all over pressed his mouth on mine.
>   The book was a Gallehault, the author as well.
>   That day we did not read another line."   138
And while she told the tale she had to tell,
>   the other wept. I fainted where I stood
>   out of pity, as if dying, and I fell   141
down on the ground the way a dead man would.

Notes

line 4   Minos, the son of Zeus and Europa, was king of Crete. Virgil describes him and his brother Rhadamanthus as judges of souls in the underworld (*Aeneid*, Book VI).

line 34   For the explanation of the "ruin" so casually mentioned here, see Canto XII, lines 32–45.

lines 52–60   Semiramis, legendary queen of Assyria, was reputed to have legalized incest to exculpate her sexual relationship with her son.

lines 61–62   Dido, widow of King Sichaeus of Tyre, was queen of Tyre and then of Carthage. By her affair with Aeneas, she broke her vow to remain faithful to her husband's memory; his abandonment of her led to her suicide. The story of Dido and Aeneas is told in Book IV of the *Aeneid*, the best-known and most celebrated part of the epic.

line 63   Cleopatra, queen of Egypt, was the mistress of Julius Caesar and of Mark Antony.

lines 64–66   Helen was the wife of Menelaus, king of Sparta; her abduction by Paris, son of King Priam of Troy, caused the Trojan War. According to a medieval legend not found in Homer, Achilles fell in love with Priam's daughter Polyxena and, in hope of an assignation with her, was lured into a fatal ambush by Paris.

line 67   Tristan was the lover of Iseult, the wife of his uncle, King Mark of Cornwall. Their tragic affair is told in a number of medieval romances.

line 97   Ravenna, the city where Dante died in exile and is buried, was the birthplace of Francesca da Rimini, whom Dante calls by name at line 117. Around 1275, a marriage was arranged between her and the physically deformed Gianciotto Malatesta; according to Boccaccio, she was tricked into believing that his handsome younger brother Paolo was her prospective husband. Sometime between 1283 and 1286, Gianciotto found his wife and brother in an adulterous liaison and killed them both. Omitted in Francesca's highly self-serving account are the facts that Paolo was also married and that both he and Francesca had children.

line 107   Caïna, described in Canto XXXII, is the first round of Cocytus, the ninth and last circle of hell; named for Cain, it punishes sinners who betrayed family. Caïna "awaits" Gianciotto because his death did not occur until 1304.

line 127   In the Old French romance *Lancelot du Lac*, Lancelot, one of the knights of the Round Table, fell in love with Guinevere, wife of King Arthur. He lost his purity through their ensuing affair and thus became incapable of discovering the Holy Grail.

line 137   Because Gallehault, Lancelot's friend and fellow knight, acted as go-between for Lancelot and Guinevere, his name had come to signify "panderer."

Canto VI

Al tornar de la mente, che si chiuse
    dinanzi a la pietà d'i due cognati,
    che di trestizia tutto mi confuse,   3
novi tormenti e novi tormentati
    mi veggio intorno, come ch'io mi mova
    e ch'io mi volga, e come che io guati.   6
Io sono al terzo cerchio, de la piova
    etterna, maladetta, fredda e greve;
    regola e qualità mai non l'è nova.   9
Grandine grossa, acqua tinta e neve
    per l'aere tenebroso si riversa;
    pute la terra che questo riceve.   12
Cerbero, fiera crudele e diversa,
    con tre gole caninamente latra
    sovra la gente che quivi è sommersa.   15
Li occhi ha vermigli, la barba unta e atra,
    e 'l ventre largo, e unghiate le mani;
    graffia li spirti ed iscoia ed isquatra.   18
Urlar li fa la pioggia come cani;
    de l'un de' lati fanno a l'altro schermo;
    volgonsi spesso i miseri profani.   21
Quando ci scorse Cerbero, il gran vermo,
    le bocche aperse e mostrocci le sanne;
    non avea membro che tenesse fermo.   24
E 'l duca mio distese le sue spanne,
    prese la terra, e con piene le pugna
    la gittò dentro a le bramose canne.   27

Canto VI

With my sense restored, which had deserted me
 at the pitiful condition of that pair
 of kinsfolk, stunned by their sad history,   3
I start to see new torments everywhere
 and new tormented souls, wherever I range
 or turn myself, wherever I may stare.   6
I have come to the third circle, where the strange
 damned freezing rainfall endlessly pours down,
 whose quality and measure never change.   9
A mass of hail and snow and filthy brown
 water comes streaming through the murky air,
 and as it lands it putrefies the ground.   12
The weird and savage Cerberus is there,
 his three throats barking doglike at the dead
 who lie submerged and sodden everywhere.   15
With a black and greasy beard, eyes burning red,
 gross belly and huge clawlike hands, he flogs
 and flays and quarters and rips them all to shreds.   18
The constant rainfall makes them howl like dogs.
 One side provides the other one's defense
 as the wretches twist and turn inside their bogs.   21
The great worm Cerberus saw us and at once
 bared the fangs of his three mouths, and never ceased
 moving his limbs, all quivering and tense.   24
My master stretched his open hands and seized
 great clumps of earth, and quickly flung the foul
 gobbets right down the throats of the greedy beast.   27

Qual è quel cane ch'abbaiando agogna,
    e si racqueta poi che 'l pasto morde,
    ché solo a divorarlo intende e pugna,   30
cotai si fecer quelle facce lorde
    de lo demonio Cerbero, che 'ntrona
    l'anime sì, ch'esser vorrebber sorde.   33
Noi passavam su per l'ombre che adona
    la greve pioggia, e ponavam le piante
    sovra lor vanità che par persona.   36
Elle giacean per terra tutte quante,
    fuor d'una ch'a seder si levò, ratto
    ch'ella ci vide passarsi davante.   39
«O tu che se' per questo 'nferno tratto»,
    mi disse, «riconoscimi, se sai:
    tu fosti, prima ch'io disfatto, fatto».   42
E io a lui: «L'angoscia che tu hai
    forse ti tira fuor de la mia mente,
    sì che non par ch'i' ti vedessi mai.   45
Ma dimmi chi tu se' che 'n sì dolente
    loco se' messo, e hai sì fatta pena,
    che, s'altra è maggio, nulla è sì spiacente».   48
Ed elli a me: «La tua città, ch'è piena
    d'invidia sì che già trabocca il sacco,
    seco mi tenne in la vita serena.   51
Voi cittadini mi chiamaste Ciacco:
    per la dannosa colpa de la gola,
    come tu vedi, a la pioggia mi fiacco.   54
E io anima trista non son sola,
    ché tutte queste a simil pena stanno
    per simil colpa». E più non fé parola.   57
Io li rispuosi: «Ciacco, il tuo affanno
    mi pesa sì, ch'a lagrimar mi 'nvita;
    ma dimmi, se tu sai, a che verranno   60

Just as a hungry hound begins to howl
  and then grows quiet when his food is thrown
  to him, and strains at it with a low growl,   30
so too the demon Cerberus's own
  smeared faces hushed, that otherwise would roar
  to make the dead wish they were deaf as stone.   33
Where shades were flattened by the hard downpour,
  we set our steps upon the emptiness
  that still looked like the men they'd been before.   36
All of the shapes were lying in the mess,
  except for one that lifted up its head
  and sat itself upright to watch us pass.   39
"O you who are being led through hell," he said,
  "come close to me and name me if you can,
  for you were made before I was unmade."   42
"It may be that your suffering," I began,
  "has driven you from my memory, because
  you seem to me to be an unknown man.   45
But tell me who you are, set in such loss
  and desolation that, although there might
  be greater torments, none could be more gross." 48
He said: "Your native city, stuffed so tight
  with envy that the sack has overflowed,
  contained me too, back in the days of light.   51
Ciacco's the name you citizens bestowed
  on me. For my damned sin of gluttony
  I'm pounded by the rainfall's filthy load.   54
Nor am I the only one. These that you see
  pay the same price for the same sin, one and all
  forever." And he said no more to me.   57
"Ciacco," I said, "your miseries appall,
  stirring my heart till I could weep for pity.
  But tell me, if you know, what will befall   60

li cittadin de la città partita;
>s'alcun v'è giusto; e dimmi la cagione
>per che l'ha tanta discordia assalita».   63

E quelli a me: «Dopo lunga tencione
>verranno al sangue, e la parte selvaggia
>caccerà l'altra con molta offensione.   66

Poi appresso convien che questa caggia
>infra tre soli, e che l'altra sormonti
>con la forza di tal che testé piaggia.   69

Alte terrà lungo tempo le fronti,
>tenendo l'altra sotto gravi pesi,
>come che di ciò pianga o che n'aonti.   72

Giusti son due, e non vi sono intesi;
>superbia, invidia e avarizia sono
>le tre faville c'hanno i cuori accesi».   75

Qui puose fine al lagrimabil suono.
>E io a lui: «Ancor vo' che mi 'nsegni
>e che di più parlar mi facci dono.   78

Farinata e 'l Tegghiaio, che fuor sì degni,
>Iacopo Rusticucci, Arrigo e 'l Mosca
>e li altri ch'a ben far puoser li 'ngegni,   81

dimmi ove sono e fa ch'io li conosca;
>ché gran disio mi stringe di savere
>se 'l ciel li addolcia o lo 'nferno li attosca».   84

E quelli: «Ei son tra l'anime più nere;
>diverse colpe giù li grava al fondo:
>se tanto scendi, là i potrai vedere.   87

Ma quando tu sarai nel dolce mondo,
>priegoti ch'a la mente altrui mi rechi:
>più non ti dico e più non ti rispondo».   90

Li diritti occhi torse allora in biechi;
>guardommi un poco e poi chinò la testa:
>cadde con essa a par de li altri ciechi.   93

the citizens of our divided city,
> and if there be one just man, and why the knife
> of discord has so rent its soul already." 63
He answered: "Blood will follow after strife,
> the rustic sect will drive the other one
> out of the city, with much loss of life. 66
Before the third full circle of the sun
> the vanquished will turn vanquishers. Through dint
> of one upon the fence, this will be done. 69
Their standard will be long in the ascent.
> They'll oppress the others, who will not be freed
> however much they bristle and lament. 72
Two men are just, but no one pays them heed.
> Those people's hearts are set aflame by three
> sparks only—envy, arrogance, and greed." 75
Thus far he spoke his doleful prophecy.
> I told him: "I would hear more. Once again
> with the great gift of your words enlighten me. 78
Of Tegghiaio and Farinata, worthy men,
> Arrigo, Mosca, Rusticucci, as well
> as many another benevolent citizen, 81
I want to hear whatever you can tell,
> for I truly wish to discover if they share
> the honey of heaven or taste the venom of hell." 84
"Their separate sins," he said, "have dragged them where
> some of the very blackest spirits stay.
> Keep going down and you will see them there. 87
But when you see the sweet world again, I pray
> that you bring me to men's memory once more.
> Nothing else will I answer, nothing will I say." 90
His eyes, that had looked so steadily, now wore
> a squint. He stared at me, then bent his head
> and lay down with the other blind ones as before. 93

E 'l duca disse a me: «Più non si desta
    di qua dal suon de l'angelica tromba,
    quando verrà la nimica podesta: 96
ciascun rivederà la trista tomba,
    ripiglierà sua carne e sua figura,
    udirà quel ch'in etterno rimbomba».   99
Sì trapassammo per sozza mistura
    de l'ombre e de la pioggia, a passi lenti,
    toccando un poco la vita futura;   102
per ch'io dissi: «Maestro, esti tormenti
    cresterann' ei dopo la gran sentenza,
    o fier minori, o saran sì cocenti?».   105
Ed elli a me: «Ritorna a tua scïenza,
    che vuol, quanto la cosa è più perfetta,
    più senta il bene, e così la doglienza.   108
Tutto che questa gente maladetta
    in vera perfezion già mai non vada,
    di là più che di qua essere aspetta».   111
Noi aggirammo a tondo quella strada,
    parlando più assai ch'i' non ridico;
    venimmo al punto dove si digrada: 114
quivi trovammo Pluto, il gran nemico.

"He will not stir again," my leader said,
    "until the angelic trump, when he will see
    that angry power that all the wicked dread.   96

Each will return to his sad tomb to be
    united with his substance and his form
    and hear the sounding of eternity."   99

Thus we moved slowly through the sodden scum,
    the filthy mix of spirits and of rain,
    talking a little of the life to come.   102

I asked him: "Master, will this burning pain
    be even greater come the judgment day,
    or stay just as it is, or will it wane?"   105

And he replied: "What does your science say?
    The more a thing approaches to perfection,
    more pleasure or more pain will come its way.   108

Because these people suffer God's rejection,
    they never can be perfect, but are meant
    in future to be moved in that direction."   111

Along the circle of the path we went,
    speaking of more than I repeat, till we
    arrived at where it started its descent.   114

There we met Plutus, the great enemy.

Notes

line 13   In classical mythology, Cerberus, the fierce three-headed dog, guards the entrance to Hades. In Book VI of the *Aeneid*, the Sybil distracts him with honeyed cake, allowing the living Aeneas to elude his vigilance. The mixture of human attributes with canine ones is Dante's invention.

line 52   Attempts have been made to identify this character with a poet called Ciacco dell'Anguillaia, but there is nothing to support the connection beyond the coincidence of names. The text suggests that Ciacco was a nickname, one he did not especially enjoy. Since *ciacco* connotes "pig" or "hog," it is tempting to assume that he was so called because of his gluttony, but it is not clear whether the word had this meaning before Dante's use of it.

lines 64–75   This is the first of the prophecies made by condemned souls at various points in the poem. Ciacco predicts events that were still in the future in April 1300, but that occurred, of course, before the writing of the *Inferno.* After driving the Ghibellines out of Florence in 1289, the Guelph party had split into rival factions, the White ("the rustic sect," to which Dante belonged, so called because its leaders, the Cerchi family, were from outside the city) and the Black ("the other one"); their rivalry flared into open warfare on May 1, 1300, and the Blacks were expelled the following year. The temporizer of line 69 is almost certainly the reviled Pope Boniface VIII, whose support of the Blacks enabled them to retake the city in 1302, sending the Whites into exile— an exile which for Dante would prove permanent. The identities of the two just men, who are in any event insufficient for the city's salvation, have not been positively established.

lines 79–87   As Ciacco suggests he will, Dante subsequently encounters Farinata degli Uberti (Canto X, line 32), Tegghiaio Aldobrandi and Jacopo Rusticucci (Canto XVI, lines 40–45), and Mosca dei Lamberti (Canto XXVIII, line 106). Oddly, Arrigo, who has never been positively identified, makes no appearance in the *Inferno* and is not mentioned again.

line 106   The science in question is the philosophy of Aristotle, in his *De anima,* and the commentary on it by Thomas Aquinas in the *Summa theologica.*

line 115   The reference is either to Pluto, the god of the underworld (also known as Hades), or to Plutus, the god of wealth—or possibly to both, since even in classical times they were often thought of in terms of one another. Obviously, in Dantean terms either one would qualify as a "great enemy" of humanity.

Canto VII

«*Pape Satàn, pape Satàn aleppe!*»,

    cominciò Pluto con la voce chioccia;

    e quel savio gentil, che tutto seppe,   3

disse per confortarmi: «Non ti noccia

    la tua paura; ché, poder ch'elli abbia,

    non ci torrà lo scender questa roccia».   6

Poi si rivolse a quella 'nfiata labbia,

    e disse: «Taci, maladetto lupo!

    consuma dentro te con la tua rabbia.   9

Non è sanza cagion l'andare al cupo:

    vuolsi ne l'alto, là dove Michele

    fé la vendetta del superbo strupo».   12

Quali dal vento le gonfiate vele

    caggiono avvolte, poi che l'alber fiacca,

    tal cadde a terra la fiera crudele.   15

Così scendemmo ne la quarta lacca,

    pigliando più de la dolente ripa

    che 'l mal de l'universo tutto insacca.   18

Ahi giustizia di Dio! tante chi stipa

    nove travaglie e pene quant' io viddi?

    e perché nostra colpa sì ne scipa?   21

Come fa l'onda là sovra Cariddi,

    che si frange con quella in cui s'intoppa,

    così convien che qui la gente riddi.   24

Qui vid' i' gente più ch'altrove troppa,

    e d'una parte e d'altra, con grand' urli,

    voltando pesi per forza di poppa.   27

Canto VII

"Pape Satàn, pape Satàn aleppe!"
    Plutus began to cry with a harsh cluck.
    That gentle and all-knowing sage then kept me   3
from losing heart: "Do not let terror block
    your purpose. Whatever power he has, he will
    never prevent our climbing down this rock."   6
And then he said: "Acc: Accuséd wolf, be still!"
    as he turned to face that bloated countenance.
    "Aim your rage inward and eat up your fill.   9
Not without reason do we now advance
    to the depths. It is willed on high, in the lofty skies
    where Michael avenged the arrogant offense."   12
As sails that are swollen when the winds arise
    collapse into a heap when the mast is cracked,
    so the cruel beast collapsed before our eyes.   15
Going down to the fourth hollow now, we tracked
    further along that mournful shore where all
    the evil of the universe is sacked.   18
Justice of God above! Who stuffs it full
    with these new pains and punishments? How can
    we let guilt waste us so? As with the pull   21
of waves that swirl above Charybdis, when
    they crash with counterwaves, forevermore
    these souls must dance their turn and turn again.   24
Now greater than what I had seen before
    were the numbers of the damned on either side,
    chests straining to push great weights, with a mighty roar.   27

Percotëansi 'ncontro; e poscia pur lì
   si rivolgea ciascun, voltando a retro,
   gridando: «Perché tieni?» e «Perché burli?».   30
Così tornavan per lo cerchio tetro
   da ogne mano a l'opposito punto,
   gridandosi anche loro ontoso metro;   33
poi si volgea ciascun, quand' era giunto,
   per lo suo mezzo cerchio a l'altra giostra.
   E io, ch'avea lo cor quasi compunto,   36
dissi: «Maestro mio, or mi dimostra
   che gente è questa, e se tutti fuor cherci
   questi chercuti a la sinistra nostra».   39
Ed elli a me: «Tutti quanti fuor guerci
   sì de la mente in la vita primaia,
   che con misura nullo spendio ferci.   42
Assai la voce lor chiaro l'abbaia,
   quando vegnono a' due punti del cerchio
   dove colpa contraria li dispaia.   45
Questi fuor cherci, che non han coperchio
   piloso al capo, e papi e cardinali,
   in cui usa avarizia il suo soperchio».   48
E io: «Maestro, tra questi cotali
   dovre' io ben riconoscere alcuni
   che furo immondi di cotesti mali».   51
Ed elli a me: «Vano pensiero aduni:
   la sconoscente vita che i fé sozzi,
   ad ogne conoscenza or li fa bruni.   54
In etterno verranno a li due cozzi:
   questi resurgeranno del sepulcro
   col pugno chiuso, e questi coi crin mozzi.   57
Mal dare e mal tener lo mondo pulcro
   ha tolto loro, e posti a questa zuffa:
   qual ella sia, parole non ci appulcro.   60

They all would come together and collide,

    then each wheeled round and rolled his weight along.

      "Why pinch it?" and "Why throw it away?" they cried.   30

Around the somber circle moved the throng

    till their previous positions were reversed,

      rebuking each other with their scornful song.   33

When each arrived where he had been at first,

    he retraced his semicircle to joust again.

      Feeling as if my heart were about to burst,   36

"Master, who are these people?" I said then.

    "The tonsured ones amassed on our left side,

      is it possible they all were clergymen?"   39

"When they were in the first life," he replied,

    "because they all had squinting intellects,

      in money matters moderation died.   42

Their howling clearly shows you the effects,

    when they come to the two points of the circle where

      their opposite sins divide them into sects.   45

The ones with heads that lack a hood of hair

    were priests and cardinals and popes. With ease

      avarice finds its full expression there."   48

"Master," I said, "among such souls as these

    must be a few that I would recognize,

      who were all polluted by this same disease."   51

And he: "It would be an empty enterprise.

    The filthy, undiscerning life they led

      makes their features indiscernible to our eyes.   54

Forever they will collide and crash. These dead

    will leave the grave with fists squeezed rigidly,

      and each of those will rise with a close-cropped head.   57

Wasting and hoarding, they lost eternity

    in the lovely world for this scuffle and this strife.

      This picture needs no prettied words from me.   60

Or puoi, figliuol, veder la corta buffa
    d'i ben che son commessi a la fortuna,
      per che l'umana gente si rabbuffa;   63
ché tutto l'oro ch'è sotto la luna
    e che già fu, di quest' anime stanche
      non poterebbe farne posare una».   66
«Maestro mio», diss' io, «or mi dì anche:
    questa fortuna di che tu mi tocche,
      che è, che i ben del mondo ha sì tra branche?».   69
E quelli a me: «Oh creature sciocche,
    quanta ignoranza è quella che v'offende!
      Or vo' che tu mia sentenza ne 'mbocche.   72
Colui lo cui saver tutto trascende,
    fece li cieli e diè lor chi conduce
      sì, ch'ogne parte ad ogne parte splende,   75
distribuendo igualmente la luce.
    Similemente a li splendor mondani
      ordinò general ministra e duce   78
che permutasse a tempo li ben vani
    di gente in gente e d'uno in altro sangue,
      oltre la difension d'i senni umani;   81
per ch'una gente impera e l'altra langue,
    seguendo lo giudicio di costei,
      che è occulto come in erba l'angue.   84
Vostro saver non ha contasto a lei:
    questa provede, giudica, e persegue
      suo regno come il loro li altri dèi.   87
Le sue permutazion non hanno triegue:
    necessità la fa esser veloce;
      sì spesso vien chi vicenda consegue.   90
Quest' è colei ch'è tanto posta in croce
    pur da color che le dovrien dar lode,
      dandole biasmo a torto e mala voce;   93

Here you see, my son, the brief ridiculous life
      of those goods in Fortune's keeping, for which the race
      of men compete and squabble and connive.   63
Not all the gold beneath the moon's bright face,
      or that ever was, could bring rest to as much as
      one of the weary spirits in this place."   66
"Of this Fortune, upon whom your discourse touches,
      Master, please tell me more" was my response.
      "Who is she, who has the world's goods in her clutches?"   69
"O foolish creatures, what vast ignorance
      oppresses you," he said. "Let me impart
      my judgment, so you may take it in at once.   72
He whose wisdom transcends all, at the very start
      made the heavens and gave guides to lead them right,
      so that every part would shine to every part,   75
thus equally distributing the light.
      For worldly splendors he likewise put in place
      a general guide and minister who might   78
transfer those empty goods through time and place,
      beyond all human wit to intervene,
      from blood to blood, from one to another race.   81
One state grows fat with power, another grows lean,
      according to her judgments as she deigns,
      which like a snake in the grass cannot be seen.   84
Your knowledge cannot counter her. She reigns,
      providing, judging, making calculations,
      as do the other gods in their domains.   87
No truce may interrupt her permutations.
      Necessity demands that she not pause.
      Man's lot is one of constant variations.   90
And this is she whom men put on the cross.
      Even the ones who ought to hold her dear
      revile her name and blame her without cause.   93

ma ella s'è beata e ciò non ode:

    con l'altre prime creature lieta

    volve sua spera e beata si gode.   96

Or discendiamo omai a maggior pieta;

    già ogne stella cade che saliva

    quand' io mi mossi, e 'l troppo star si vieta».   99

Noi ricidemmo il cerchio a l'altra riva

    sovr' una fonte che bolle e riversa

    per un fossato che da lei deriva.   102

L'acqua era buia assai più che persa;

    e noi, in compagnia de l'onde bige,

    intrammo giù per una via diversa.   105

In la palude va c'ha nome Stige

    questo tristo ruscel, quand' è disceso

    al piè de le maligne piagge grige.   108

E io, che di mirare stava inteso,

    vidi genti fangose in quel pantano,

    ignude tutte, con sembiante offeso.   111

Queste si percotean non pur con mano,

    ma con la testa e col petto e coi piedi,

    troncandosi co' denti a brano a brano.   114

Lo buon maestro disse: «Figlio, or vedi

    l'anime di color cui vinse l'ira;

    e anche vo' che tu per certo credi   117

che sotto l'acqua è gente che sospira,

    e fanno pullular quest' acqua al summo,

    come l'occhio ti dice, u' che s'aggira.   120

Fitti nel limo dicon: "Tristi fummo

    ne l'aere dolce che dal sol s'allegra,

    portando dentro accidïoso fummo: 123

or ci attristiam ne la belletta negra".

    Quest' inno si gorgoglian ne la strozza,

    ché dir nol posson con parola integra».   126

But she is blesséd and she does not hear.
    With the other primal creatures happily
    she rejoices in her bliss and turns her sphere.   96
Now we go down to greater misery.
    The stars that rose when I set out for you
    have now begun to sink, and by decree   99
we must not tarry." We crossed the circle to
    the other shore, above a boiling spring
    that spilled into a ditch it had cut through.   102
Darker than perse was the water. Following
    the downward track where the black current went,
    we found a strange road for our journeying.   105
When this sad stream completes its long descent
    at the base of the malign gray slopes, its path
    ends in the Stygian marsh, where I stared, intent,   108
at the scene before me. In that filthy bath
    was a crowd of muddy people, filling it,
    all naked, all with faces full of wrath.   111
They hit each other with their fists, and hit
    each other with both feet, and chest, and head,
    and chewed each other to pieces bit by bit.   114
"My son, you see now," my good master said,
    "the souls that anger overwhelmed, and I
    would have you know for certain that more dead   117
are down there, underwater, where they sigh
    and make the surface bubble with their breath,
    as you can tell wherever you turn your eye.   120
Set in the slime, they say: 'We were sullen, with
    no pleasure in the sweet, sun-gladdened air,
    carrying in our souls the fumes of sloth.   123
Now we are sullen in this black ooze'—where
    they hymn this in their throats with a gurgling sound
    because they cannot form the words down there."   126

Così girammo de la lorda pozza
    grand' arco tra la ripa secca e 'l mézzo,
    con li occhi vòlti a chi del fango ingozza.   129
Venimmo al piè d'una torre al da sezzo.

Between the marsh and dry shore, we walked round

    the scummy pool, with our eyes turned toward the place

    where the souls were gulping mud, and crossed the ground   129

till we arrived at a tall tower's base.

Notes

line 1	Discussion of the meaning of this line has been extensive and wide-ranging. Some claim that it is mere gibberish, but that interpretation seems implausible: the third line suggests that Virgil understands what Plutus is saying, and the terms Plutus uses do resemble recognizable words. The most common interpretation is that Plutus is invoking Satan as father or pope. With *aleppe*, which suggests the Hebrew *aleph*, he might be either claiming the primacy of Satan or crying out a variation on *alas*.
line 12	Lucifer's rebellion against God led to the expulsion of the rebel angels from heaven by the archangel Michael.
line 22	In Book XII of the *Odyssey*, Odysseus must navigate around the whirlpool Charybdis, located in the Strait of Messina. Dante would have been more familiar with Charybdis through references in Ovid, Lucan, and the *Aeneid*.
line 38	The placement of the avaricious on the left side suggests that their sin is worse than that of their opposites, the spendthrifts.
lines 98–99	Virgil's words indicate that it is now past midnight.

Canto VIII

Io dico, seguitando, ch'assai prima
    che noi fossimo al piè de l'alta torre,
    li occhi nostri n'andar suso a la cima   3
per due fiammette che i vedemmo porre,
    e un'altra da lungi render cenno,
    tanto ch'a pena il potea l'occhio tòrre.   6
E io mi volsi al mar di tutto 'l senno;
    dissi: «Questo che dice? e che risponde
    quell' altro foco? e chi son quei che 'l fenno?».   9
Ed elli a me: «Su per le sucide onde
    già scorgere puoi quello che s'aspetta,
    se 'l fummo del pantan nol ti nasconde».   12
Corda non pinse mai da sé saetta
    che sì corresse via per l'aere snella,
    com' io vidi una nave piccioletta   15
venir per l'acqua verso noi in quella,
    sotto 'l governo d'un sol galeoto,
    che gridava: «Or se' giunta, anima fella!».   18
«Flegïàs, Flegïàs, tu gridi a vòto»,
    disse lo mio segnore, «a questa volta:
    più non ci avrai che sol passando il loto».   21
Qual è colui che grande inganno ascolta
    che li sia fatto, e poi se ne rammarca,
    fecesi Flegïàs ne l'ira accolta.   24
Lo duca mio discese ne la barca,
    e poi mi fece intrare appresso lui;
    e sol quand' io fui dentro parve carca.   27

Canto VIII

I say, continuing, before our stop
    at the base of that tall tower, our eyes were turned
    to something gleaming at its very top.   3
There at the summit two small fires burned
    and another signaled back from far away,
    so distant it could barely be discerned.   6
I turned to the sea of all wisdom: "What does it say,
    that flame? And what is meant by the answering light?
    And the ones who lit these fires, who are they?"   9
He said: "What they await is heading right
    across the foul waves already, as you can see
    unless the marsh's fumes hide it from sight."   12
Never did arrow move so rapidly,
    shot whistling through the air from a bowman's string,
    as did a boat that I saw suddenly,   15
coming straight toward where we waited, hastening
    with only a lone rower at the oar,
    who called: "I have you now, accurséd thing!"   18
"Phlegyas, Phlegyas, I fear this time you roar
    for nothing," my master said. "You have us as long
    as it will take to reach the other shore."   21
Like someone who has heard that a great wrong
    was done to him, and smolders helplessly,
    so Phlegyas glared at us, with all his strong   24
anger held back. My leader instructed me
    to follow him in the boat, and I complied.
    Only when I was aboard did it seem to be   27

Tosto che 'l duca e io nel legno fui,
  segando se ne va l'antica prora
  de l'acqua più che non suol con altrui.   30

Mentre noi corravam la morta gora,
  dinanzi mi si fece un pien di fango,
  e disse: «Chi se' tu che vieni anzi ora?».   33

E io a lui: «S'i' vegno, non rimango;
  ma tu chi se', che sì se' fatto brutto?».
  Rispuose: «Vedi che son un che piango».   36

E io a lui: «Con piangere e con lutto,
  spirito maladetto, ti rimani;
  ch'i' ti conosco, ancor sie lordo tutto».   39

Allor distese al legno ambo le mani;
  per che 'l maestro accorto lo sospinse,
  dicendo: «Via costà con li altri cani!».   42

Lo collo poi con le braccia mi cinse;
  basciommi 'l volto e disse: «Alma sdegnosa,
  benedetta colei che 'n te s'incinse!   45

Quei fu al mondo persona orgogliosa;
  bontà non è che sua memoria fregi:
  così s'è l'ombra sua qui furïosa.   48

Quanti si tegnon or là sù gran regi
  che qui staranno come porci in brago,
  di sé lasciando orribili dispregi!».   51

E io: «Maestro, molto sarei vago
  di vederlo attuffare in questa broda
  prima che noi uscissimo del lago».   54

Ed elli a me: «Avante che la proda
  ti si lasci veder, tu sarai sazio:
  di tal disïo convien che tu goda».   57

Dopo ciò poco vid' io quello strazio
  far di costui a le fangose genti,
  che Dio ancor ne lodo e ne ringrazio.   60

carrying weight. When we were both inside,
    the ancient prow moved forward, cutting through
    the water more deeply than when others ride.   30
We slipped through that dead channel. "Who are you,"
    cried a muddy shape that lifted up its head,
    "who come down here before your time is due?"   33
"If I come, it is not to stay here with the dead.
    But who are you, so covered with this mess?"
    "You see that I am one who weeps," he said.   36
And I: "In weeping and in wretchedness
    may you remain, damned soul, for even when
    you are bathed in filth, I know you nonetheless."   39
He stretched his two hands toward the boat just then,
    but my wary master gave him a sharp thrust,
    saying: "Back down with the other dogs again!"   42
Then he put his arms around my neck and kissed
    my face. "Indignant soul," he said to me,
    "the mother who carried you is truly blest!   45
In the world he was arrogant. To his memory
    not a scrap of goodness clings, so his spirit stays
    down in the mire seething furiously.   48
How many who think themselves great kings these days
    will lie like pigs in the muck here, and they will
    leave behind names of horrible dispraise."   51
"Master," I said to him, "while we are still
    on the lake, it would please me greatly if I might
    see him dipped down once more into the swill."   54
And he: "Before the shore has come in sight,
    you will have satisfaction straightaway.
    To grant a wish like that is only right."   57
And soon the muddy mob began to flay
    the shade so wildly that for what I saw
    I still give thanks and praise God to this day.   60

Tutti gridavano: «A Filippo Argenti!»;
   e 'l fiorentino spirito bizzarro
   in sé medesmo si volvea co' denti.   63

Quivi il lasciammo, che più non ne narro;
   ma ne l'orecchie mi percosse un duolo,
   per ch'io avante l'occhio intento sbarro.   66

Lo buon maestro disse: «Omai, figliuolo,
   s'appressa la città c'ha nome Dite,
   coi gravi cittadin, col grande stuolo».   69

E io: «Maestro, già le sue meschite
   là entro certe ne la valle cerno,
   vermiglie come se di foco uscite   72

fossero». Ed ei mi disse: «Il foco etterno
   ch'entro l'affoca le dimostra rosse,
   come tu vedi in questo basso inferno».   75

Noi pur giugnemmo dentro a l'alte fosse
   che vallan quella terra sconsolata:
   le mura mi parean che ferro fosse.   78

Non sanza prima far grande aggirata,
   venimmo in parte dove il nocchier forte
   «Usciteci», gridò: «qui è l'intrata».   81

Io vidi più di mille in su le porte
   da ciel piovuti, che stizzosamente
   dicean: «Chi è costui che sanza morte   84

va per lo regno de la morta gente?».
   E 'l savio mio maestro fece segno
   di voler lor parlar segretamente.   87

Allor chiusero un poco il gran disdegno
   e disser: «Vien tu solo, e quei sen vada
   che sì ardito intrò per questo regno.   90

Sol si ritorni per la folle strada:
   pruovi, se sa; ché tu qui rimarrai,
   che li ha' iscorta sì buia contrada».   93

"Let's get Filippo Argenti!" came the raw
    cry of the crowd, and the raging Florentine
    turned his teeth upon himself and began to gnaw.   63
Enough of him. He was no longer seen.
    But my ears were hit with a wave of lamentation
    and I strained my eyes to see what it might mean.   66
Said my guide: "My son, we are nearing the location
    of the city whose name is Dis, inhabited
    by a huge brigade and a somber population."   69
"Now, master, I can clearly see," I said,
    "there in the valley, all its mosques aglow
    as if taken from the furnace, fiery red."   72
And he: "They look that way because they show
    the flame that burns inside them eternally
    here in the part of hell that lies below."   75
We had reached the deep moats on the periphery
    of that disconsolate city with its immense
    walls made of iron, as it seemed to me.   78
When we had sailed a broad circumference,
    we came to a place where I heard the boatman shout:
    "Here's the gate! Get out!" Before the battlements   81
more than a thousand of those who had been cast out
    and rained from heaven, looked at us and cried:
    "Who is this man who dares to traipse about   84
through the kingdom of the dead without having died?"
    And my wise master made a sign to say
    that it was his wish to speak with them aside.   87
They tempered their scorn a bit: "Well, come you may,
    but come alone. As for him who has the face
    to breach this kingdom, let him go away.   90
All alone, if he can do it, let him retrace
    his fool's road. You'll stay here, you who have been
    his guide on his dark pathway to this place."   93

Pensa, lettor, se io mi sconfortai

nel suon de le parole maladette,

ché non credetti ritornarci mai.   96

«O caro duca mio, che più di sette

volte m'hai sicurtà renduta e tratto

d'alto periglio che 'ncontra mi stette,   99

non mi lasciar», diss' io, «così disfatto;

e se 'l passar più oltre ci è negato,

ritroviam l'orme nostre insieme ratto».   102

E quel segnor che lì m'avea menato,

mi disse: «Non temer; ché 'l nostro passo

non ci può tòrre alcun: da tal n'è dato.   105

Ma qui m'attendi, e lo spirito lasso

conforta e ciba di speranza buona,

ch'i' non ti lascerò nel mondo basso».   108

Così sen va, e quivi m'abbandona

lo dolce padre, e io rimagno in forse,

che sì e no nel capo mi tenciona.   111

Udir non potti quello ch'a lor porse;

ma ei non stette là con essi guari,

che ciascun dentro a pruova si ricorse.   114

Chiuser le porte que' nostri avversari

nel petto al mio segnor, che fuor rimase

e rivolsesi a me con passi rari.   117

Li occhi a la terra e le ciglia avea rase

d'ogne baldanza, e dicea ne' sospiri:

«Chi m'ha negate le dolenti case!».   120

E a me disse: «Tu, perch' io m'adiri,

non sbigottir, ch'io vincerò la prova,

qual ch'a la difension dentro s'aggiri.   123

Questa lor tracotanza non è nova;

ché già l'usaro a men segreta porta,

la qual sanza serrame ancor si trova.   126

Reader, decide for yourself if I did not then
    lose heart at what those demons shouted, for
    I thought I would never come back here again.   96
"O my dear leader, seven times and more,"
    I said, "you have restored my confidence
    and drawn me back from danger. I implore   99
that you not leave me here with no defense.
    And if our going forward is denied,
    then side by side let us go back at once."   102
The lord who had brought me to that place replied:
    "Do not be afraid. No one can interfere
    with our progress, when its warrant is supplied   105
by such a one. You will await me here.
    Let your weary soul be comforted and fed
    with hope. I will not leave you, never fear,   108
alone in the low world." So the sweet father said,
    and I remained in doubt while he walked away,
    with yes and no contending in my head.   111
I could not overhear what he had to say,
    but only a moment seemed to pass before
    they were fighting to get back inside, where they,   114
our enemies, immediately shut the door
    against my master, slamming it in his face.
    Then with slow steps he walked toward me once more.   117
He sighed, with eyes cast down, with every trace
    of self-assertion shriveled from his brow:
    "Who dares deny me sorrow's dwelling place?"   120
And to me: "Though I am vexed, do not allow
    your soul to falter, for I shall win through,
    however they may plot to stop us now.   123
This arrogance of theirs is nothing new.
    It was flaunted once at a less secret gate,
    unbolted despite all that they could do.   126

Sovr' essa vedestù la scritta morta:

    e già di qua da lei discende l'erta,

    passando per li cerchi sanza scorta,   129

tal che per lui ne fia la terra aperta».

You read its deadly inscription. Coming straight
    past it and through the circles without a guide,
    there is one who is on his way to where we wait,   129
by whom the city will be opened wide."

Notes

line 1   From Boccaccio in the fourteenth century to Giorgio Padoan (*Il lungo cammino del "Poema sacro": studi danteschi,* Florence) in 1993, the opening of this canto has led commentators to speculate that some time elapsed between the writing of the first seven cantos and a resumption at this point; such arguments have not drawn much support. Dante does, however, pursue an unusual narrative strategy here, an extended flashback until line 80, when Virgil and Dante arrive at the tower mentioned in the last line of Canto VII.

line 19   Phlegyas is here the boatman of the river Styx. In classical mythology, he was the son of the war god Ares and a human mother, and was the father of Coronis, who was seduced by Apollo. To avenge his daughter, Phlegyas burned the temple of Apollo at Delphi, for which the god killed him and condemned him to punishment in the underworld. As a shade, he appears briefly in Book VI of the *Aeneid,* warning others against such rashness toward the gods. John Ciardi notes: "Dante's choice of a ferryman is especially apt. Phlegyas is the link between the Wrathful (to whom his paternity relates him) and the Rebellious Angels who menaced God (as he menaced Apollo)" (*The Inferno,* Rutgers, 1954).

line 61   Filippo de Cavicciuoli was a member of the Adimari family, who were of the Black faction of the Guelphs (see note to Canto VI, lines 64–75). Of great wealth and short temper, he was supposedly called "Argenti" because he had his horse shod with silver. According to early accounts, his brother came into possession of some of Dante's property after the poet's exile from Florence.

lines 68–69   Dis was another name for Pluto, the Roman god of the underworld, equivalent to the Greek Hades, and by further equivalence another name for Lucifer or Satan. The "huge brigade" are the angels who followed Lucifer in his rebellion against God and were "cast out / and rained from heaven" (lines 82–83).

line 71   The mosques suggest the medieval Christian view of Islam as a heresy, a rebellion against God. Also, as Bernard Lewis says of medieval and

Renaissance references to Islam: "In poetry and polemic, in history and literature, they reflect the consciousness of a Christian Europe besieged and threatened by a mighty and expanding Islamic world, a Europe that in a sense was defined and delimited by the frontiers of Muslim power in the east, the southeast, and the south" (*Cultures in Conflict*, Oxford, 1995).

line 96   "Here" is the earth, where Dante is writing his account.

lines 125–27 The "less secret gate" is the entrance to hell described at the beginning of Canto III. Christ forced open the outer portal in his harrowing of hell (see note to Canto IV, lines 52–63), despite the opposition of Satan and his followers. The "inscription" is lines 1–9 of Canto III.

Canto IX

Quel color che viltà di fuor mi pinse
    veggendo il duca mio tornare in volta,
    più tosto dentro il suo novo ristrinse.   3
Attento si fermò com' uom ch'ascolta;
    ché l'occhio nol potea menare a lunga
    per l'aere nero e per la nebbia folta.   6
«Pur a noi converrà vincer la punga»,
    cominciò el, «se non . . . Tal ne s'offerse.
    Oh quanto tarda a me ch'altri qui giunga!».   9
I' vidi ben sì com' ei ricoperse
    lo cominciar con l'altro che poi venne,
    che fur parole a le prime diverse;   12
ma nondimen paura il suo dir dienne,
    perch' io traeva la parola tronca
    forse a peggior sentenzia che non tenne.   15
«In questo fondo de la trista conca
    discende mai alcun del primo grado,
    che sol per pena ha la speranza cionca?».   18
Questa question fec' io; e quei «Di rado
    incontra», mi rispuose, «che di noi
    faccia il cammino alcun per qual io vado.   21
Ver è ch'altra fïata qua giù fui,
    congiurato da quella Eritón cruda
    che richiamava l'ombre a' corpi sui.   24
Di poco era di me la carne nuda,
    ch'ella mi fece intrar dentr' a quel muro,
    per trarne un spirto del cerchio di Giuda.   27

Canto IX

Seeing the color cowardice gave to me,
      painting my face when I saw my guide turn back,
      he repressed his own new color instantly.   3
He stood like someone listening, for lack
      of light enough to let his vision cross
      the thick fog and the air that was nearly black.   6
"Still, we were meant to be victorious,
      or else . . . ," he said. "She promised us such aid!
      How long it seems till someone comes to us."   9
I clearly saw how his last words overlaid
      the first part of his speech, how their intent
      reversed the first impression he had made.   12
But the phrase that he had left unfinished sent
      a new fear through me as my mind supplied
      more dire conclusions than he might have meant.   15
"Does anyone ever come down," I inquired,
      "to this dismal pit from the first circle, where
      the only punishment is hope denied?"   18
"Indeed," he said, "the instances are rare
      that a journey like this one of mine has been
      taken by anyone who dwells up there.   21
I myself have come here once before. It was when
      I was conjured by cruel Erichtho, who designed
      to join souls to their bodies once again.   24
When newly stripped of my flesh, I was assigned
      at her command to breach that wall and bring
      a soul from the place where Judas is confined,   27

Quell' è 'l più basso loco e 'l più oscuro,
    e 'l più lontan dal ciel che tutto gira:
    ben so 'l cammin; però ti fa sicuro.   30
Questa palude che 'l gran puzzo spira
    cigne dintorno la città dolente,
    u' non potemo intrare omai sanz' ira».   33
E altro disse, ma non l'ho a mente;
    però che l'occhio m'avea tutto tratto
    ver' l'alta torre a la cima rovente,   36
dove in un punto furon dritte ratto
    tre furïe infernal di sangue tinte,
    che membra feminine avieno e atto,   39
e con idre verdissime eran cinte;
    serpentelli e ceraste avien per crine,
    onde le fiere tempie erano avvinte.   42
E quei, che ben conobbe le meschine
    de la regina de l'etterno pianto,
    «Guarda», mi disse, «le feroci Erine.   45
Quest' è Megera dal sinistro canto;
    quella che piange dal destro è Aletto;
    Tesifón è nel mezzo»; e tacque a tanto.   48
Con l'unghie si fendea ciascuna il petto;
    battiensi a palme e gridavan sì alto,
    ch'i' mi strinsi al poeta per sospetto.   51
«Vegna Medusa: sì 'l farem di smalto»,
    dicevan tutte riguardando in giuso;
    «mal non vengiammo in Tesëo l'assalto».   54
«Volgiti 'n dietro e tien lo viso chiuso;
    ché se 'l Gorgón si mostra e tu 'l vedessi,
    nulla sarebbe di tornar mai suso».   57
Così disse 'l maestro; ed elli stessi
    mi volse, e non si tenne a le mie mani,
    che con le sue ancor non mi chiudessi.   60

the lowest, darkest, and most distant ring
     from the all-encircling heaven. I know this ground.
     Fear not, I know the road we are following.   30
This powerfully reeking marsh runs all around
     the dolorous city, where we cannot go
     without provoking wrath." I heard the sound   33
of further words, and yet I do not know
     what he said next, because my eyes were steered
     to the summit of the high tower, with its glow,   36
for on that spot had suddenly appeared
     three hellish Furies, who in shape and mien
     resembled women, but they were blood-smeared   39
and girdled with hydras of the deepest green.
     They had horned vipers and small snakes for hair,
     round their fierce temples. Handmaids of the queen   42
of eternal lamentation, all three were
     well known to him who turned and said to me:
     "Behold the ferocious Erinyes up there.   45
That is Megaera on the left, and she
     is Alecto who is wailing on the right.
     The one in the center is Tisiphone."   48
They were clawing at their breasts with all their might,
     beating themselves and shrieking. I tried to hold
     as close as I could to the poet in my fright.   51
"Now let Medusa come! He'll be stone cold
     when she gets done!" they cried. "It was a poor
     revenge we took when Theseus was so bold!"   54
"Turn round and keep your eyes shut tight! Be sure
     that if the Gorgon shows herself to you
     and you look at her, you will see the world no more!"   57
So my master cried, and with his own hands too
     he covered my eyes when he had turned me round,
     as if not trusting what my hands could do.   60

O voi ch'avete li 'ntelletti sani,
    mirate la dottrina che s'asconde
    sotto 'l velame de li versi strani.   63
E già venìa su per le torbide onde
    un fracasso d'un suon, pien di spavento,
    per cui tremavano amendue le sponde,   66
non altrimenti fatto che d'un vento
    impetüoso per li avversi ardori,
    che fier la selva e sanz' alcun rattento   69
li rami schianta, abbatte e porta fori;
    dinanzi polveroso va superbo,
    e fa fuggir le fiere e li pastori.   72
Li occhi mi sciolse e disse: «Or drizza il nerbo
    del viso su per quella schiuma antica
    per indi ove quel fummo è più acerbo».   75
Come le rane innanzi a la nimica
    biscia per l'acqua si dileguan tutte,
    fin ch'a la terra ciascuna s'abbica,   78
vid' io più di mille anime distrutte
    fuggir così dinanzi ad un ch'al passo
    passava Stige con le piante asciutte.   81
Dal volto rimovea quell' aere grasso,
    menando la sinistra innanzi spesso;
    e sol di quell' angoscia parea lasso.   84
Ben m'accorsi ch'elli era da ciel messo,
    e volsimi al maestro; e quei fé segno
    ch'i' stessi queto ed inchinassi ad esso.   87
Ahi quanto mi parea pien di disdegno!
    Venne a la porta e con una verghetta
    l'aperse, che non v'ebbe alcun ritegno.   90
«O cacciati del ciel, gente dispetta»,
    cominciò elli in su l'orribil soglia,
    «ond' esta oltracotanza in voi s'alletta?   93

O you who have intelligence that is sound,
      look through the veil of these strange lines and see
      to where the hidden doctrine may be found.   63

Now along the muddy waves there came to me
      a terrifying crash that made the shore
      on either side start shaking violently,   66

like one of those wild winds born with a roar
      when two conflicting heats clash in the air,
      that tears through forests sweeping all before,   69

smashing the branches, stripping the trees bare,
      driving on proudly in a cloud of dust,
      scattering beasts and herdsmen everywhere.   72

My master said, removing the hands still pressed
      around my eyes: "Point the beam of your sight beyond,
      where the fumes from this ancient scum are bitterest."   75

As frogs dart through the water to abscond
      from their enemy the serpent, till they lie
      all huddled at the bottom of the pond,   78

so I saw many wasted souls slip by,
      more than a thousand, fleeing from one who strode
      across the Styx with feet that were still dry.   81

He fanned his left hand often, to clear the load
      of fetid air with which the place was full.
      This was the only weariness he showed.   84

I knew that he had come at heaven's will.
      I turned to my master then, who signified
      that I should bow before him and keep still.   87

With high disdain, he opened the gate wide
      with a little wand he carried in his hand,
      and there was no resistance from inside.   90

"Outcasts of heaven, miserable band,"
      he called to those within from the terrible sill,
      "why do you make so insolent a stand?   93

Perché recalcitrate a quella voglia
    a cui non puote il fin mai esser mozzo,
    e che più volte v'ha cresciuta doglia?   96
Che giova ne le fata dar di cozzo?
    Cerbero vostro, se ben vi ricorda,
    ne porta ancor pelato il mento e 'l gozzo».   99
Poi si rivolse per la strada lorda,
    e non fé motto a noi, ma fé sembiante
    d'omo cui altra cura stringa e morda   102
che quella di colui che li è davante;
    e noi movemmo i piedi inver' la terra,
    sicuri appresso le parole sante.   105
Dentro li 'ntrammo sanz' alcuna guerra;
    e io, ch'avea di riguardar disio
    la condizion che tal fortezza serra,   108
com' io fui dentro, l'occhio intorno invio:
    e veggio ad ogne man grande campagna,
    piena di duolo e di tormento rio.   111
Sì come ad Arli, ove Rodano stagna,
    sì com' a Pola, presso del Carnaro
    ch'Italia chiude e suoi termini bagna,   114
fanno i sepulcri tutt' il loco varo,
    così facevan quivi d'ogne parte,
    salvo che 'l modo v'era più amaro;   117
ché tra li avelli fiamme erano sparte,
    per le quali eran sì del tutto accesi,
    che ferro più non chiede verun' arte.   120
Tutti li lor coperchi eran sospesi,
    e fuor n'uscivan sì duri lamenti,
    che ben parean di miseri e d'offesi.   123
E io: «Maestro, quai son quelle genti
    che, seppellite dentro da quell' arche,
    si fan sentir coi sospiri dolenti?».   126

Why are you so recalcitrant toward the will
  that can never be balked, that has added to the weight
  of your pain many times? Have you not had your fill?   96
What do you gain by butting against fate?
  The still-peeled throat and chin of your Cerberus
  should tell you what those who try can anticipate."   99
He turned away without a word to us.
  Seeming like one who was preoccupied
  much more with other matters than he was   102
with our affairs, he crossed the filthy tide.
  Safe in the holy words and unafraid,
  we approached the city and we went inside.   105
No one opposed the progress that we made.
  I was eager to observe the way things fare
  behind such fortress walls, so my eyes strayed   108
in all directions once I entered there.
  There was an enormous plain, where I could see
  great pain and savage torments everywhere.   111
Just as at Arles, where the Rhône flows sluggishly,
  as at Pola, with Quarnaro lying near
  to hem Italy in and bathe her boundary,   114
where sepulchers make all the ground appear
  uneven, with some lower and some higher,
  so it was here, but so much harsher here.   117
Surrounded as they were by scattered fire,
  the tombs glowed with a heat much more intense
  than any human purpose could require.   120
Their lids were raised, and from them came laments
  so wretched as to make me realize
  these souls paid horribly for their offense.   123
"Master," I said, "who are these who agonize
  inside the arks, and in voices so abject
  fill up the air with so many doleful sighs?"   126

E quelli a me: «Qui son li eresïarche
      con lor seguaci, d'ogne setta, e molto
      più che non credi son le tombe carche.   129
Simile qui con simile è sepolto,
      e i monimenti son più e men caldi».
      E poi ch'a la man destra si fu vòlto,   132
passammo tra i martìri e li alti spaldi.

And he: "The heresiarchs of every sect

 lie here with their followers. Every sepulcher

 is packed more fully than you would suspect.   129

They are buried like with like. The temperature

 from tomb to tomb displays great variance."

 He made a turn to the right, and soon we were   132

between the tortures and the battlements.

Notes

line 23   In Book VI of Lucan's *Pharsalia,* Erichtho, a sorceress of Thessaly, reanimates a dead soldier of Pompey's army at the behest of the general's son, Sextus, who wishes to learn in advance the outcome of the campaign against Caesar (48 B.C.E.). There is no known source for the incident that Virgil describes in lines 22–27, and it is generally assumed to be of Dante's invention.

line 27   Judecca is the fourth and last region of the ninth and last circle of hell (see Canto XXXIV).

lines 38–48   The Furies, also known as Erinyes or Eumenides, appear in many classical works, most notably the *Oresteia* of Aeschylus, as avengers of crimes, especially those that violate the bonds of kinship. They are presented as the gatekeepers of the city of Dis in Book VI of the *Aeneid.*

line 52   The Gorgons were three sisters, of whom the beautiful Medusa was the youngest. After her rape by Neptune (Ovid's *Metamorphoses,* Book IV), the goddess Minerva gave her serpents for hair, making her appearance so horrifying that all who saw her were turned to stone.

lines 53–54   In the version followed by Dante, Theseus, king of Athens, entered the underworld to carry off Proserpine, wife of Hades, and was imprisoned there until Hercules rescued him.

lines 61–63   Commentators are divided on the meaning of these lines, not only in their interpretations of "the hidden doctrine" but also on whether the "strange lines" are the ones preceding or following this address to the reader.

lines 98–99   When Hercules came to hell to rescue Theseus (see note to lines 53–54), he chained Cerberus and dragged him on the ground.

lines 112–16   These lines refer to ancient Roman cemeteries, with sarcophagi of varying heights, in Provence and in Istria (Croatia).

CANTO X

Ora sen va per un secreto calle,
    tra 'l muro de la terra e li martìri,
    lo mio maestro, e io dopo le spalle.   3
«O virtù somma, che per li empi giri
    mi volvi», cominciai, «com' a te piace,
    parlami, e sodisfammi a' miei disiri.   6
La gente che per li sepolcri giace
    potrebbesi veder? già son levati
    tutt' i coperchi, e nessun guardia face».   9
E quelli a me: «Tutti saran serrati
    quando di Iosafàt qui torneranno
    coi corpi che là sù hanno lasciati.   12
Suo cimitero da questa parte hanno
    con Epicuro tutti suoi seguaci,
    che l'anima col corpo morta fanno.   15
Però a la dimanda che mi faci
    quinc' entro satisfatto sarà tosto,
    e al disio ancor che tu mi taci».   18
E io: «Buon duca, non tegno riposto
    a te mio cuor se non per dicer poco,
    e tu m'hai non pur mo a ciò disposto».   21
«O Tosco che per la città del foco
    vivo ten vai così parlando onesto,
    piacciati di restare in questo loco.   24
La tua loquela ti fa manifesto
    di quella nobil patrïa natio,
    a la qual forse fui troppo molesto».   27

Canto X

My master walked a secret path that led
 between the great wall and the agonies
 of the tortured souls. I followed him, and said: 3
"O highest virtue, revolving me as you please
 through all the unholy circles, satisfy
 my wishes now and speak to me of these. 6
Is it possible to see the ones who lie
 in the sepulchers? The lids are raised, I see,
 and nowhere is any watchman standing by." 9
"When they come from Jehoshaphat," he answered me,
 "with the bodies they left above at their demise,
 the tombs will all be sealed eternally. 12
Here in this section Epicurus lies,
 surrounded by his followers, all those
 who make the soul die when the body dies. 15
And therefore to the question that you pose
 you will soon have satisfaction, and have it too
 to the other wish that you do not disclose." 18
And I: "I do not hide my heart from you,
 dear guide, except to speak in briefer space,
 as you have inclined me previously to do." 21
"O living Tuscan, speaking with such grace
 and honesty as you go walking here
 in the city of flame, will you please stop in this place? 24
You are a native son, as your speech makes clear,
 of that noble fatherland to which I have done
 much damage, and perhaps was too severe." 27

Subitamente questo suono uscìo
    d'una de l'arche; però m'accostai,
    temendo, un poco più al duca mio.   30
Ed el mi disse: «Volgiti! Che fai?
    Vedi là Farinata che s'è dritto:
    da la cintola in sù tutto 'l vedrai».   33
Io avea già il mio viso nel suo fitto;
    ed el s'ergea col petto e con la fronte
    com' avesse l'inferno a gran dispitto.   36
E l'animose man del duca e pronte
    mi pinser tra le sepulture a lui,
    dicendo: «Le parole tue sien conte».   39
Com' io al piè de la sua tomba fui,
    guardommi un poco, e poi, quasi sdegnoso,
    mi dimandò: «Chi fuor li maggior tui?».   42
Io ch'era d'ubidir disideroso,
    non gliel celai, ma tutto gliel' apersi;
    ond' ei levò le ciglia un poco in suso;   45
poi disse: «Fieramente furo avversi
    a me e a miei primi e a mia parte,
    sì che per due fiate li dispersi».   48
«S'ei fur cacciati, ei tornar d'ogne parte»,
    rispuos' io lui, «d'una e l'altra fiata;
    ma i vostri non appreser ben quell' arte».   51
Allor surse a la vista scoperchiata
    un'ombra, lungo questa, infino al mento:
    credo che s'era in ginocchie levata.   54
Dintorno mi guardò, come talento
    avesse di veder s'altri era meco;
    e poi che 'l sospecciar fu tutto spento,   57
piangendo disse: «Se per questo cieco
    carcere vai per altezza d'ingegno,
    mio figlio ov' è? e perché non è teco?».   60

This sound arising suddenly from one
    of the nearby arks so scared me that I drew
    close to the side of my leader, whereupon   30
he said: "What are you doing? Turn round and view
    Farinata who has risen now, upright.
    From head to waist he stands in front of you."   33
His gaze and mine already were locked tight.
    He stood with chest thrown out and upturned head
    as if hell itself were contemptible in his sight.   36
By my leader's bold and quick hands I was sped
    between the tombs toward him. "Now you must be
    appropriate in your speech," my master said.   39
When I reached the foot of his tomb, he looked at me
    for just a moment, and then I heard him say,
    as if disdainful, "Who were your family?"   42
And I, since I was eager to obey,
    held nothing back, but told him everything.
    I saw his brows go up a little way,   45
then he said: "They were fierce foes, bedevilling
    my party, my house, and me. But on the attack
    two separate times I sent them scattering."   48
"Though driven out, they managed to come back
    both times from where they were dispersed," I said,
    "an art that those of your kind seem to lack."   51
Beside him rose another of the dead
    just then. This one was on his knees, I thought,
    for all that he was showing was his head.   54
His eyes went all around, as if he sought
    someone else who might be there, but when he knew
    that all his expectation was for naught,   57
he wept, and said: "If high genius lets you through
    to wander this prison where the light has died,
    where is my son? and why is he not with you?"   60

E io a lui: «Da me stesso non vegno:
    colui ch'attende là, per qui mi mena
    forse cui Guido vostro ebbe a disdegno».   63

Le sue parole e 'l modo de la pena
    m'avean di costui già letto il nome;
    però fu la risposta così piena.   66

Di sùbito drizzato gridò: «Come?
    dicesti "elli ebbe"? non viv' elli ancora?
    non fiere li occhi suoi lo dolce lume?».   69

Quando s'accorse d'alcuna dimora
    ch'io facëa dinanzi a la risposta,
    supin ricadde e più non parve fora.   72

Ma quell' altro magnanimo, a cui posta
    restato m'era, non mutò aspetto,
    né mosse collo, né piegò sua costa;   75

e sé continüando al primo detto,
    «S'elli han quell' arte», disse, «male appresa,
    ciò mi tormenta più che questo letto.   78

Ma non cinquanta volte fia raccesa
    la faccia de la donna che qui regge,
    che tu saprai quanto quell' arte pesa.   81

E se tu mai nel dolce mondo regge,
    dimmi: perché quel popolo è sì empio
    incontr' a' miei in ciascuna sua legge?».   84

Ond' io a lui: «Lo strazio e 'l grande scempio
    che fece l'Arbia colorata in rosso,
    tal orazion fa far nel nostro tempio».   87

Poi ch'ebbe sospirando il capo mosso,
    «A ciò non fu' io sol», disse, «né certo
    sanza cagion con li altri sarei mosso.   90

Ma fu' io solo, là dove sofferto
    fu per ciascun di tòrre via Fiorenza,
    colui che la difesi a viso aperto».   93

"I have come not of myself. He who stands aside
        leads me through here to one that, it may be,
        your Guido had disdain for," I replied.   63
His words and the nature of his penalty
        had given his identity away
        and allowed me to respond so thoroughly.   66
He suddenly stood up straight. "What's that you say?
        He 'had'? Is he no longer living then?
        Are his eyes not struck by the sweet light of day?"   69
Noticing how I hesitated when
        he expected me to answer him, he dropped
        down in his tomb and did not rise again.   72
That great soul at whose urging I had stopped,
        who had neither changed his look nor moved his head
        nor turned to watch, once more picked up our cropped   75
discussion where it had been cut, and said:
        "An art they seem to lack? If that is the case,
        I find it more tormenting than this bed.   78
But before the lady who reigns here has her face
        relit another fifty times, you will know
        all about that art and just how much it weighs.   81
And explain to me, so may you once more go
        to the sweet world, why your people's laws have spurned
        my kind, and why you all despise us so."   84
"The carnage and the savagery that turned
        the Arbia's current crimson," I replied,
        "are the reason for the prayers that we have learned   87
to pray in our temple." He shook his head and sighed:
        "I was not alone in that, and would not have thrown
        in with the rest were it not justified.   90
But there was a time when with open face I alone
        dared defend Florence when the rest agreed
        to raze the city down to the last stone."   93

«Deh, se riposi mai vostra semenza»,
  prega' io lui, «solvetemi quel nodo
  che qui ha 'nviluppata mia sentenza.   96

El par che voi veggiate, se ben odo,
  dinanzi quel che 'l tempo seco adduce,
  e nel presente tenete altro modo».   99

«Noi veggiam, come quei c'ha mala luce,
  le cose», disse, «che ne son lontano;
  cotanto ancor ne splende il sommo duce. 102

Quando s'appressano o son, tutto è vano
  nostro intelletto; e s'altri non ci apporta,
  nulla sapem di vostro stato umano.   105

Però comprender puoi che tutta morta
  fia nostra conoscenza da quel punto
  che del futuro fia chiusa la porta».   108

Allor, come di mia colpa compunto,
  dissi: «Or direte dunque a quel caduto
  che 'l suo nato è co' vivi ancor congiunto; 111

e s'i' fui, dianzi, a la risposta muto,
  fate i saper che 'l fei perché pensava
  già ne l'error che m'avete soluto».   114

E già 'l maestro mio mi richiamava;
  per ch'i' pregai lo spirto più avaccio
  che mi dicesse chi con lu' istava.   117

Dissemi: «Qui con più di mille giaccio:
  qua dentro è 'l secondo Federico
  e 'l Cardinale; e de li altri mi taccio». 120

Indi s'ascose; e io inver' l'antico
  poeta volsi i passi, ripensando
  a quel parlar che mi parea nemico.   123

Elli si mosse; e poi, così andando,
  mi disse: «Perché se' tu sì smarrito?».
  E io li sodisfeci al suo dimando.   126

"And now," I said, "so may peace find your seed,
        I beg you to resolve this knot for me
        so that my understanding may be freed.   96
You seem to know of the things that are yet to be
        delivered by time, if what I hear is right,
        but the present moment, that you cannot see."   99
He said: "We are like those with squinting sight.
        When things are far away, we see them clear.
        The lord supreme still grants us that much light.   102
Our minds are dark when things are close, or here.
        As for the present, we know nothing but
        what we are told about your human sphere.   105
Now, therefore, you may comprehend just what
        our future holds. Our knowledge will go dead
        that moment when the door of time is shut."   108
It was compunction for my fault that led
        to my next words: "That other shade who fell,
        tell him his son is still alive," I said.   111
"As for why I did not answer him, please tell
        of how my thought was wholly occupied
        in that error you have clarified so well."   114
And now my master called me to his side,
        so to the shade I hastily appealed
        to learn who were there with him, and he replied: 117
"More than a thousand in this part of the field,
        the second Frederick and the Cardinal . . .
        The names of all the rest I leave concealed."   120
And he hid himself. I turned toward the venerable
        poet my master, thinking anxiously
        about those words that seemed to mean me ill.   123
We moved along, and then he said to me:
        "What has occurred to make you so unnerved?"
        And I satisfied his curiosity.   126

«La mente tua conservi quel ch'udito
    hai contra te», mi comandò quel saggio;
    «e ora attendi qui», e drizzò 'l dito: 129
«quando sarai dinanzi al dolce raggio
    di quella il cui bell' occhio tutto vede,
    da lei saprai di tua vita il vïaggio».   132
Appresso mosse a man sinistra il piede:
    lasciammo il muro e gimmo inver' lo mezzo
    per un sentier ch'a una valle fiede,   135
che 'nfin là sù facea spiacer suo lezzo.

"Let the words that were said against you be preserved
 in memory, but take heed," the sage commanded,
 and then he raised his finger as he observed: 129
"When you stand in her sweet radiance whose splendid
 eyes can see all, then you will learn from her
 the whole journey of your life till it is ended."   132
We turned to the left, from the walled perimeter
 to a central path on which we were to go
 down into a valley. High up as we were,   135
we were sickened by the vile stench from below.

Notes

lines 10–12 According to Joel 3.2, Jehoshaphat, a valley between Jerusalem and the Mount of Olives, will be the site of the last judgment, when all will reclaim their bodies and return with them to heaven or hell.

line 13 The Greek philosopher Epicurus (342–270 B.C.E.) maintained that all events are subject to natural, not supernatural, explanation, and that the greatest good is pleasure (not sensuality, but freedom from pain and anxiety), which is achieved through virtue, temperance, and harmony of mind and body. His philosophy denied divine intervention and punishment and the immortality of the soul.

line 32 Manente degli Uberti, called Farinata, was born early in the thirteenth century, and in 1239 became leader of the Ghibellines, who expelled the Guelphs from Florence in 1248. The Guelphs returned three years later and in 1258 expelled the Ghibellines, who drove them out once again in 1260 at the bloody battle of Montaperti, near the river Arbia (see lines 85–86). After the battle, a council was held in Empoli, at which Farinata argued successfully against the intention of the Pisan Ghibellines to destroy Florence (see lines 91–93). Farinata died in 1264, the year before Dante's birth. In 1283, he and his wife, who had disbelieved in the resurrection of Christ, were posthumously branded heretics.

line 63 The shade to whom Dante is speaking is Cavalcante de' Cavalcanti (died c. 1280), a leader of the Guelphs. His son was the poet Guido Cavalcanti (whose works were translated by Dante Gabriel Rossetti and Ezra Pound). In *La vita nuova*, Dante had earlier described Guido as his "first friend." In an effort to heal political strife, Guido Cavalcanti was married to Farinata's daughter Beatrice. Farinata's later remarks (lines 100–105) explain why Cavalcante is unaware that his son Guido is alive in April 1300 (and that he will die in August of that year), while Farinata can apparently tell the future. Lines 61–63 are ambiguous, no doubt deliberately so. Even the syntax is not entirely clear, since the object of Guido's disdain can be either Virgil or, in the reading I have followed, the one to whom Virgil is conducting Dante—which can mean either Beatrice or God. The heretical views of the Cavalcanti family would seem to support the latter interpretation.

lines 79–81   "The lady who reigns here" is Hecate, or Proserpine, wife of Hades; she was commonly identified with the moon. Fifty months or so after this prophecy, in the summer of 1304, the Whites made their last, futile attempt to reenter Florence, after which Dante saw no prospect of the end of his exile.

lines 107–8   After the last judgment, time will no longer exist.

line 119   Frederick II (1194–1250), king of Sicily and Naples, Holy Roman Emperor, was known as *stupor mundi*, "the wonder of the world," for his political skills, his intellectual accomplishments and fostering of learning, and his open mind and humanistic spirit. Although himself a scourge of heretics, he was suspected of Epicureanism by the Guelphs; the latter part of his reign was marked by constant struggles with the papacy, and he was excommunicated. The Cardinal is Ottaviano degli Ubaldini (d. 1273), who was suspected of unbelief and is reputed to have said, "If I have a soul, I have lost it a thousand times for the Ghibellines." His nephew Archbishop Ruggieri is among the most deeply damned (see Canto XXXIII and note to line 13).

Canto XI

In su l'estremità d'un'alta ripa
  che facevan gran pietre rotte in cerchio,
  venimmo sopra più crudele stipa;   3
e quivi, per l'orribile soperchio
  del puzzo che 'l profondo abisso gitta,
  ci raccostammo, in dietro, ad un coperchio   6
d'un grand' avello, ov' io vidi una scritta
  che dicea: 'Anastasio papa guardo,
  lo qual trasse Fotin de la via dritta'.   9
«Lo nostro scender conviene esser tardo,
  sì che s'ausi un poco in prima il senso
  al tristo fiato; e poi no i fia riguardo».   12
Così 'l maestro; e io «Alcun compenso»,
  dissi lui, «trova che 'l tempo non passi
  perduto». Ed elli: «Vedi ch'a ciò penso».   15
«Figliuol mio, dentro da cotesti sassi»,
  cominciò poi a dir, «son tre cerchietti
  di grado in grado, come que' che lassi.   18
Tutti son pien di spirti maladetti;
  ma perché poi ti basti pur la vista,
  intendi come e perché son costretti.   21
D'ogne malizia, ch'odio in cielo acquista,
  ingiuria è 'l fine, ed ogne fin cotale
  o con forza o con frode altrui contrista.   24
Ma perché frode è de l'uom proprio male,
  più spiace a Dio; e però stan di sotto
  li frodolenti, e più dolor li assale.   27

CANTO XI

At the edge of a high bank formed by a ring
    of enormous broken rocks, we came to a halt
    and looked down on a crueler gathering.   3
Choked by the overpowering assault
    of noxious stink that rose from the deep abyss,
    we drew back to the lid of a large vault   6
on which I saw an inscription that said this:
    "Herein I hold Pope Anastasius, drawn
    by Photinus from the path of righteousness."   9
"We must tarry here before we can go on,"
    my master said, "till the sense has been resigned
    to the foul breath, and the odor will seem gone." 12
"So the time will not be wasted, can we find
    some compensation?" I inquired of him,
    and he replied: "That is what I have in mind."   15
So he thus began: "My son, inside the rim
    of the rocks, three smaller, narrowing circles lie,
    like the ones through which we have already come. 18
All are filled up with damned spirits. So that I
    need only show them to you in due course,
    I will tell you now how they are held and why.   21
The intent of every malice that heaven abhors
    is an injustice, and the result of it
    is to do another harm, by fraud or force.   24
Because only human beings can commit
    a fraud, this is the sin God most resents.
    These sinners endure more pain, in the lower pit. 27

Di vïolenti il primo cerchio è tutto;
 ma perché si fa forza a tre persone,
 in tre gironi è distinto e costrutto. 30

A Dio, a sé, al prossimo si pòne
 far forza, dico in loro e in lor cose,
 come udirai con aperta ragione. 33

Morte per forza e ferute dogliose
 nel prossimo si danno, e nel suo avere
 ruine, incendi e tollette dannose; 36

onde omicide e ciascun che mal fiere,
 guastatori e predon, tutti tormenta
 lo giron primo per diverse schiere. 39

Puote omo avere in sé man vïolenta
 e ne' suoi beni; e però nel secondo
 giron convien che sanza pro si penta 42

qualunque priva sé del vostro mondo,
 biscazza e fonde la sua facultade,
 e piange là dov' esser de' giocondo. 45

Puossi far forza ne la deïtade,
 col cor negando e bestemmiando quella,
 e spregiando natura e sua bontade; 48

e però lo minor giron suggella
 del segno suo e Soddoma e Caorsa
 e chi, spregiando Dio col cor, favella. 51

La frode, ond' ogne coscïenza è morsa,
 può l'omo usare in colui che 'n lui fida
 e in quel che fidanza non imborsa. 54

Questo modo di retro par ch'incida
 pur lo vinco d'amor che fa natura;
 onde nel cerchio secondo s'annida 57

ipocresia, lusinghe e chi affattura,
 falsità, ladroneccio e simonia,
 ruffian, baratti e simile lordura. 60

The first circle holds the violent. Since violence
    may have three objects, the circle is split in three
    and has one ring for each kind of offense.   30
To God or self or neighbor one may be
    violent, against his person or possession,
    as I will now unfold it logically.   33
Wounding and death come of violent aggression
    on a neighbor's self. On his property one may bring
    ruin, arson, or extortionate oppression.   36
You will see in separate groups in the first ring
    despoilers, plunderers, murderers, everyone
    who used malicious force on man or thing.   39
To one's own person violence may be done,
    or to one's own goods. To the second ring are sent
    all those who now must uselessly atone   42
for robbing themselves of the world, all those who went
    through their property with dice or dissipation,
    all those who wept when they should have been content.   45
They are violent against God who feel negation
    and blasphemy at heart, who in bitterness
    hate nature and the bounty of creation.   48
And thus the smallest ring with its impress
    seals Sodom and Cahors, and those who say
    evil of God within the heart's recess.   51
Fraud gnaws at every conscience, and a man may
    use fraud on one who trusts him or one who invests
    no special confidence. In the latter way   54
he breaks the natural bond of love that exists
    among all humanity, and thus is sent
    to the second circle, which contains the nests   57
of hypocrites, flatterers, thieves, those who were bent
    on sorcery, simoniacs and cheats,
    swindlers and pimps and all such excrement.   60

Per l'altro modo quell' amor s'oblia
    che fa natura, e quel ch'è poi aggiunto,
    di che la fede spezïal si cria;   63
onde nel cerchio minore, ov' è 'l punto
    de l'universo in su che Dite siede,
    qualunque trade in etterno è consunto».   66
E io: «Maestro, assai chiara procede
    la tua ragione, e assai ben distingue
    questo baràtro e 'l popol ch'e' possiede.   69
Ma dimmi: quei de la palude pingue,
    che mena il vento, e che batte la pioggia,
    e che s'incontran con sì aspre lingue,   72
perché non dentro da la città roggia
    sono ei puniti, se Dio li ha in ira?
    e se non li ha, perché sono a tal foggia?».   75
Ed elli a me «Perché tanto delira»,
    disse, «lo 'ngegno tuo da quel che sòle?
    o ver la mente dove altrove mira?   78
Non ti rimembra di quelle parole
    con le quai la tua Etica pertratta
    le tre disposizion che 'l ciel non vole,   81
incontenenza, malizia e la matta
    bestialitade? e come incontenenza
    men Dio offende e men biasimo accatta?   84
Se tu riguardi ben questa sentenza,
    e rechiti a la mente chi son quelli
    che sù di fuor sostegnon penitenza,   87
tu vedrai ben perché da questi felli
    sien dipartiti, e perché men crucciata
    la divina vendetta li martelli».   90
«O sol che sani ogne vista turbata,
    tu mi contenti sì quando tu solvi,
    che, non men che saver, dubbiar m'aggrata.   93

But in the former way he violates
      not just this natural love, but what is worse,
      a special bond and the trust that it creates.   63
Thus at the center of the universe
      is the seat of Dis, the smallest circle, where
      all traitors are ravaged by the eternal curse."   66
"Master, your lucid words make me aware,"
      I said, "of how the abyss has been laid out
      and the kinds of people that are kept down there.   69
But those in the thick marsh, those who are driven about
      by the wind, those in the rainfall and its mess,
      and those who crash together and harshly shout,   72
why does the red-hot city not oppress
      those souls with pain, if they have earned God's hate?
      If not, why are they set in such distress?"   75
"Why does your understanding deviate
      so far afield?" he said. "Has your mind been driven
      by stray thoughts into some distracted state?   78
Do you forget the explanation given,
      in the pages of your *Ethics*, of the three
      dispositions that offend the will of heaven,   81
incontinence, malice, and mad bestiality?
      How it says there that incontinence will incur
      less blame, offending God less grievously?   84
If you contemplate that saying and you stir
      your wits to recollect the souls you saw
      punished above, just who and what they were,   87
you will see why justice has seen fit to draw
      a line between them and the evil souls below,
      why they are less fiercely battered by God's law." 90
"O sun that clears the mists, your answers so
      content me that I am as gratified
      to be perplexed by doubt as I am to know.   93

Ancora in dietro un poco ti rivolvi»,

    diss' io, «là dove di' ch'usura offende

    la divina bontade, e 'l groppo solvi».   96

«Filosofia», mi disse, «a chi la 'ntende,

    nota, non pure in una sola parte,

    come natura lo suo corso prende   99

dal divino 'ntelletto e da sua arte;

    e se tu ben la tua Fisica note,

    tu troverai, non dopo molte carte,   102

che l'arte vostra quella, quanto pote,

    segue, come 'l maestro fa 'l discente;

    sì che vostr' arte a Dio quasi è nepote.   105

Da queste due, se tu ti rechi a mente

    lo Genesì dal principio, convene

    prender sua vita e avanzar la gente;   108

e perché l'usuriere altra via tene,

    per sé natura e per la sua seguace

    dispregia, poi ch'in altro pon la spene.   111

Ma seguimi oramai che 'l gir mi piace;

    ché i Pesci guizzan su per l'orizzonta,

    e 'l Carro tutto sovra 'l Coro giace,   114

e 'l balzo via là oltra si dismonta».

But please go back," I said, "to where you implied
    that one who practices usury offends
    God's bounty. I would like that knot untied."   96
"Philosophy, to one who comprehends,
    makes clear," he said, "and not only in one part,
    that the course of nature totally depends   99
upon divine intelligence and its art.
    If you read your *Physics* carefully, then you
    will find, not many pages from the start,   102
that art follows nature, as well as it can do,
    like a pupil with his master. It may be said
    that your art is God's grandchild. It is by these two,   105
as you will recollect from having read
    the beginning of Genesis, that humans were
    enjoined to make their way and earn their bread.   108
By taking another road, the usurer
    puts his hope elsewhere, and in doing so
    despises nature and her follower.   111
But now come follow me, for I wish to go.
    The Wain has crossed over Caurus the north wind,
    on the horizon the Fish begin to glow,   114
and before us waits the cliff we must descend."

Notes

lines 8–9   There is a possible confusion here between Pope Anastasius II (496–498) and the emperor Anastasius I (491–518). Photinus, a deacon of Thessalonica, is believed to have persuaded the emperor to the heresy of Acacius, which denied the divinity of Christ. On the other hand, Robert and Jean Hollander point out that Isidore of Seville, a possible source for Dante's lines, says that Pope Anastasius was converted by Photinus, bishop of Sirmium, to the Ebionite heresy, which claimed that Jesus was the purely human child of Mary and Joseph (*Dante Alighieri: Inferno*, Doubleday, 2000).

line 50   The reference to Sodom connotes sodomy. Cahors, a city in southern France, was notorious in the Middle Ages for usury.

line 80   Aristotle's *Nicomachean Ethics* is cited. For Aristotle, "bestiality," or brutishness, is a category that transcends the normal range of human evil to encompass such things as cannibalism; since the *Inferno* groups violence and fraud under malice, there has been much debate over what Dante intends by the term.

line 101   The reference is to the *Physics* of Aristotle, although this discussion of usury more likely derives from the commentary of Aquinas on Aristotle's *Politics*.

lines 107–8   See Genesis 3.19: "In the sweat of thy face shalt thou eat bread, till thou return unto the ground."

lines 113–15   The Wain is the Big Dipper, and the Fish are the constellation Pisces. It is now about four o'clock in the morning, and ten of the journey's twenty-four hours have elapsed.

Canto XII

Era lo loco ov' a scender la riva
    venimmo, alpestro e, per quel che v'er' anco,
      tal, ch'ogne vista ne sarebbe schiva.   3
Qual è quella ruina che nel fianco
    di qua da Trento l'Adice percosse,
      o per tremoto o per sostegno manco,   6
che da cima del monte, onde si mosse,
    al piano è sì la roccia discoscesa,
      ch'alcuna via darebbe a chi sù fosse: 9
cotal di quel burrato era la scesa;
    e 'n su la punta de la rotta lacca
      l'infamïa di Creti era distesa   12
che fu concetta ne la falsa vacca;
    e quando vide noi, sé stesso morse,
      sì come quei cui l'ira dentro fiacca.   15
Lo savio mio inver' lui gridò: «Forse
    tu credi che qui sia 'l duca d'Atene,
      che sù nel mondo la morte ti porse?   18
Pàrtiti, bestia, ché questi non vene
    ammaestrato da la tua sorella,
      ma vassi per veder le vostre pene».   21
Qual è quel toro che si slaccia in quella
    c'ha ricevuto già 'l colpo mortale,
      che gir non sa, ma qua e là saltella,   24
vid' io lo Minotauro far cotale;
    e quello accorto gridò: «Corri al varco;
      mentre ch'e' 'nfuria, è buon che tu ti cale».   27

Canto XII

The place was of an alpine nature where
    we were to go down, a place to be abhorred
    by every eye because of what was there.   3
As with the devastation that was poured
    on the bank of the Adige this side of Trent
    by a quake or by the land's being badly shored,   6
where down the mountainside the turbulent
    rockslide has formed a pathway to allow
    the traveler to make a rough descent,   9
such was the slope that we had come to now.
    And stretched out near the shattered chasm's edge
    lay the thing that was conceived in the false cow,   12
the infamy of Crete. Like one whose rage
    is tearing at his insides, he began
    to bite himself at the sight of us. My sage   15
called out to him: "Perhaps you think this man
    is the Duke of Athens, he who struck you dead
    in the world above, coming after you again.   18
Beast, get away from here! He is not led
    by your sister's guidance, but has come to see
    the punishments inflicted on your head."   21
And like a bull that suddenly breaks free
    when it takes its deathblow, and from side to side
    it leaps and wheels, careening crazily,   24
the Minotaur jumped up, and my wary guide
    called out to me: "Run for the opening there
    while his mad fury has him occupied!"   27

Così prendemmo via giù per lo scarco
    di quelle pietre, che spesso moviensi
    sotto i miei piedi per lo novo carco.   30
Io gia pensando; e quei disse: «Tu pensi
    forse a questa ruina, ch'è guardata
    da quell' ira bestial ch'i' ora spensi.   33
Or vo' che sappi che l'altra fïata
    ch'i' discesi qua giù nel basso inferno,
    questa roccia non era ancor cascata.   36
Ma certo poco pria, se ben discerno,
    che venisse colui che la gran preda
    levò a Dite del cerchio superno,   39
da tutte parti l'alta valle feda
    tremò sì, ch'i' pensai che l'universo
    sentisse amor, per lo qual è chi creda   42
più volte il mondo in caòsso converso;
    e in quel punto questa vecchia roccia,
    qui e altrove, tal fece riverso.   45
Ma ficca li occhi a valle, ché s'approccia
    la riviera del sangue in la qual bolle
    qual che per vïolenza in altrui noccia».   48
Oh cieca cupidigia e ira folle,
    che sì ci sproni ne la vita corta,
    e ne l'etterna poi sì mal c'immolle!   51
Io vidi un'ampia fossa in arco torta,
    come quella che tutto 'l piano abbraccia,
    secondo ch'avea detto la mia scorta;   54
e tra 'l piè de la ripa ed essa, in traccia
    corrien centauri, armati di saette,
    come solien nel mondo andare a caccia.   57
Veggendoci calar, ciascun ristette,
    e de la schiera tre si dipartiro
    con archi e asticciuole prima elette;   60

We picked our way down the scattered rockpile, where
    the stones beneath my feet were moved about
    by the unaccustomed load I made them bear.   30
I was walking lost in thought, till he spoke out:
    "Are you thinking about this ruin, guarded by
    that beastly wrath I just now put to rout?   33
You should be aware that the other time that I
    delved down into the deep hell's lowest ring,
    this crag had not yet fallen from on high.   36
Not long before he came, by my reckoning,
    who carried off from Dis the great spoils of
    the highest circle through his harrowing,   39
the deep and reeking pit so shook—above,
    below, on every side—that I began
    to think the universe was moved by love,   42
by which, some say, the world has often been
    convulsed to chaos. These ancient rocks, both here
    and elsewhere, all came crashing down just then.   45
But look to the valley. All who interfere
    with others by violence, doing them injury,
    are boiled in the river of blood that is coming near."   48
O senseless rage and blind cupidity,
    that in the short life stimulate us so
    and in the eternal one drench us wretchedly!   51
I saw a broad ditch bending like a bow,
    just as my guide had said, with its wide embrace
    surrounding the whole plain that lay below.   54
I saw a single file of centaurs race,
    with arrows armed, between the ditch and hill,
    as in the world they had galloped to the chase.   57
When they saw us coming down, they all stood still.
    Selecting arrows, three began to go
    away from the others, approaching us, until   60

e l'un gridò da lungi: «A qual martiro
  venite voi che scendete la costa?
  Ditel costinci; se non, l'arco tiro».   63

Lo mio maestro disse: «La risposta
  farem noi a Chirón costà di presso:
  mal fu la voglia tua sempre sì tosta».   66

Poi mi tentò, e disse: «Quelli è Nesso,
  che morì per la bella Deianira,
  e fé di sé la vendetta elli stesso.   69

E quel di mezzo, ch'al petto si mira,
  è il gran Chirón, il qual nodrì Achille;
  quell' altro è Folo, che fu sì pien d'ira.   72

Dintorno al fosso vanno a mille a mille,
  saettando qual anima si svelle
  del sangue più che sua colpa sortille».   75

Noi ci appressammo a quelle fiere isnelle:
  Chirón prese uno strale, e con la cocca
  fece la barba in dietro a le mascelle.   78

Quando s'ebbe scoperta la gran bocca,
  disse a' compagni: «Siete voi accorti
  che quel di retro move ciò ch'el tocca?   81

Così non soglion far li piè d'i morti».
  E 'l mio buon duca, che già li er' al petto,
  dove le due nature son consorti,   84

rispuose: «Ben è vivo, e sì soletto
  mostrar li mi convien la valle buia;
  necessità 'l ci 'nduce, e non diletto.   87

Tal si partì da cantare alleluia
  che mi commise quest' officio novo:
  non è ladron, né io anima fuia.   90

Ma per quella virtù per cu' io movo
  li passi miei per sì selvaggia strada,
  danne un de' tuoi, a cui noi siamo a provo,   93

one called from afar. "You there! We want to know
    what punishment you are going to," he said.
    "Tell us from there, or else I draw the bow." 63
My master answered: "We will reply instead
    to Chiron beside you, when we come down there.
    You have always harmed yourself with your hot head." 66
He nudged me. "That is Nessus, who died for the fair
    Deïanira, having managed first to stage
    revenge for himself upon his very slayer. 69
In the center, gazing at his chest, is sage
    Chiron, who taught Achilles. The other one
    is Pholus, who was always full of rage. 72
They patrol the ditch in thousands, arrows drawn
    to pierce any spirit who rises from the blood
    higher than guilt allows." Then we moved on, 75
approaching where those nimble creatures stood.
    Chiron took up an arrow, and with its notch
    he brushed his beard aside until his broad 78
mouth was uncovered, and told the others: "Watch
    the one who walks behind. Look, do you see it,
    the way his feet are moving what they touch? 81
I have never seen that done by dead men's feet."
    My good leader, who now stood before his breast,
    that part of him where his two natures meet, 84
replied: "He is alive, as I'll attest.
    Alone I must show him the dark vale, not for my
    or his pleasure, but at necessity's behest. 87
One who was singing alleluia on high
    came where I was, to give me this new command.
    He is no thief, no cutpurse soul am I. 90
But by the power that through so wild a land
    moves all my steps, I ask you now to spare
    one who can guide us, a member of your band 93

e che ne mostri là dove si guada,

    e che porti costui in su la groppa,

    ché non è spirto che per l'aere vada».   96

Chirón si volse in su la destra poppa,

    e disse a Nesso: «Torna, e sì li guida,

    e fa cansar s'altra schiera v'intoppa».   99

Or ci movemmo con la scorta fida

    lungo la proda del bollor vermiglio,

    dove i bolliti facieno alte strida.   102

Io vidi gente sotto infino al ciglio;

    e 'l gran centauro disse: «E' son tiranni

    che dier nel sangue e ne l'aver di piglio.   105

Quivi si piangon li spietati danni;

    quivi è Alessandro, e Dïonisio fero

    che fé Cicilia aver dolorosi anni.   108

E quella fronte c'ha 'l pel così nero,

    è Azzolino; e quell' altro ch'è biondo,

    è Opizzo da Esti, il qual per vero   111

fu spento dal figliastro sù nel mondo».

    Allor mi volsi al poeta, e quei disse:

    «Questi ti sia or primo, e io secondo».   114

Poco più oltre il centauro s'affisse

    sovr' una gente che 'nfino a la gola

    parea che di quel bulicame uscisse.   117

Mostrocci un'ombra da l'un canto sola,

    dicendo: «Colui fesse in grembo a Dio

    lo cor che 'n su Tamisi ancor si cola».   120

Poi vidi gente che di fuor del rio

    tenean la testa e ancor tutto 'l casso;

    e di costoro assai riconobb' io.   123

Così a più a più si facea basso

    quel sangue, sì che cocea pur li piedi;

    e quindi fu del fosso il nostro passo.   126

to walk beside us and to show us where
    the crossing is, and carry him astride,
    for he is no spirit who can fly through air."   96
Chiron told Nessus: "Go then, be their guide,"
    as he turned on his right flank, "and if you see
    another troop, then make them move aside."   99
With our trusty escort we walked the boundary
    of the boiling crimson, where we heard the cries
    of the boiled shades shrieking in their agony.   102
With some, the river rose above their eyes.
    The great centaur said: "These gave themselves to fierce
    plunder and carnage, living to tyrannize.   105
Here they lament their merciless careers.
    Here is Alexander, cruel Dionysius too
    who gave Sicily so many painful years.   108
This one upon whose head such black hair grew
    is Azzolino, and that fairhaired one
    is Opizzo d'Esti, who—and this is true—   111
was extinguished in the world by his stepson."
    I turned to the poet, who told me: "In this sphere
    he leads, I follow. Thus let it be done."   114
We approached a group whose heads and throats were clear
    of the stream. One spirit stood alone, away
    from all of the other ones. As we drew near,   117
the centaur stopped to point to him and say:
    "That one pierced through a heart, in God's own breast,
    that drips blood above the Thames to this very day."   120
Then I saw some who stood up to the chest
    out of the current, and in this crowd I spied
    many I recognized among the rest.   123
Thus more and more I saw the bloody tide
    recede, till it cooked the feet alone, so low
    that here we went across to the other side.   126

«Sì come tu da questa parte vedi

lo bulicame che sempre si scema»,

disse 'l centauro, «voglio che tu credi   129

che da quest' altra a più a più giù prema

lo fondo suo, infin ch'el si raggiunge

ove la tirannia convien che gema.   132

La divina giustizia di qua punge

quell' Attila che fu flagello in terra,

e Pirro e Sesto; e in etterno munge   135

le lagrime, che col bollor diserra,

a Rinier da Corneto, a Rinier Pazzo,

che fecero a le strade tanta guerra».   138

Poi si rivolse e ripassossi 'l guazzo.

"Just as you see the boiling river grow
  more and more shallow," the centaur said to me,
    "here in this part of the plain, I would have you know   129
that on the other side it constantly
  grows deeper till it completes its circle where
    the tyrants are groaning in their misery.   132
Heavenly justice stings Attila there,
  who was a scourge upon the earth for years,
    and Pyrrhus and Sextus. And it stings that pair—   135
the one from Corneto, and Pazzo—the two Riniers
  who turned the public roads to fields of war,
    for the bath unlocks and justice milks their tears."   138
Then he turned round and crossed the ford once more.

Notes

lines 4–6   The precipice of Slavini di Marco, south of Trent in northern Italy, was formed by a landslide, c. 883, which diverted the Adige from its course.

lines 12–13   Minos, king of Crete, failed to carry out the promised sacrifice of a bull to the sea god Poseidon, who afflicted Minos's wife, Pasiphaë, with an unnatural passion for a bull. She lured the bull by crouching inside a wooden cow covered with cowhide. From this union was born the Minotaur, which Minos kept imprisoned in an intricate labyrinth. It is usually represented as having a bull's head and a human body.

lines 17–20   Theseus, king of Athens, killed the Minotaur with the assistance of Ariadne, daughter of Minos and Pasiphaë, who provided him with a sword and a long thread by which to find his way back out of the labyrinth.

lines 37–45   In Matthew 27.50–53, the earth is convulsed by a mighty earthquake at the moment of Christ's death upon the cross.

line 55   The original centaurs, one hundred in number, were passionate and violent creatures, half man, half horse. They were born when Ixion, seeking to possess Hera, instead assaulted a cloud that Zeus had fashioned to resemble her, and the drops of his seed fell to the earth.

line 65   Chiron was the son of Philyra and of Kronos, the sun god, who had turned himself into a horse to elude his wife's jealousy. Wise and just, Chiron was the tutor of Achilles, Jason, Asclepius, and others.

lines 67–69   Nessus, one of the sons of Ixion, carried Deianira, wife of Hercules, across a stream. Attempting to rape her, he was shot by Hercules with a poisoned arrow. Dying, the centaur told her to keep some of his blood, which, he claimed, when smeared on a garment, would cause its wearer to love her. Hercules later fell in love with Iole, Deianira gave him the garment, and its poison caused him such horrible suffering that he committed suicide (Ovid, *Metamorphoses*, Book IX).

line 72   Pholus, another of Ixion's sons, died accidentally when he dropped one of Hercules' poisoned arrows on his foot.

line 107   The likeliest identifications are Alexander of Macedonia, the Great (356–323 B.C.E.), and Dionysus the Elder, who ruled Syracuse from 405 to 367 B.C.E.

line 110   Ezzelino III da Romano (1194–1259), son-in-law of Frederick II, was a Ghibelline leader who committed atrocities, especially against the Paduans.

line 111   Obizzo II d'Este (1247–1293), lord of Ferrara and a Guelph, is believed to have been smothered by his son and successor, Azzo VIII. Various attempts have been made to explain "stepson": some see it as a hint at the infidelity of Obizzo's wife, others as a suggestion of the unnaturalness of his son's crime.

lines 119–20   "That one" is Guy de Montfort (c. 1243–1298), of royal English blood. To avenge his father, Simon de Montfort, killed at the battle of Evesham in 1265 by the future Edward I, Guy stabbed Edward's cousin, Prince Henry of Cornwall, at mass in the church of San Silvestro in Viterbo in 1271. According to one source, Henry's heart was placed in a golden casket on a pillar at the end of London Bridge. It continues to drip because Henry's murder remains unavenged.

line 133   Attila (c. 406–453), king of the Huns c. 433–453, was known as the Scourge of God.

line 135   Both identifications are disputed, but Pyrrhus is probably the king of Epirus (318–272 B.C.E.) whose defeat of the Romans at Asculum in 279 was the original Pyrrhic victory, and Sextus is most likely Sextus Pompeius Magnus (d. 35 B.C.E.), younger son of Pompey the Great.

line 136   Rinier da Corneto and Rinier Pazzo were highway robbers of Dante's time, the former near Rome and the latter south of Florence.

CANTO XIII

Non era ancor di là Nesso arrivato,
    quando noi ci mettemmo per un bosco
    che da neun sentiero era segnato.   3

Non fronda verde, ma di color fosco;
    non rami schietti, ma nodosi e 'nvolti;
    non pomi v'eran, ma stecchi con tòsco.   6

Non han sì aspri sterpi né sì folti
    quelle fiere selvagge che 'n odio hanno
    tra Cecina e Corneto i luoghi cólti.   9

Quivi le brutte Arpie lor nidi fanno,
    che cacciar de le Strofade i Troiani
    con tristo annunzio di futuro danno.   12

Ali hanno late, e colli e visi umani,
    piè con artigli, e pennuto 'l gran ventre;
    fanno lamenti in su li alberi strani.   15

E 'l buon maestro «Prima che più entre,
    sappi che se' nel secondo girone»,
    mi cominciò a dire, «e sarai mentre   18
che tu verrai ne l'orribil sabbione.
    Però riguarda ben; sì vederai
    cose che torrien fede al mio sermone».   21

Io sentia d'ogne parte trarre guai
    e non vedea persona che 'l facesse;
    per ch'io tutto smarrito m'arrestai.   24
Cred' ïo ch'ei credette ch'io credesse
    che tante voci uscisser, tra quei bronchi,
    da gente che per noi si nascondesse.   27

Canto XIII

Not yet had Nessus finished crossing there
  when we began to walk into a grim
  forest without a pathway anywhere.   3
Not bright green leaves, but foliage dark and dim,
  not sturdy branches, but each a twisted bough,
  not fruits, but poisoned thorns on every limb.   6
Not even the beasts that hate the lands men plow
  between Corneto and Cécina can roam
  through such rough, tangled brush as I saw now.   9
This wood is the foul, nesting Harpies' home,
  who drove the Trojans from the Strophades
  with dread predictions of approaching doom.   12
With talons, broad wings, gross feathered paunches, these
  human-faced things sit uttering their lay
  of lamentation in the twisted trees.   15
"Before going any further on the way,"
  said my good master, "I would have you know
  you are in the second ring, where you will stay   18
till the horrid sand. Look closely as we go.
  Here are things that you would call impossible
  if you had heard me tell you they were so."   21
I could hear wailing, deep and pitiful,
  but there was no one anywhere about,
  and I grew so perplexed that I stood still.   24
I think that he was thinking that I thought
  that all those voices came from people who,
  on seeing us approach, had quickly sought   27

Però disse 'l maestro: «Se tu tronchi
    qualche fraschetta d'una d'este piante,
    li pensier c'hai si faran tutti monchi».   30

Allor porsi la mano un poco avante
    e colsi un ramicel da un gran pruno;
    e 'l tronco suo gridò: «Perché mi schiante?».   33

Da che fatto fu poi di sangue bruno,
    ricominciò a dir: «Perché mi scerpi?
    non hai tu spirto di pietade alcuno?   36

Uomini fummo, e or siam fatti sterpi:
    ben dovrebb' esser la tua man più pia,
    se state fossimo anime di serpi».   39

Come d'un stizzo verde ch'arso sia
    da l'un de' capi, che da l'altro geme
    e cigola per vento che va via,   42

sì de la scheggia rotta usciva insieme
    parole e sangue; ond' io lasciai la cima
    cadere, e stetti come l'uom che teme.   45

«S'elli avesse potuto creder prima»,
    rispuose 'l savio mio, «anima lesa,
    ciò c'ha veduto pur con la mia rima,   48

non averebbe in te la man distesa;
    ma la cosa incredibile mi fece
    indurlo ad ovra ch'a me stesso pesa.   51

Ma dilli chi tu fosti, sì che 'n vece
    d'alcun' ammenda tua fama rinfreschi
    nel mondo sù, dove tornar li lece».   54

E 'l tronco: «Sì col dolce dir m'adeschi,
    ch'i' non posso tacere; e voi non gravi
    perch' ïo un poco a ragionar m'inveschi.   57

Io son colui che tenni ambo le chiavi
    del cor di Federigo, e che le volsi,
    serrando e diserrando, sì soavi,   60

to hide themselves. And so he said: "If you
  break off a little branch, you will soon see
  that what you are thinking will be broken too."   30
Then I reached out, and from a great thorn tree
  I tugged a branch until it snapped apart,
  and the stem cried out: "Why are you tearing me?"   33
Where it was broken, I saw dark blood start.
  "Why are you mangling me?" it cried again.
  "Have you no spirit of pity in your heart?   36
Now we are turned to stumps, but we were men
  when we were on the earth. Truly, your hand
  should show more mercy, even if we had been   39
the souls of serpents." Just as a green brand
  will burn at one end, and the escaping air
  will hiss as sap drips from the other end,   42
so from the stump words mixed with blood flowed where
  I had broken it. I dropped it suddenly,
  and like someone terror-stricken I stood there.   45
"O wounded soul," my sage replied, "if he
  could have believed what previously he had met
  only in the pages of my poetry,   48
he would not have raised his hand to you, and yet
  the thing was so incredible that I came
  to urge him on, which I myself regret.   51
So that he may make amends, let him know your name,
  that when, as he will be allowed to do,
  he returns to earth, he may refresh your fame."   54
Said the stem: "Allured by such sweet words from you,
  I cannot stay silent. May it not displease
  if I am enticed to speak a word or two.   57
I was the man who carried both the keys
  to Frederick's heart. I turned them expertly,
  locking, unlocking with such tender ease   60

che dal secreto suo quasi ogn' uom tolsi;
    fede portai al glorïoso offizio,
    tanto ch'i' ne perde' li sonni e ' polsi.   63

La meretrice che mai da l'ospizio
    di Cesare non torse li occhi putti,
    morte comune e de le corti vizio,   66

infiammò contra me li animi tutti;
    e li 'nfiammati infiammar sì Augusto,
    che ' lieti onor tornaro in tristi lutti.   69

L'animo mio, per disdegnoso gusto,
    credendo col morir fuggir disdegno,
    ingiusto fece me contra me giusto.   72

Per le nove radici d'esto legno
    vi giuro che già mai non ruppi fede
    al mio segnor, che fu d'onor sì degno.   75

E se di voi alcun nel mondo riede,
    conforti la memoria mia, che giace
    ancor del colpo che 'nvidia le diede».   78

Un poco attese, e poi «Da ch'el si tace»,
    disse 'l poeta a me, «non perder l'ora;
    ma parla, e chiedi a lui, se più ti piace».   81

Ond' ïo a lui: «Domandal tu ancora
    di quel che credi ch'a me satisfaccia;
    ch'i' non potrei, tanta pietà m'accora».   84

Perciò ricominciò: «Se l'om ti faccia
    liberamente ciò che 'l tuo dir priega,
    spirito incarcerato, ancor ti piaccia   87

di dirne come l'anima si lega
    in questi nocchi; e dinne, se tu puoi,
    s'alcuna mai di tai membra si spiega».   90

Allor soffiò il tronco forte, e poi
    si convertì quel vento in cotal voce:
    «Brievemente sarà risposto a voi.   93

that scarcely any shared his intimacy.

> True to the glorious office in my care,
>
> I gave up sleep and my vitality. 63

That whore who never turns aside her stare,

> keeping her sluttish eyes on Caesar's hall,
>
> common vice and death of royal courts everywhere, 66

inflamed all minds against me, and they all,

> once so inflamed, then so inflamed Augustus
>
> that my glad honors turned to mortal gall. 69

My mind, so filled with scorn and with disgust, was

> thinking through death to escape their scorn for me,
>
> so myself to my just self did great injustice. 72

But I swear by the new and strange roots of this tree

> that I never once betrayed my lord, who so
>
> deserved all honor and all loyalty. 75

If it is true that one of you will go

> back to earth, restore my memory, which still
>
> lies fallen from the force of envy's blow." 78

The poet paused for a little while, until

> he said: "Since he is silent, you should start
>
> to use the time, and ask him what you will." 81

And I replied: "Now you must take my part

> and speak for me. I am unable to,
>
> with so much pity tearing through my heart." 84

So he began: "That this man may freely do

> what you have begged, then satisfy his mind,
>
> imprisoned spirit, if it pleases you 87

to tell us how the gnarled wood comes to bind

> the souls, and if you know whether one may be
>
> set free again once it has been confined." 90

When he had done, the branch puffed mightily

> and then these words were fashioned from that breath:
>
> "I will briefly answer what you ask of me. 93

Quando si parte l'anima feroce
 dal corpo ond' ella stessa s'è disvelta,
 Minòs la manda a la settima foce.   96
Cade in la selva, e non l'è parte scelta;
 ma là dove fortuna la balestra,
 quivi germoglia come gran di spelta.   99
Surge in vermena e in pianta silvestra:
 l'Arpie, pascendo poi de le sue foglie,
 fanno dolore, e al dolor fenestra.   102
Come l'altre verrem per nostre spoglie,
 ma non però ch'alcuna sen rivesta,
 ché non è giusto aver ciò ch'om si toglie.   105
Qui le strascineremo, e per la mesta
 selva saranno i nostri corpi appesi,
 ciascuno al prun de l'ombra sua molesta».   108
Noi eravamo ancora al tronco attesi,
 credendo ch'altro ne volesse dire,
 quando noi fummo d'un romor sorpresi,   111
similemente a colui che venire
 sente 'l porco e la caccia a la sua posta,
 ch'ode le bestie, e le frasche stormire.   114
Ed ecco due da la sinistra costa,
 nudi e graffiati, fuggendo sì forte,
 che de la selva rompieno ogne rosta.   117
Quel dinanzi: «Or accorri, accorri, morte!».
 E l'altro, cui pareva tardar troppo,
 gridava: «Lano, sì non furo accorte   120
le gambe tue a le giostre dal Toppo!».
 E poi che forse li fallia la lena,
 di sé e d'un cespuglio fece un groppo.   123
Di rietro a loro era la selva piena
 di nere cagne, bramose e correnti
 come veltri ch'uscisser di catena.   126

When the ferocious soul is finished with
    the flesh from which it rooted itself out,
      Minos sends it to the seventh hole in his wrath.   96

It falls into the forest, blown about
    where fortune flings it. After its descent
      it roots at random. Like spelt it starts to sprout.   99

It grows to a sapling, then to a wild plant.
    The Harpies, feasting on its foliage then,
      both give it pain and give the pain a vent.   102

We will come for our remains like other men,
    but not to wear them. It would not be fit
      that what we steal from ourselves we have again.   105

We will drag our bodies here to this desolate
    forest, where they will hang forevermore,
      each on the tree of the shade that murdered it."   108

We waited, thinking that he might say more,
    but then we were startled by a clamorous sound,
      as when a hunter senses the wild boar   111

and the hounds hot on its heels as they all pound
    toward where he stands in wait, and hears the blare
      of the beasts, and branches crashing all around.   114

And hard upon our left we saw a pair
    of scratched and naked figures running by
      so fast they smashed the tangles everywhere.   117

"Come quickly, death, come quickly!" came the cry
    from the leader. Losing ground, the other one
      called out: "Ah, Lano, your legs were not so spry   120

in the jousting at the Toppo!" Whereupon
    he knotted himself with a bush, as if to hide,
      perhaps because his breath was nearly gone.   123

A swarm of great black mastiffs in full stride
    filled up the wood behind them, like a pack
      of starving swift greyhounds who have been untied.   126

In quel che s'appiattò miser li denti,
  e quel dilaceraro a brano a brano;
  poi sen portar quelle membra dolenti.   129
Presemi allor la mia scorta per mano,
  e menommi al cespuglio che piangea
  per le rotture sanguinenti in vano.   132
«O Iacopo», dicea, «da Santo Andrea,
  che t'è giovato di me fare schermo?
  che colpa ho io de la tua vita rea?».   135
Quando 'l maestro fu sovr' esso fermo,
  disse: «Chi fosti, che per tante punte
  soffi con sangue doloroso sermo?».   138
Ed elli a noi: «O anime che giunte
  siete a veder lo strazio disonesto
  c'ha le mie fronde sì da me disgiunte,   141
raccoglietele al piè del tristo cesto.
  I' fui de la città che nel Batista
  mutò 'l primo padrone; ond' ei per questo   144
sempre con l'arte sua la farà trista;
  e se non fosse che 'n sul passo d'Arno
  rimane ancor di lui alcuna vista,   147
que' cittadin che poi la rifondarno
  sovra 'l cener che d'Attila rimase,
  avrebber fatto lavorare indarno.   150
Io fei gibetto a me de le mie case».

They reached the bush and fell to the attack.

    They tore the one who crouched there limb from limb,

    then seized the wretched pieces and ran back.   129

My escort took my hand, and I walked with him

    to stand before the torn bush where it bled,

    weeping uselessly through every broken stem.   132

"O Jacopo de Sant'Andrea," it said,

    "you made me your screen, and what good did it do?

    How am I to blame for the evil life you led?"   135

Then my master stood above it. "Who were you,"

    he asked, "who have words and blood now blowing out

    through so many limbs that have been snapped in two?"   138

"O souls who arrived to see this shameful rout,"

    it told us, "that has ripped the foliage from

    my boughs, please bring the leaves that are strewn about   141

to the foot of this unhappy bush. My home

    was the city that chose the Baptist to replace

    its ancient patron, who for all time to come   144

will therefore use his art to afflict our race.

    And if the Arno bridge did not still contain

    some semblance of his visage at its base,   147

then those who made the city rise again

    out of the ashes left by Attila when he

    destroyed it would have done their work in vain.   150

I turned my house into my gallows tree."

Notes

line 8   The reference is to the rough terrain of the Maremma in Tuscany, bounded on the north by the river Cecina and on the south by the Marta, on which the town of Corneto is situated.

lines 10–15   The Harpies, daughters of Thaumas and Electra, were usually represented as birds with the faces of women and as defilers of food. In

Book III of the *Aeneid*, they chase the Trojans from the Strophades islands with prophecies of famine and starvation.

lines 47–48   In Book III of the *Aeneid*, Aeneas breaks the branch of a myrtle bush, and from it comes the voice of the murdered Polydorus, a son of King Priam, who is buried beneath the plant.

lines 58–59   The speaker is Pier delle Vigne (c. 1190–1249), a trusted counselor and minister of Emperor Frederick II. After a long and successful career, he was accused of treachery, blinded, and thrown into prison, where he committed suicide. His speech in this canto reflects the rhetorically ornate style both of his official documents, written in Latin, and of his vernacular poetry.

line 64   The reference is to envy.

lines 115–23   Arcolano Maconi of Siena and Giacomo da Sant'Andrea of Padua were notorious spendthrifts and squanderers of their property. Maconi died in 1288 in a bloody encounter between the Sienese and the Aretines at the crossing of the Pieve del Toppo, reputedly choosing to die in battle rather than to escape and live in poverty.

lines 139–51   The speaker of these lines has not been positively identified. According to legend as reported in the early commentaries, in pagan times the Florentines chose Mars, the god of war, as their patron. When the city was converted to Christianity, Mars was replaced by Saint John the Baptist, but the statue of Mars was preserved in a tower, in order to avoid the god's displeasure. When Florence was destroyed by Attila in 450, the tower—and the statue—fell into the Arno. When the city was rebuilt by Charlemagne early in the ninth century, the statue was recovered and placed on a pillar by the river, where it remained until it was swept away by a flood in 1333.

line 149   Florence was in fact besieged by Totila, king of the Ostrogoths, in 542, not by Attila nearly a century earlier. There is no evidence that the city was destroyed by Totila—or by Attila or by anyone else—and then rebuilt by Charlemagne.

Canto XIV

Poi che la carità del natio loco
    mi strinse, raunai le fronde sparte
    e rende'le a colui, ch'era già fioco.   3

Indi venimmo al fine ove si parte
    lo secondo giron dal terzo, e dove
    si vede di giustizia orribil arte.   6

A ben manifestar le cose nove,
    dico che arrivammo ad una landa
    che dal suo letto ogne pianta rimove.   9

La dolorosa selva l'è ghirlanda
    intorno, come 'l fosso tristo ad essa;
    quivi fermammo i passi a randa a randa.   12

Lo spazzo era una rena arida e spessa,
    non d'altra foggia fatta che colei
    che fu da' piè di Caton già soppressa.   15

O vendetta di Dio, quanto tu dei
    esser temuta da ciascun che legge
    ciò che fu manifesto a li occhi mei!   18

D'anime nude vidi molte gregge
    che piangean tutte assai miseramente,
    e parea posta lor diversa legge.   21

Supin giacea in terra alcuna gente,
    alcuna si sedea tutta raccolta,
    e altra andava continüamente.   24

Quella che giva 'ntorno era più molta,
    e quella men che giacëa al tormento,
    ma più al duolo avea la lingua sciolta.   27

Canto XIV

By the love of my native land I was bestirred
    to gather up the scattered leaves for him,
    whose voice had grown too feeble to be heard.   3
From there we moved on, coming to the rim
    that marks the second from the third ring, where
    the hand of justice is horrible and grim.   6
To explain these new things, I must now declare
    that we had come upon a plain which would
    permit no plant to root or flower there.   9
The plain is garlanded by the sad wood,
    just as the wood is girded by the band
    of the miserable ditch. We paused, and stood   12
at the very edge. I saw the ground was sand,
    arid and deep, and in its quality
    like that where Cato marched with his command.   15
O vengeance of God almighty, they should be
    quaking in terror now who read of these
    horrors that were made manifest to me!   18
I saw naked souls bewailing their miseries,
    ranged in many herds, and every group seemed bound
    to suffer a separate set of penalties.   21
Some of them lay stretched out along the ground,
    some of them crouched and squatted, and others went
    unendingly meandering around.   24
Those who wandered were the largest complement.
    Fewer in number were the ones who lay
    on the ground, but they were loudest in lament.   27

Sovra tutto 'l sabbion, d'un cader lento,
    piovean di foco dilatate falde,
    come di neve in alpe sanza vento.   30
Quali Alessandro in quelle parti calde
    d'Indïa vide sopra 'l süo stuolo
    fiamme cadere infino a terra salde,   33
per ch'ei provide a scalpitar lo suolo
    con le sue schiere, acciò che lo vapore
    mei si stingueva mentre ch'era solo: 36
tale scendeva l'etternale ardore;
    onde la rena s'accendea, com' esca
    sotto focile, a doppiar lo dolore.   39
Sanza riposo mai era la tresca
    de le misere mani, or quindi or quinci
    escotendo da sé l'arsura fresca.   42
I' cominciai: «Maestro, tu che vinci
    tutte le cose, fuor che ' demon duri
    ch'a l'intrar de la porta incontra uscinci, 45
chi è quel grande che non par che curi
    lo 'ncendio e giace dispettoso e torto,
    sì che la pioggia non par che 'l marturi?». 48
E quel medesmo, che si fu accorto
    ch'io domandava il mio duca di lui,
    gridò: «Qual io fui vivo, tal son morto. 51
Se Giove stanchi 'l suo fabbro da cui
    crucciato prese la folgore aguta
    onde l'ultimo dì percosso fui;   54
o s'elli stanchi li altri a muta a muta
    in Mongibello a la focina negra,
    chiamando "Buon Vulcano, aiuta, aiuta!", 57
sì com' el fece a la pugna di Flegra,
    e me saetti con tutta sua forza:
    non ne potrebbe aver vendetta allegra». 60

Enormous flakes of fire made their way
 through the air, falling slowly over the whole expanse,
 like snow in the mountains on a windless day.   30
And just as Alexander in the intense
 broiling heat of India saw fireballs fall
 to earth, intact, upon his regiments,   33
and had his men begin to trample all
 the soil around them, so as to contain
 the flames while they were separate and small,   36
so I saw now with the everlasting rain.
 Just as flint will kindle tinder, it ignited
 the sand and thus redoubled all the pain.   39
Here, there, the wretched hands danced an excited
 and constant dance as they brushed away the spate
 of fiery flakes that endlessly alighted.   42
I said: "O master, you who eliminate
 all obstacles except that obstinate breed
 of demons at the entrance to the gate,   45
who is that great one who seems not to heed
 the flame, lying there with a scornful scowl instead,
 who despite the rain remains an unripened seed?"   48
That very shade immediately said,
 knowing he was the one alluded to:
 "What I was when I was alive, I still am, dead!   51
Though Jove wear out his smith, from whom he drew
 the sharpened bolt that on my final day
 was hurled at me in rage and ran me through,   54
though he wear out one by one the whole array
 of dark Mongibello's blacksmiths with the call
 of 'Help me, good Vulcan, help me,' just the way   57
he did at the field of Phlegra, and then with all
 his might fall down upon me, I guarantee
 that his pleasure in his vengeance will be small."   60

Allora il duca mio parlò di forza
    tanto, ch'i' non l'avea sì forte udito:
    «O Capaneo, in ciò che non s'ammorza   63
la tua superbia, se' tu più punito;
    nullo martiro, fuor che la tua rabbia,
    sarebbe al tuo furor dolor compito».   66
Poi si rivolse a me con miglior labbia,
    dicendo: «Quei fu l'un d'i sette regi
    ch'assiser Tebe; ed ebbe e par ch'elli abbia   69
Dio in disdegno, e poco par che 'l pregi;
    ma, com' io dissi lui, li suoi dispetti
    sono al suo petto assai debiti fregi.   72
Or mi vien dietro, e guarda che non metti,
    ancor, li piedi ne la rena arsiccia;
    ma sempre al bosco tien li piedi stretti».   75
Tacendo divenimmo là 've spiccia
    fuor de la selva un picciol fiumicello,
    lo cui rossore ancor mi raccapriccia.   78
Quale del Bulicame esce ruscello
    che parton poi tra lor le peccatrici,
    tal per la rena giù sen giva quello.   81
Lo fondo suo e ambo le pendici
    fatt' era 'n pietra, e ' margini dallato;
    per ch'io m'accorsi che 'l passo era lici.   84
«Tra tutto l'altro ch'i' t'ho dimostrato,
    poscia che noi intrammo per la porta
    lo cui sogliare a nessuno è negato,   87
cosa non fu da li tuoi occhi scorta
    notabile com' è 'l presente rio,
    che sovra sé tutte fiammelle ammorta».   90
Queste parole fuor del duca mio;
    per ch'io 'l pregai che mi largisse 'l pasto
    di cui largito m'avëa il disio.   93

And then my leader spoke more forcefully
    than I had ever heard him speak, and cried:
    "Capaneus, your punishment's intensity   63
grows stronger with your unextinguished pride.
    No torment could be more appropriate
    than your ravings, for the rage you have inside."   66
Then he turned to me, with his face less sternly set.
    "He was one of the seven kings, and with the rest
    besieged Thebes. He held God—and seems to yet—   69
in high disdain, in low esteem at best.
    But his own rantings, as you heard me say,
    are the fittest decorations for his breast.   72
Now follow me, and be careful not to stray
    to the burning sand, but let your feet be led
    close to the forest the entire way."   75
We walked in silence till we reached the bed
    of a stream that spurted from the woods, whose look
    makes me shudder even now, it was so red.   78
Down from the Bulicame comes a brook
    that the sinful women share, just like the flow
    of this rivulet that through the hot sands took   81
its steady course. Its bed was stone, and so
    were both its banks and both its margins too,
    and I saw that this was the path we were to go.   84
"Of all the things that I have shown to you
    since we crossed the threshold of the wide gate where
    no one is ever stopped from coming through,   87
not one among those marvels can compare
    to this stream that has the power to quench the fire
    that comes raining down upon it through the air."   90
So my leader said, which led me to inquire
    if he would have the grace to furnish me
    with the food for which he had furnished the desire.   93

«In mezzo mar siede un paese guasto»,
    diss' elli allora, «che s'appella Creta,
    sotto 'l cui rege fu già 'l mondo casto.   96
Una montagna v'è che già fu lieta
    d'acqua e di fronde, che si chiamò Ida;
    or è diserta come cosa vieta.   99
Rëa la scelse già per cuna fida
    del suo figliuolo, e per celarlo meglio,
    quando piangea, vi facea far le grida.   102
Dentro dal monte sta dritto un gran veglio,
    che tien volte le spalle inver' Dammiata
    e Roma guarda come süo speglio.   105
La sua testa è di fin oro formata,
    e puro argento son le braccia e 'l petto,
    poi è di rame infino a la forcata;   108
da indi in giuso è tutto ferro eletto,
    salvo che 'l destro piede è terra cotta;
    e sta 'n su quel, più che 'n su l'altro, eretto.   111
Ciascuna parte, fuor che l'oro, è rotta
    d'una fessura che lagrime goccia,
    le quali, accolte, fóran quella grotta.   114
Lor corso in questa valle si diroccia;
    fanno Acheronte, Stige e Flegetonta;
    poi sen van giù per questa stretta doccia,   117
infin, là ove più non si dismonta,
    fanno Cocito; e qual sia quello stagno
    tu lo vedrai, però qui non si conta».   120
E io a lui: «Se 'l presente rigagno
    si diriva così dal nostro mondo,
    perché ci appar pur a questo vivagno?».   123
Ed elli a me: «Tu sai che 'l loco è tondo;
    e tutto che tu sie venuto molto,
    pur a sinistra, giù calando al fondo,   126

"There is a land in the middle of the sea,
 a wasteland now, called Crete," my lord replied,
 "under whose king the world lived virtuously.   96

It has a mountain, Ida, once supplied
 with plants and water bright beneath the sky,
 deserted now like something cast aside.   99

There Rhea hid her son in days gone by,
 concealed in his safe cradle, and had each priest
 make a loud clamor when the child would cry.   102

In the mountain is a huge old man encased,
 who looks toward Rome as in a looking glass,
 with his back to Damietta in the east.   105

His head is made of gold of the finest class,
 of purest silver are his arms and breast,
 to where the legs fork he is solid brass.   108

From there he is choice iron, the very best,
 except for his right foot, which is baked clay.
 On this, more than the other, his weight is pressed.   111

All the parts of him except the gold display
 great fissures. Constant tears seep from each crack
 and cut through the floor of the cavern. Slipping away   114

to this valley as they drip from rock to rock,
 they form the Acheron, Styx, and Phlegethon.
 Then they descend along this narrow track   117

till, where no more descending can be done,
 they form Cocytus. I will not speak to you
 of that pool, which your own eyes will look upon."   120

I asked him then: "And yet, if it is true
 that this stream starts up above, where the living are,
 why does it only now come into view?"   123

"You know," he said, "that the place is circular,
 and going toward the bottom with your feet
 turned always to the left, you have come far,   126

non se' ancor per tutto 'l cerchio vòlto;

    per che, se cosa n'apparisce nova,

    non de' addur maraviglia al tuo volto».   129

E io ancor: «Maestro, ove si trova

    Flegetonta e Letè? ché de l'un taci,

    e l'altro di' che si fa d'esta piova».   132

«In tutte tue question certo mi piaci»,

    rispuose, «ma 'l bollor de l'acqua rossa

    dovea ben solver l'una che tu faci.   135

Letè vedrai, ma fuor di questa fossa,

    là dove vanno l'anime a lavarsi

    quando la colpa pentuta è rimossa».   138

Poi disse: «Omai è tempo da scostarsi

    dal bosco; fa che di retro a me vegne:

    li margini fan via, che non son arsi,   141

e sopra loro ogne vapor si spegne».

but the whole circle is not yet complete.

    So there needn't be such astonishment upon

    your face at every new thing that we meet." 129

And I said: "Master, where are Phlegethon

    and Lethe? You have told me that one is fed

    by this rain, and say nothing of the other one." 132

"All of your questions please me well," he said,

    "but you should find one solution in the roll

    of the stream before you as it boils blood-red. 135

And you will see Lethe too, not in this hole

    but far from here, in the place where spirits go

    to wash when penance has purged guilt from the soul. 138

It is time for you to leave the wood, and so

    you must follow me closely through the fiery sand

    on the margins, which do not burn, because the flow 141

quenches all the flames above it before they land."

Notes

line 15	Cato the Younger (95–46 B.C.E.) led his army through the northern Sahara in Libya to escape Caesar's forces after the defeat of Pompey. Dante adapts a reference from Lucan's *Pharsalia*, in which Cato refuses to be carried, as was customary, and instead marches on foot with his soldiers.
line 31	Dante here cites the *De meteoris* of Albertus Magnus (c. 1200–1280), who misrecalls an incident in the (probably spurious) *Epistoli Alexandri*, in which Alexander the Great supposedly describes to his tutor, Aristotle, how he had ordered his soldiers to trample the snow.
line 46	Capaneus was one of the seven against Thebes, as recounted in the *Thebaid*, an epic poem by Statius (Publius Papinius Statius, c. 40–96 C.E.). With the aid of an army and seven mighty champions, Polynices, son of Oedipus, besieged the city when his brother Eteocles refused to relinquish power to him as previously agreed. As he scaled the city wall, Capaneus defied Jove, who slew him with a thunderbolt.
line 56	Mongibello is Mount Etna in Sicily, where Vulcan had his forge.

line 58	At Phlegra, Jove defeated the giants who were storming Mount Olympus.
line 79	The Bulicame is a hot spring, near Viterbo, where a spa developed. According to Boccaccio, a stream was diverted from the spring to serve the needs of the many local prostitutes, who were not allowed to use the public baths.
line 95	The Mediterranean island of Crete was once believed to be the center of the world. According to the *Aeneid*, it was the source of Trojan—and therefore of Roman—civilization. Its king was Saturn (equivalent to the Greek Kronos).
lines 100—102	Saturn devoured each of his children to prevent the fulfillment of the prophecy that he would be overthrown by one of them. His wife, Rhea, hid their son Jupiter (or Jove) to spare him this fate.
lines 103—5	The statue is derived from the dream of Nebuchadnezzar (Daniel 2.31—35), but its placement within Mount Ida is apparently Dante's invention. According to Charles S. Singleton, the Egyptian city of Damietta may have been identified in the Middle Ages with Memphis, the seat of the Pharaohs (*Dante Alighieri: The Divine Comedy. Inferno 2: Commentary*. Princeton, 1970).
line 119	Cocytus is the frozen lake at the pit of hell (Cantos XXXIII–XXXIV).
lines 136—38	In Latin poetry, Lethe is the river of forgetfulness, whose waters are drunk by souls about to be reincarnated. Dante places it at the summit of the Mount of Purgatory.

Canto XV

Ora cen porta l'un de' duri margini;
    e 'l fummo del ruscel di sopra aduggia,
    sì che dal foco salva l'acqua e li argini.   3
Quali Fiamminghi tra Guizzante e Bruggia,
    temendo 'l fiotto che 'nver' lor s'avventa,
    fanno lo schermo perché 'l mar si fuggia;   6
e quali Padoan lungo la Brenta,
    per difender lor ville e lor castelli,
    anzi che Carentana il caldo senta: 9
a tale imagine eran fatti quelli,
    tutto che né sì alti né sì grossi,
    qual che si fosse, lo maestro félli.   12
Già eravam da la selva rimossi
    tanto, ch'i' non avrei visto dov' era,
    perch' io in dietro rivolto mi fossi,   15
quando incontrammo d'anime una schiera
    che venian lungo l'argine, e ciascuna
    ci riguardava come suol da sera   18
guardare uno altro sotto nuova luna;
    e sì ver' noi aguzzavan le ciglia
    come 'l vecchio sartor fa ne la cruna.   21
Così adocchiato da cotal famiglia,
    fui conosciuto da un, che mi prese
    per lo lembo e gridò: «Qual maraviglia!».   24
E io, quando 'l suo braccio a me distese,
    ficcaï li occhi per lo cotto aspetto,
    sì che 'l viso abbrusciato non difese   27

Canto XV

Now the solid margin bears us as we go,
    and the vapor from the stream creates a shade
    that keeps the flames from the banks and from the flow.   3
As Flemings from Wissant to Bruges, afraid
    of the rising tide as it rushes in headlong,
    repel it with the bulwarks they have made,   6
and as the Paduans who live along
    the Brenta keep their towns and castles free
    from the Carentana thaw when the sun grows strong—   9
whoever the master builder here might be,
    he had made these walls, though not as high or wide,
    with similar design and artistry.   12
We had moved so far along that, had I tried
    turning round and looking back where we had been,
    I could not have seen the forest. Alongside   15
the embankment appeared a group of shades just then,
    and each one stared at us as they passed by
    the way that men will stare at other men   18
at nightfall, with the new moon in the sky.
    Each knit his brows as an old tailor does
    when he attempts to thread a needle's eye.   21
Looked over by the lot of them, I was
    recognized by one, who reached out suddenly
    and grasped my hem and cried: "How marvelous!"   24
And I, when he held out his arm toward me,
    scanned his scorched visage and began to peer
    at the baked features, till my memory   27

la conoscenza süa al mio 'ntelletto;

    e chinando la mano a la sua faccia,

      rispuosi: «Siete voi qui, ser Brunetto?».   30

E quelli: «O figliuol mio, non ti dispiaccia

    se Brunetto Latino un poco teco

      ritorna 'n dietro e lascia andar la traccia».   33

I' dissi lui: «Quanto posso, ven preco;

    e se volete che con voi m'asseggia,

      faròl, se piace a costui che vo seco».   36

«O figliuol», disse, «qual di questa greggia

    s'arresta punto, giace poi cent' anni

      sanz' arrostarsi quando 'l foco il feggia.   39

Però va oltre: i' ti verrò a' panni;

    e poi rigiugnerò la mia masnada,

      che va piangendo i suoi etterni danni».   42

Io non osava scender de la strada

    per andar par di lui; ma 'l capo chino

      tenea com' uom che reverente vada.   45

El cominciò: «Qual fortuna o destino

    anzi l'ultimo dì qua giù ti mena?

      e chi è questi che mostra 'l cammino?».   48

«Là sù di sopra, in la vita serena»,

    rispuos' io lui, «mi smarri' in una valle,

      avanti che l'età mia fosse piena.   51

Pur ier mattina le volsi le spalle:

    questi m'apparve, tornand' ïo in quella,

      e reducemi a ca per questo calle».   54

Ed elli a me: «Se tu segui tua stella,

    non puoi fallire a glorïoso porto,

      se ben m'accorsi ne la vita bella;   57

e s'io non fossi sì per tempo morto,

    veggendo il cielo a te così benigno,

      dato t'avrei a l'opera conforto.   60

allowed their original image to come clear,

    and then I stretched my hand down toward his face

    and answered: "Ser Brunetto, are you here?"   30

"Let it not displease you if for a little space

    Brunetto Latini turns back with you, my son,"

    he said, "and lets his band move on apace."   33

"With all my heart," I said, "let it be done,

    or I will sit with you, if you desire,

    if it pleases him with whom I journey on."   36

"My son, if one stops for a second, the laws require

    that he lie for a hundred years on the burning plain,

    forbidden to brush away the falling fire.   39

I will follow at your hem, and then regain

    my company where they wander in their woe,

    loudly bewailing their eternal pain."   42

I did not dare to leave the path and go

    to his level, but like one in reverence

    I walked beside him with my head bowed low.   45

And he began: "What destiny or chance

    brings you down here before your dying day,

    and who points out the road by which you advance?"   48

I said: "In the pleasant life I lost my way

    before the fullness of my age had come.

    It was in a valley that I went astray.   51

Yesterday morning I was fleeing from

    that place when I turned back, and he came to me.

    And now along this path he leads me home."   54

"Follow your star and you will certainly

    come to a glorious harbor, if it is true

    that in the sweet life I had power to see,"   57

he said, "and seeing heaven so kind to you,

    if I had not died so soon, I surely would

    have sustained you in the work you seek to do.   60

Ma quello ingrato popolo maligno
    che discese di Fiesole *ab* antico,
    e tiene ancor del monte e del macigno,   63
ti si farà, per tuo ben far, nimico;
    ed è ragion, ché tra li lazzi sorbi
    si disconvien fruttare al dolce fico.   66
Vecchia fama nel mondo li chiama orbi;
    gent' è avara, invidiosa e superba:
    dai lor costumi fa che tu ti forbi.   69
La tua fortuna tanto onor ti serba,
    che l'una parte e l'altra avranno fame
    di te; ma lungi fia dal becco l'erba.   72
Faccian le bestie fiesolane strame
    di lor medesme, e non tocchin la pianta,
    s'alcuna surge ancora in lor letame,   75
in cui riviva la sementa santa
    di que' Roman che vi rimaser quando
    fu fatto il nido di malizia tanta».   78
«Se fosse tutto pieno il mio dimando»,
    rispuos' io lui, «voi non sareste ancora
    de l'umana natura posto in bando;   81
ché 'n la mente m'è fitta, e or m'accora,
    la cara e buona imagine paterna
    di voi quando nel mondo ad ora ad ora   84
m'insegnavate come l'uom s'etterna:
    e quant' io l'abbia in grado, mentr' io vivo
    convien che ne la mia lingua si scerna.   87
Ciò che narrate di mio corso scrivo,
    e serbolo a chiosar con altro testo
    a donna che saprà, s'a lei arrivo.   90
Tanto vogl' io che vi sia manifesto,
    pur che mia coscïenza non mi garra,
    ch'a la Fortuna, come vuol, son presto.   93

But that people of malice and ingratitude
    who came down from Fiesole so long ago,
      though the mountain and the rock still rule their blood,   63
will despise you for your good work—rightly so,
    for it is not fit that the sweet fig should abide
      and bear its fruit where bitter sorb trees grow.   66
A race of envy, avarice, and pride,
    they are blind, as the world has said since olden days.
      Of their customs let yourself be purified.   69
The honors fortune holds for you will raise
    a hunger in both factions for your doom,
      but the grass grows far from where the goat will graze.   72
Let the wild beasts from Fiesole consume
    themselves for fodder, and let them not molest
      that plant—if any bit of it still bloom   75
in their manure—that preserves the best,
    the sacred seed of the Romans who chose to stay
      when the city was turned into corruption's nest."   78
"If I could have the things for which I pray,"
    I said to him, "then you would not yet be
      banished from our humanity this way.   81
Forever fixed in poignant memory
    is the kind, paternal, loving face I knew
      when in the world above you instructed me   84
from time to time in what a man must do
    to become eternal. I must proclaim with pride,
      for as long as I still live, my debt to you.   87
I will write what you have told of my fortune's tide
    with another text, which a lady will understand
      and make clear to me, if I ever reach her side.   90
But know this much: as long as I can stand
    upright, with conscience clear, I will undergo
      unafraid whatever Fortune may have planned.   93

Non è nuova a li orecchi miei tal arra:
    però giri Fortuna la sua rota
    come le piace, e 'l villan la sua marra».   96
Lo mio maestro allora in su la gota
    destra si volse in dietro e riguardommi;
    poi disse: «Bene ascolta chi la nota».   99
Né per tanto di men parlando vommi
    con ser Brunetto, e dimando chi sono
    li suoi compagni più noti e più sommi.   102
Ed elli a me: «Saper d'alcuno è buono;
    de li altri fia laudabile tacerci,
    ché 'l tempo saria corto a tanto suono.   105
In somma sappi che tutti fur cherci
    e litterati grandi e di gran fama,
    d'un peccato medesmo al mondo lerci.   108
Priscian sen va con quella turba grama,
    e Francesco d'Accorso anche; e vedervi,
    s'avessi avuto di tal tigna brama,   111
colui potei che dal servo de' servi
    fu trasmutato d'Arno in Bacchiglione,
    dove lasciò li mal protesi nervi.   114
Di più direi; ma 'l venire e 'l sermone
    più lungo esser non può, però ch'i' veggio
    là surger nuovo fummo del sabbione.   117
Gente vien con la quale esser non deggio.
    Sieti raccomandato il mio Tesoro,
    nel qual io vivo ancora, e più non cheggio».   120
Poi si rivolse, e parve di coloro
    che corrono a Verona il drappo verde
    per la campagna; e parve di costoro   123
quelli che vince, non colui che perde.

This prophecy is not new to me, and so
  let Fortune turn her wheel as she sees fit
  and let the peasant likewise turn his hoe."   96
At these last words my master turned a bit
  round to his right and looked at me and said:
  "He listens well who makes a note of it."   99
I did not give an answer, but instead
  asked Ser Brunetto who were the most renowned
  and the highest born in that circle of the dead.   102
"It is good to learn of some who share this ground,"
  he said, "but the rest require reticence,
  for the time for so much talk cannot be found.   105
In short, they all were men of great eminence,
  all of them clerics and men of letters who
  were one and all befouled by the same offense.   108
Here Priscian moves amid the wretched crew,
  with Francesco d'Accorso also among the reviled,
  and had you a taste for mange, you might see too   111
the one whom the servant of servants had exiled
  from the Arno to the Bacchiglione, where
  he left the distended nerves he had defiled.   114
There is more that I could say, but I do not dare
  speak or stay with you longer, for I see
  a new smoke rising from the sand out there.   117
People are coming with whom I must not be.
  But let my *Treasure*, where I still live on—
  I ask no more—live in your memory."   120
Then he doubled back, like one of those who run
  for the green cloth at Verona, and as my eyes
  followed him, he seemed not to be the one   123
who loses, but the one who wins the prize.

Notes

lines 4–9   Wissant and Bruges are in Flanders. Chiarentana is a mountainous region north of Padua. In both areas, dikes were constructed to prevent flooding.

line 30   Brunetto Latini (c. 1220–1294) was a notary (hence the title *Ser*) and a prominent Guelph. He lived in France from 1260 to 1266, during a Ghibelline ascendancy, and was afterward active in public affairs in Florence. His principal volume was *Li Livres dou Tresor*, an encyclopedic work in French prose. His *Tesoretto* is a long allegorical and didactic poem in Italian, which influenced Dante in the writing of the *Comedy*. There is no other surviving or known source for the identification of Brunetto as a homosexual.

lines 61–78   As did Farinata in Canto X, Brunetto prophesies Dante's exile from Florence. These lines draw upon the legend, retold by Brunetto in his *Tresor*, that Florence was founded by the Romans after the siege of nearby Fiesole, where Catiline had fled after the failure of his conspiracy (63 B.C.E.), and that the Fiesolans, including Catiline's followers, intermingled with the Roman settlers.

lines 89–90   The other text is the prophecy of Farinata; the lady is Beatrice.

line 109   Priscian was a celebrated Latin grammarian of the early sixth century. The little that survives concerning him says nothing about homosexuality.

line 110   Francesco d'Accorso (1225–1293) was born in Bologna, where he became—as his father had been in Florence—a lawyer and a professor of civil law. In 1273, he went to England at the invitation of Edward I, and was for a time a lecturer at Oxford.

lines 112–14   Andrea de' Mozzi was bishop of Florence from 1287 to 1295, when he was transferred to Vicenza on the Bacchiglione because of his scandalous ways. He died in February 1296. Since the pope who transferred him was Boniface VIII, the traditional description of the pontiff as "the servant of servants" has a satirical application here.

lines 121–24   The race in question, in which the runners competed naked, was established in 1207 and held on the first Sunday in Lent.

Canto XVI

Già era in loco onde s'udia 'l rimbombo
    de l'acqua che cadea ne l'altro giro,
    simile a quel che l'arnie fanno rombo,   3

quando tre ombre insieme si partiro,
    correndo, d'una torma che passava
    sotto la pioggia de l'aspro martiro.   6

Venian ver' noi, e ciascuna gridava:
    «Sòstati tu ch'a l'abito ne sembri
    esser alcun di nostra terra prava».   9

Ahimè, che piaghe vidi ne' lor membri,
    ricenti e vecchie, da le fiamme incese!
    Ancor men duol pur ch'i' me ne rimembri.   12

A le lor grida il mio dottor s'attese;
    volse 'l viso ver' me, e «Or aspetta»,
    disse, «a costor si vuole esser cortese.   15

E se non fosse il foco che saetta
    la natura del loco, i' dicerei
    che meglio stesse a te che a lor la fretta».   18

Ricominciar, come noi restammo, ei
    l'antico verso; e quando a noi fuor giunti,
    fenno una rota di sé tutti e trei.   21

Qual sogliono i campion far nudi e unti,
    avvisando lor presa e lor vantaggio,
    prima che sien tra lor battuti e punti,   24

così rotando, ciascuno il visaggio
    drizzava a me, sì che 'n contraro il collo
    faceva ai piè continüo vïaggio.   27

Canto XVI

In that place to which we had already come,
    the water falling into the next ring
    resounded like a beehive's steady hum,   3
when all at once three shades came hurrying
    across the sand as they broke free from the rest
    of a band beneath the rain's tormenting sting.   6
All three cried out with one voice as they pressed
    toward where we were: "Stop, you who seem to be
    from our wicked land, by the way that you are dressed."   9
Alas, what old and fresh wounds I could see
    burned in their members, etched into their skin.
    Remembering it now still saddens me.   12
My teacher attended to their cries, and then
    turned to me, saying: "Here courtesy is due.
    You must wait, and be respectful to these men.   15
Were it not for all the flames that fly here through
    the nature of this place, then I would feel
    this haste suits them much less than it suits you."   18
They resumed their old refrain as we turned heel
    to wait for them. They reached us, and at once
    all three combined themselves into a wheel.   21
As oiled and naked wrestling champions
    circle warily, seeking grip and vantage place
    before the thrusting and the blows commence,   24
so each one fixed his eyes upon my face,
    and his head and feet as he was turning there
    went in opposite directions with each pace.   27

E «Se miseria d'esto loco sollo
      rende in dispetto noi e nostri prieghi»,
      cominciò l'uno, «e 'l tinto aspetto e brollo,   30
la fama nostra il tuo animo pieghi
      a dirne chi tu se', che i vivi piedi
      così sicuro per lo 'nferno freghi.   33
Questi, l'orme di cui pestar mi vedi,
      tutto che nudo e dipelato vada,
      fu di grado maggior che tu non credi: 36
nepote fu de la buona Gualdrada;
      Guido Guerra ebbe nome, e in sua vita
      fece col senno assai e con la spada.   39
L'altro, ch'appresso me la rena trita,
      è Tegghiaio Aldobrandi, la cui voce
      nel mondo sù dovria esser gradita.   42
E io, che posto son con loro in croce,
      Iacopo Rusticucci fui, e certo
      la fiera moglie più ch'altro mi nuoce».   45
S'i' fossi stato dal foco coperto,
      gittato mi sarei tra lor di sotto,
      e credo che 'l dottor l'avria sofferto;   48
ma perch' io mi sarei brusciato e cotto,
      vinse paura la mia buona voglia
      che di loro abbracciar mi facea ghiotto.   51
Poi cominciai: «Non dispetto, ma doglia
      la vostra condizion dentro mi fisse,
      tanta che tardi tutta si dispoglia,   54
tosto che questo mio segnor mi disse
      parole per le quali i' mi pensai
      che qual voi siete, tal gente venisse.   57
Di vostra terra sono, e sempre mai
      l'ovra di voi e li onorati nomi
      con affezion ritrassi e ascoltai.   60

One said: "If our charred faces, singed of hair,
    and the misery of this barren sand compel
    contempt for us and for our every prayer,   30
then let our fame prevail on you to tell
    who you are, who walk with living feet that show
    such confidence upon the floor of hell.   33
This one whose steps I trample must now go
    naked and peeled, but in the days that were
    he was of higher station than you know.   36
The good Gualdrada was his grandmother.
    He was Guido Guerra. His good works combined
    the deeds of a counselor and those of a warrior.   39
The other one, who treads the sand behind,
    is Tegghiaio Aldobrandi. Wise words from him
    the world above would have done well to mind.   42
And I, who am set upon the cross with them,
    was Iacopo Rusticucci. The savagery
    of my wife did much to bring me where I am."   45
Could I have braved the flames without injury,
    I would have flung myself down from the wall,
    and I think my guide would not have hindered me,   48
but since I would have burnt and baked, the pall
    of fear held back my good will from achieving
    its greedy impulse to embrace them all.   51
Then I began: "It was not contempt, but grieving
    for your eternal misery that lay—
    so heavily it will be a long time leaving—   54
upon my heart when I heard my master say
    respectful words that conveyed the eminence
    of the men that we saw hurrying our way.   57
I am from your land. With what fond sentiments
    I have always loved to hear and to retell
    your honored names and high accomplishments.   60

Lascio lo fele e vo per dolci pomi

    promessi a me per lo verace duca;

    ma 'nfino al centro pria convien ch'i' tomi».   63

«Se lungamente l'anima conduca

    le membra tue», rispuose quelli ancora,

    «e se la fama tua dopo te luca,   66

cortesia e valor dì se dimora

    ne la nostra città sì come suole,

    o se del tutto se n'è gita fora;   69

ché Guiglielmo Borsiere, il qual si duole

    con noi per poco e va là coi compagni,

    assai ne cruccia con le sue parole».   72

«La gente nuova e i sùbiti guadagni

    orgoglio e dismisura han generata,

    Fiorenza, in te, sì che tu già ten piagni».   75

Così gridai con la faccia levata;

    e i tre, che ciò inteser per risposta,

    guardar l'un l'altro com' al ver si guata.   78

«Se l'altre volte sì poco ti costa»,

    rispuoser tutti, «il satisfare altrui,

    felice te se sì parli a tua posta!   81

Però, se campi d'esti luoghi bui

    e torni a riveder le belle stelle,

    quando ti gioverà dicere "I' fui",   84

fa che di noi a la gente favelle».

    Indi rupper la rota, e a fuggirsi

    ali sembiar le gambe loro isnelle.   87

Un amen non saria possuto dirsi

    tosto così com' e' fuoro spariti;

    per ch'al maestro parve di partirsi.   90

Io lo seguiva, e poco eravam iti,

    che 'l suon de l'acqua n'era sì vicino,

    che per parlar saremmo a pena uditi.   93

I will leave the gall, to go where sweet fruits dwell,

as my honest leader promised me, although

I must first go down to the very core of hell." 63

"So may your body for a long time go

still guided by your soul," that one replied,

"so may your fame even afterward still glow, 66

tell us if valor and courtesy abide

in our city as they did in olden days,

or if such customs have been cast aside. 69

Guiglielmo Borsiere, walking in these ways

of pain as a newcomer to our band,

has told us things that fill us with malaise." 72

"New people and sudden wealth have brought your land

so much excess and so much vanity,

O Florence, the time of weeping is at hand," 75

I cried with my face uplifted. And all three

took this to be my answer, and began

exchanging looks that men wear when they see 78

the truth. They said: "If at other times you can

speak with so little cost and with such flair

to satisfy others, you are a happy man. 81

And if you escape these dark lands to go where

you may gaze upon the lovely stars again,

when you take pleasure in saying 'I was there,' 84

be sure to speak of us to living men."

And then they broke their circle, whereupon

they fled on legs that seemed like wings. *Amen* 87

could not be said by the time that they were gone

from sight, so quickly did they disappear.

My master thought it best that we move on. 90

I followed, and in a short time we could hear

the sound of water falling with such force

that, if we spoke, not one word would be clear. 93

Come quel fiume c'ha proprio cammino
 prima dal Monte Viso 'nver' levante,
 da la sinistra costa d'Apennino,   96
che si chiama Acquacheta suso, avante
 che si divalli giù nel basso letto,
 e a Forlì di quel nome è vacante,   99
rimbomba là sovra San Benedetto
 de l'Alpe per cadere ad una scesa
 ove dovea per mille esser recetto;   102
così, giù d'una ripa discoscesa,
 trovammo risonar quell' acqua tinta,
 sì che 'n poc' ora avria l'orecchia offesa.   105
Io avea una corda intorno cinta,
 e con essa pensai alcuna volta
 prender la lonza a la pelle dipinta.   108
Poscia ch'io l'ebbi tutta da me sciolta,
 sì come 'l duca m'avea comandato,
 porsila a lui aggroppata e ravvolta.   111
Ond' ei si volse inver' lo destro lato,
 e alquanto di lunge da la sponda
 la gittò giuso in quell' alto burrato.   114
'E' pur convien che novità risponda',
 dicea fra me medesmo, 'al novo cenno
 che 'l maestro con l'occhio sì seconda'.   117
Ahi quanto cauti li uomini esser dienno
 presso a color che non veggion pur l'ovra,
 ma per entro i pensier miran col senno!   120
El disse a me: «Tosto verrà di sovra
 ciò ch'io attendo e che il tuo pensier sogna;
 tosto convien ch'al tuo viso si scovra».   123
Sempre a quel ver c'ha faccia di menzogna
 de' l'uom chiuder le labbra fin ch'el puote,
 però che sanza colpa fa vergogna;   126

As that river (the Acquacheta at its source,

    but at Forlì it leaves that name behind)

    which is the very first to take its course   96

from Monte Viso eastward and to wind

    down the Apennines' left slope to its low bed,

    at floodtide when the waters are combined   99

above San Benedetto dell'Arpe is sped

    so mightily that it makes one cataract where

    there might otherwise be a thousand rills instead,   102

here too there was such a roaring in the air

    of dark water dropping steeply that the din

    would have hurt our ears if we had lingered there.   105

Wrapped around me was a cord which I had been

    hoping to make good use of previously,

    to catch the leopard with the painted skin.   108

My leader ordered me to work it free.

    I passed the cord from my hand into his

    wound in a coil, and taking it from me   111

he flung it well beyond the precipice

    when he had turned a little to his right,

    and down it fell into the deep abyss.   114

"This strange signal that he follows with his sight,"

    I told myself, "now in response to it

    surely some strange new thing will come to light."   117

How careful men should be with those whose wit

    can see not only what we say and do

    but has the power to pluck the intimate   120

thoughts from our heads! He said: "The thing that you

    are dreaming in your mind, the thing that I

    am looking for, will soon come into view."   123

When the truth he wants to tell has the face of a lie,

    a man should be silent. Though he does no wrong,

    some shame will still attach to him thereby.   126

ma qui tacer nol posso; e per le note
    di questa comedìa, lettor, ti giuro,
      s'elle non sien di lunga grazia vòte,   129
ch'i' vidi per quell' aere grosso e scuro
    venir notando una figura in suso,
      maravigliosa ad ogne cor sicuro,   132
sì come torna colui che va giuso
    talora a solver l'àncora ch'aggrappa
      o scoglio o altro che nel mare è chiuso,   135
che 'n sù si stende e da piè si rattrappa.

But, reader, here I cannot hold my tongue.

By the notes of this very comedy, I swear—

so may the favor that it finds be long—   129

that even those of stoutest heart would stare

in amazement at the sight that greeted me,

floating up through the dark and heavy air   132

the way that one who has worked the anchor free

from a rock or another obstacle will go

back to the surface, rising through the sea   135

with arms stretched high and feet drawn in below.

Notes

line 37	Gualdrada was the daughter of Bellincione Berti, and when young supposedly impressed Emperor Otto IV with her beauty, intelligence, and modesty. Unfortunately for legend, she was married in 1180, twenty years before Otto became emperor and nearly thirty before he visited Florence.
line 38	Guido Guerra (1220–1272) was a Guelph leader on the field of battle. He advised the Florentine Guelphs against the planned Sienese campaign of 1260; his counsel was disregarded, with disastrous results.
line 41	Tegghiaio Aldobrandi was another leader of the Florentine Guelphs, who also counseled against the Sienese expedition.
line 44	Jacopo Rusticucci was apparently a middle-class merchant, and thus the social inferior of his two companions. According to early commentators, his wife was so shrewish that he sent her back to her family.
line 70	Little is known of Guiglielmo Borsiere, whose surname suggests "pursemaker." He is the protagonist of one of the tales in Boccaccio's *Decameron.*
lines 94–102	San Benedetto dell'Arpe is a monastery near the source of the Montone, a river northeast of Florence that runs to the Adriatic.

Canto XVII

«Ecco la fiera con la coda aguzza,
    che passa i monti e rompe i muri e l'armi!
    Ecco colei che tutto 'l mondo appuzza!».   3
Sì cominciò lo mio duca a parlarmi;
    e accennolle che venisse a proda,
    vicino al fin d'i passeggiati marmi.   6
E quella sozza imagine di froda
    sen venne, e arrivò la testa e 'l busto,
    ma 'n su la riva non trasse la coda.   9
La faccia sua era faccia d'uom giusto,
    tanto benigna avea di fuor la pelle,
    e d'un serpente tutto l'altro fusto;   12
due branche avea pilose insin l'ascelle;
    lo dosso e 'l petto e ambedue le coste
    dipinti avea di nodi e di rotelle.   15
Con più color, sommesse e sovraposte
    non fer mai drappi Tartari né Turchi,
    né fuor tai tele per Aragne imposte.   18
Come talvolta stanno a riva i burchi,
    che parte sono in acqua e parte in terra,
    e come là tra li Tedeschi lurchi   21
lo bivero s'assetta a far sua guerra,
    così la fiera pessima si stava
    su l'orlo ch'è di pietra e 'l sabbion serra.   24
Nel vano tutta sua coda guizzava,
    torcendo in sù la venenosa forca
    ch'a guisa di scorpion la punta armava.   27

Canto XVII

"Behold the beast with the pointed tail, who can pass
    over mountains, who breaks walls and weaponry,
    who makes the world a festering morass!"   3
These were the words my master said to me
    while beckoning him to the cliff's edge, near the place
    where the marble pathway ended suddenly.   6
Fraud's filthy image came to us apace,
    beaching head and torso at my master's sign
    but leaving his tail to dangle into space.   9
His face was the face of a just man, so benign
    was the outward aspect that it chose to wear,
    but beneath it his long trunk was serpentine.   12
To the armpits his two paws were thick with hair.
    His breast and back and both sides were arrayed
    with painted knots and ringlets everywhere.   15
Never was cloth that Turks or Tartars made
    so colorful in design and background, nor
    did Arachne ever weave such rich brocade.   18
The way a boat will lie along the shore
    half in the water and half upon the ground,
    the way the beaver settles in for its war   21
in the swilling Germans' land, was the way I found
    that worst of all beasts perched upon the ring
    of rocky ledge by which the sand is bound.   24
The entire length of his tail was quivering
    in the emptiness and lifting its forked end,
    which had its point armed like a scorpion's sting.   27

Lo duca disse: «Or convien che si torca
    la nostra via un poco insino a quella
    bestia malvagia che colà si corca».   30
Però scendemmo a la destra mammella,
    e diece passi femmo in su lo stremo,
    per ben cessar la rena e la fiammella.   33
E quando noi a lei venuti semo,
    poco più oltre veggio in su la rena
    gente seder propinqua al loco scemo.   36
Quivi 'l maestro «Acciò che tutta piena
    esperïenza d'esto giron porti»,
    mi disse, «va, e vedi la lor mena.   39
Li tuoi ragionamenti sian là corti;
    mentre che torni, parlerò con questa,
    che ne conceda i suoi omeri forti».   42
Così ancor su per la strema testa
    di quel settimo cerchio tutto solo
    andai, dove sedea la gente mesta.   45
Per li occhi fora scoppiava lor duolo;
    di qua, di là soccorrien con le mani
    quando a' vapori, e quando al caldo suolo: 48
non altrimenti fan di state i cani
    or col ceffo or col piè, quando son morsi
    o da pulci o da mosche o da tafani.   51
Poi che nel viso a certi li occhi porsi,
    ne' quali 'l doloroso foco casca,
    non ne conobbi alcun; ma io m'accorsi   54
che dal collo a ciascun pendea una tasca
    ch'avea certo colore e certo segno,
    e quindi par che 'l loro occhio si pasca.   57
E com' io riguardando tra lor vegno,
    in una borsa gialla vidi azzurro
    che d'un leone avea faccia e contegno.   60

"And now," my leader told me, "we must bend
     our way a bit so that it will bring us where
     that beast is lying." We started to descend   30
on the right side of the marble path, taking care
     to walk ten steps out on the cliff and be
     clear of the burning sand and the fiery air.   33
When we had reached the creature, I could see
     that some people sat on the sand near the abyss
     a short way off, and my master said to me: 36
"To take the whole experience of this
     circle away with you, you ought to go
     and learn from them what their situation is.   39
Speak to them briefly, and while you are doing so,
     I will see if I can persuade this one to stretch
     his mighty shoulders and carry us below."   42
So I walked on by myself along the ledge
     of the seventh circle and approached that band
     of wretched people sitting near the edge.   45
Their pain was bursting through their eyes. One hand
     or another would fly now here, now there, to stay
     the falling fire or the scorching sand,   48
in the same way that a dog on a summer day,
     with its paws in motion now, and now its snout,
     tries to drive the horseflies, fleas, or flies away.   51
There were none among those people sitting out
     under the flames that I could recognize,
     but each of them had a great purse hung about   54
his neck, and each of them seemed to feast his eyes
     upon the moneybag that he was wearing.
     Each one had its own color and device.   57
The first I saw as I moved among them, staring,
     was a yellow purse with an azure form that would
     have been a lion by its shape and bearing.   60

Poi, procedendo di mio sguardo il curro,
 vidine un'altra come sangue rossa,
 mostrando un'oca bianca più che burro. 63
E un che d'una scrofa azzurra e grossa
 segnato avea lo suo sacchetto bianco,
 mi disse: «Che fai tu in questa fossa? 66
Or te ne va; e perché se' vivo anco,
 sappi che 'l mio vicin Vitalïano
 sederà qui dal mio sinistro fianco. 69
Con questi Fiorentin son padoano:
 spesse fïate mi 'ntronan li orecchi
 gridando: "Vegna 'l cavalier sovrano, 72
che recherà la tasca con tre becchi!"».
 Qui distorse la bocca e di fuor trasse
 la lingua, come bue che 'l naso lecchi. 75
E io, temendo no 'l più star crucciasse
 lui che di poco star m'avea 'mmonito,
 torna'mi in dietro da l'anime lasse. 78
Trova' il duca mio ch'era salito
 già su la groppa del fiero animale,
 e disse a me: «Or sie forte e ardito. 81
Omai si scende per sì fatte scale;
 monta dinanzi, ch'i' voglio esser mezzo,
 sì che la coda non possa far male». 84
Qual è colui che sì presso ha 'l riprezzo
 de la quartana, c'ha già l'unghie smorte,
 e triema tutto pur guardando 'l rezzo, 87
tal divenn' io a le parole porte;
 ma vergogna mi fé le sue minacce,
 che innanzi a buon segnor fa servo forte. 90
I' m'assettai in su quelle spallacce;
 sì volli dir, ma la voce non venne
 com' io credetti: 'Fa che tu m'abbracce'. 93

Whiter than butter was the goose that stood
 on a sack a little further off, displayed
 against a background that was red as blood.   63
And one who wore a white purse, which portrayed
 a gross blue sow, saw me there and raised a cry:
 "Get out of here, whoever you are who've strayed 66
to this ditch! And know, since you have yet to die,
 that my townsman Vitaliano will appear
 and will sit here at my left side by and by.   69
I am Paduan, and all these others here
 are Florentines who keep shouting, the whole crew,
 'Let him come down, the sovereign cavalier   72
who will bring the purse with the three goats!'" Then he drew
 his mouth in a grimace and thrust out his tongue
 the way an ox that licks its nose will do.   75
I turned, and spent no further time among
 those weary souls, lest I provoke my guide,
 who had cautioned me that I should not be long. 78
I found that he already was astride
 the savage creature's rump. He said to me:
 "Be bold, and let your soul be fortified.   81
From this point on, our going down will be
 on such stairs. Mount in front, here I will sit
 to keep his tail from doing you injury."   84
As one with quartan draws so near his fit
 that his nails grow pale and shade can make him start
 to tremble at the very sight of it,   87
such terror did those words of his impart.
 But shame, which gives a servant courage when
 he stands before a good lord, reproved my heart. 90
I scaled the hideous shoulders and I began
 to try to say (though my voice did not accord
 with my intent): "Be sure you hold me then." 93

Ma esso, ch'altra volta mi sovvenne
　　ad altro forse, tosto ch'i' montai
　　con le braccia m'avvinse e mi sostenne;　　　　96
e disse: «Gerïon, moviti omai:
　　le rote larghe, e lo scender sia poco;
　　pensa la nova soma che tu hai».　　　　99
Come la navicella esce di loco
　　in dietro in dietro, sì quindi si tolse;
　　e poi ch'al tutto si sentì a gioco,　　　　102
là 'v' era 'l petto, la coda rivolse,
　　e quella tesa, come anguilla, mosse,
　　e con le branche l'aere a sé raccolse.　　　　105
Maggior paura non credo che fosse
　　quando Fetonte abbandonò li freni,
　　per che 'l ciel, come pare ancor, si cosse;　　　　108
né quando Icaro misero le reni
　　sentì spennar per la scaldata cera,
　　gridando il padre a lui «Mala via tieni!»,　　　　111
che fu la mia, quando vidi ch'i' era
　　ne l'aere d'ogne parte, e vidi spenta
　　ogne veduta fuor che de la fera.　　　　114
Ella sen va notando lenta lenta;
　　rota e discende, ma non me n'accorgo
　　se non che al viso e di sotto mi venta.　　　　117
Io sentia già da la man destra il gorgo
　　far sotto noi un orribile scroscio,
　　per che con li occhi 'n giù la testa sporgo.　　　　120
Allor fu' io più timido a lo stoscio,
　　però ch'i' vidi fuochi e senti' pianti;
　　ond' io tremando tutto mi raccoscio.　　　　123
E vidi poi, ché nol vedea davanti,
　　lo scendere e 'l girar per li gran mali
　　che s'appressavan da diversi canti.　　　　126

But he, who had at other times restored
    my heart through other dangers, gripped me tight
    and steadied me once I had climbed aboard.   96
He said: "Now, Geryon, carry us from this height.
    And, remembering the new burden that you bear,
    make great wide circles and a long, slow flight."   99
As bit by bit a boat backs out from where
    it is moored, just so did Geryon begin
    to move, and when he sensed he was in the air   102
he turned his tail round where his breast had been
    and stretched it out, and it wriggled like an eel,
    and with his paws he gathered the air in.   105
Such fear, I think, did no one ever feel,
    not Phaëthon when he dropped the reins that day
    and burned the sky with a scar still visible,   108
nor wretched Icarus when he went astray
    and the wax began to melt and his father cried:
    "You are going wrong!" and his feathers fell away.   111
Not even they could have been as terrified
    as I with nothing but the beast in view
    and nothing but thin air on every side.   114
The wind upon my face and the wind that blew
    from beneath were the only ways I had to know
    that, wheeling, dropping, Geryon slowly flew.   117
And now I heard a horrid roaring grow
    from the whirlpool underneath us, on our right,
    so I stretched out my neck to look below.   120
Then I was filled with even greater fright,
    seeing fires and hearing cries of misery,
    and, trembling in every part, I held on tight.   123
Now for the first time I could really see
    the turn and descent. On every side my eyes
    took in onrushing scenes of agony.   126

Come 'l falcon ch'è stato assai su l'ali,

    che sanza veder logoro o uccello

    fa dire al falconiere «Omè, tu cali!»,   129

discende lasso onde si move isnello,

    per cento rote, e da lunge si pone

    dal suo maestro, disdegnoso e fello;   132

così ne puose al fondo Gerïone

    al piè al piè de la stagliata rocca,

    e, discarcate le nostre persone,   135

si dileguò come da corda cocca.

As when a falcon for a long time flies
    without catching sight of any bird or lure
    ("You're already coming down?" the master cries)   129
and, after a hundred weary circles where
    it had taken off so swiftly, comes back down,
    sullen and angry, far from the falconer,   132
so, when we were discharged by Geryon
    at the very base of the jagged cliff, far below
    where we began, he turned and he was gone,   135
vanishing like an arrow from the bow.

Notes

line 1   The monster is identified as Geryon at line 97 of the canto. In classical mythology, he was the treacherous three-headed or three-bodied king of an island in the far western stream Oceanus and the possessor of a fabled herd of cattle. He was killed by Hercules as part of his tenth labor, that of the oxen of the sun. He is mentioned in the *Aeneid* and in Ovid's *Heroides*. Dante's depiction of him draws upon his tripartite nature, but incorporates details from the plague of locusts in Revelations and from the manticore as described in Pliny's *Historia naturalis* and in the *Tresor* of Brunetto Latini.

line 18   Arachne challenged the goddess Athene (Minerva to the Romans) to a weaving competition. Arachne's tapestry depicted the amours of the gods. Angered by its subject, unable to find any flaw in its craftsmanship, Minerva destroyed the design of Arachne, who hanged herself. The goddess, however, saved her and changed her into a spider. Ovid tells the story in Book VI of the *Metamorphoses*.

lines 59–60   The azure lion on a yellow background was the heraldic device of the Gianfigliazzi family of Florence, prominent Black Guelphs and accused usurers.

lines 61–63   The white goose on the blood-red field denotes the Ubriachi family, Ghibelline bankers and moneychangers.

lines 64–65   The white purse with the blue sow signifies the Scrovegni family of Padua. The speaker is usually identified as Reginaldo degli Scrovegni, who became very wealthy through the practice of usury and died around 1290.

line 68   This line is customarily understood to refer to Vitaliano del Dente, who
                 was appointed mayor of Padua in 1307, and was described as a money-
                 lender.

lines 72–73   The "sovereign cavalier" is assumed to be Giovanni Buiamonte, of the
                 Becchi family of Florence, a moneylender who was made a knight some-
                 time before 1298.

line 107   Phaëthon persuaded his father, the sun god Helios, to let him drive the
                 chariot of the sun. He was unable to control the horses, and Zeus slew
                 him with a thunderbolt to keep the earth from catching fire. The scar
                 on the sky is the Milky Way. The story is related in Book II of the *Meta-
                 morphoses.*

line 109   On a second flight, Icarus ignored the warnings of his father, Daedalus,
                 and flew too near the sun, which melted the wax that held the feathers
                 of his wings, and he fell into the sea and drowned (*Metamorphoses*, Book
                 VIII).

Canto XVIII

Luogo è in inferno detto Malebolge,
    tutto di pietra di color ferrigno,
    come la cerchia che dintorno il volge.   3
Nel dritto mezzo del campo maligno
    vaneggia un pozzo assai largo e profondo,
    di cui *suo loco* dicerò l'ordigno.   6
Quel cinghio che rimane adunque è tondo
    tra 'l pozzo e 'l piè de l'alta ripa dura,
    e ha distinto in dieci valli il fondo.   9
Quale, dove per guardia de le mura
    più e più fossi cingon li castelli,
    la parte dove son rende figura,   12
tale imagine quivi facean quelli;
    e come a tai fortezze da' lor sogli
    a la ripa di fuor son ponticelli,   15
così da imo de la roccia scogli
    movien che ricidien li argini e ' fossi
    infino al pozzo che i tronca e raccogli.   18
In questo luogo, de la schiena scossi
    di Gerïon, trovammoci; e 'l poeta
    tenne a sinistra, e io dietro mi mossi.   21
A la man destra vidi nova pieta,
    novo tormento e novi frustatori,
    di che la prima bolgia era repleta.   24
Nel fondo erano ignudi i peccatori;
    dal mezzo in qua ci venien verso 'l volto,
    di là con noi, ma con passi maggiori,   27

Canto XVIII

In hell there is a region that is known
    as Malebolge. Like the cliff by which it's sealed,
    it is all made of iron-colored stone.   3
In the very center of this evil field
    is a deep, wide pit, and in the proper place
    its structure and its use will be revealed.   6
The belt descending from the high cliff's base
    to the pit is circular. Ten valleys lie
    near the bottom, just above that gaping space.   9
As the walls of a castle are protected by
    concentric rings of moats, just such a row
    of patterned circles now impressed my eye   12
as I gazed upon the scene that stretched below,
    and as lines of little bridges will project
    from the walls to the outer bank, here long crags go   15
through the ditches and embankments to connect
    the cliff to the lip of the pit, which gathers them
    and cuts them off before they intersect.   18
This is where we were when we were shaken from
    Geryon's back. Now the poet began to stride
    off to the left, and I walked after him.   21
I saw new miseries now on the right side,
    new tortures, new tormentors with long whips,
    with which the ditch was abundantly supplied.   24
The sinners were naked, moving through the depths.
    The nearer file faced us, while the others went
    the same way we did, but with longer steps,   27

come i Roman per l'essercito molto,
    l'anno del giubileo, su per lo ponte
    hanno a passar la gente modo colto,   30
che da l'un lato tutti hanno la fronte
    verso 'l castello e vanno a Santo Pietro,
    da l'altra sponda vanno verso 'l monte.   33
Di qua, di là, su per lo sasso tetro
    vidi demon cornuti con gran ferze,
    che li battien crudelmente di retro.   36
Ahi come facean lor levar le berze
    a le prime percosse! già nessuno
    le seconde aspettava né le terze.   39
Mentr' io andava, li occhi miei in uno
    furo scontrati; e io sì tosto dissi:
    «Già di veder costui non son digiuno».   42
Per ch'ïo a figurarlo i piedi affissi;
    e 'l dolce duca meco si ristette,
    e assentio ch'alquanto in dietro gissi.   45
E quel frustato celar si credette
    bassando 'l viso; ma poco li valse,
    ch'io dissi: «O tu che l'occhio a terra gette,   48
se le fazion che porti non son false,
    Venedico se' tu Caccianemico.
    Ma che ti mena a sì pungenti salse?».   51
Ed elli a me: «Mal volontier lo dico;
    ma sforzami la tua chiara favella,
    che mi fa sovvenir del mondo antico.   54
I' fui colui che la Ghisolabella
    condussi a far la voglia del marchese,
    come che suoni la sconcia novella.   57
E non pur io qui piango bolognese;
    anzi n'è questo loco tanto pieno,
    che tante lingue non son ora apprese   60

just as the Romans, for the management
    of the huge crowds in the Year of Jubilee,
    have a plan by which the opposing rows are sent   30
across the bridge, with one line constantly
    facing the mount, while their opposite numbers wind
    in the direction of Saint Peter's as they see   33
the castle before them. Here the dark rock was lined
    at stages by horned demons who drove the herd
    of sinners along by lashing them from behind.   36
With the first crack of the whip each one was spurred
    to pick his heels up! No one seemed to care
    to linger for the second or the third.   39
As I walked, one met my eyes with a moment's stare,
    and I said at once when I saw him: "I have not
    always been starved of the sight of that man there."   42
My gentle leader stopped with me on that spot
    and let me go back a bit, with steps that led
    to the one whose face I was trying to make out.   45
The scourged soul sought to hide, with lowered head,
    but it was all in vain for him to try.
    "You there with your eyes upon the ground," I said,   48
"I know you, for unless your features lie,
    Venedico Caccianemico is your name.
    You are cooked in spicy sauces now, but why?"   51
He said: "I can hear the world from which I came
    in your plain speech, and though I would keep still,
    I feel compelled to answer all the same.   54
I was the one—however they may tell
    the vile tale—who brought Ghisolabella to
    the marchese, so that she might do his will.   57
I am far from the only Bolognese who
    laments here. There are more of us than they breed
    to say *sipa* from the Sàvena clear through   60

a dicer 'sipa' tra Sàvena e Reno;

    e se di ciò vuoi fede o testimonio,

    rècati a mente il nostro avaro seno».   63

Così parlando il percosse un demonio

    de la sua scurïada, e disse: «Via,

    ruffian! qui non son femmine da conio».   66

I' mi raggiunsi con la scorta mia;

    poscia con pochi passi divenimmo

    là 'v' uno scoglio de la ripa uscia.   69

Assai leggeramente quel salimmo;

    e vòlti a destra su per la sua scheggia,

    da quelle cerchie etterne ci partimmo.   72

Quando noi fummo là dov' el vaneggia

    di sotto per dar passo a li sferzati,

    lo duca disse: «Attienti, e fa che feggia   75

lo viso in te di quest' altri mal nati,

    ai quali ancor non vedesti la faccia

    però che son con noi insieme andati».   78

Del vecchio ponte guardavam la traccia

    che venìa verso noi da l'altra banda,

    e che la ferza similmente scaccia.   81

E 'l buon maestro, sanza mia dimanda,

    mi disse: «Guarda quel grande che vene,

    e per dolor non par lagrime spanda: 84

quanto aspetto reale ancor ritene!

    Quelli è Iasón, che per cuore e per senno

    li Colchi del monton privati féne.   87

Ello passò per l'isola di Lenno

    poi che l'ardite femmine spietate

    tutti li maschi loro a morte dienno.   90

Ivi con segni e con parole ornate

    Isifile ingannò, la giovinetta

    che prima avea tutte l'altre ingannate.   93

to the Reno. If it's assurance that you need,
>some token or testimony, just keep clear
>in your mind that we are famous for our greed." 63
And as he spoke, a demon standing near
>lashed him and cried: "Keep moving, panderer!
>There are no women for the coining here!" 66
I soon rejoined my escort, and we were,
>in a few steps, at a place where from the ledge
>a reef was jutting outward like a spur. 69
With easy steps we climbed onto that bridge.
>We left the eternal circlings, and we made
>a turn to the right across the jagged ridge. 72
The ditch was wide to make room for all the flayed.
>My leader said, as we watched them from on high:
>"Stop here and let this opposite parade 75
of misbegotten wretches strike your eye.
>Their faces will be new to you, for they
>were going the same way as you and I." 78
From the old bridge we could see the whole array
>as they came toward us, and like the opposing row
>these spirits were being flogged along their way. 81
Before I had even asked what I wished to know,
>my guide said: "See that great one there, and see
>how he seems to shed no tear for all his woe. 84
His face still wears an air of majesty.
>That is Jason, who purloined the Colchian
>ram through his cunning and his bravery. 87
On his way, he sailed to the isle of Lemnos, when
>the bold and merciless women of that place
>had all laid murderous hands upon their men. 90
There, with love tokens and with words of grace
>he deceived Hypsipyle, the maiden who
>had deceived the other women of her race. 93

Lasciolla quivi, gravida, soletta;
  tal colpa a tal martiro lui condanna;
  e anche di Medea si fa vendetta.   96

Con lui sen va chi da tal parte inganna;
  e questo basti de la prima valle
  sapere e di color che 'n sé assanna».   99

Già eravam là 've lo stretto calle
  con l'argine secondo s'incrocicchia,
  e fa di quello ad un altr' arco spalle.   102

Quindi sentimmo gente che si nicchia
  ne l'altra bolgia e che col muso scuffa,
  e sé medesma con le palme picchia.   105

Le ripe eran grommate d'una muffa,
  per l'alito di giù che vi s'appasta,
  che con li occhi e col naso facea zuffa.   108

Lo fondo è cupo sì, che non ci basta
  loco a veder sanza montare al dosso
  de l'arco, ove lo scoglio più sovrasta.   111

Quivi venimmo; e quindi giù nel fosso
  vidi gente attuffata in uno sterco
  che da li uman privadi parea mosso.   114

E mentre ch'io là giù con l'occhio cerco,
  vidi un col capo sì di merda lordo,
  che non parëa s'era laico o cherco.   117

Quei mi sgridò: «Perché se' tu sì gordo
  di riguardar più me che li altri brutti?».
  E io a lui: «Perché, se ben ricordo,   120

già t'ho veduto coi capelli asciutti,
  e se' Alessio Interminei da Lucca:
  però t'adocchio più che li altri tutti».   123

Ed elli allor, battendosi la zucca:
  «Qua giù m'hanno sommerso le lusinghe
  ond' io non ebbi mai la lingua stucca».   126

He left her pregnant and bereft. Here you
    may see the punishments such vices cause,
    and here Medea has her vengeance too.   96
All such deceivers move here without pause.
    That is all you need to know of this first ditch
    and of all the souls that are gripped within its jaws."   99
And while he spoke, we came to the point at which
    our narrow path reached the next embankment, where
    it arched once more to form another bridge,   102
over the next pouch. We heard people there
    hitting themselves and uttering loud cries
    and snuffling with their muzzles at the air.   105
From down inside this ditch rank vapors rise
    that cling to the rockface, causing mold to grow,
    and that wage a constant war with nose and eyes.   108
Here the bottom is so deep that we had to go
    up to the bridge's highest point, between
    the embankments, so that we could see below.   111
From that great height we stared down at the scene
    of a swarm of people plunged into a mess
    that looked as if it came from a latrine.   114
My eyes, as they went picking through that press,
    saw one whose head was so besmeared with shit,
    whether he was priest or layman, who could guess?   117
He called to me: "Your greedy eyeballs sit
    on me more than the other pigs here. Why?"
    And I: "Because, if I remember it   120
rightly, I saw you when your hair was dry,
    and you are Alessio Interminei
    from Lucca. That is why you caught my eye."   123
Then he began to smack his gourd and say:
    "How have I sunk to this disgusting place
    through the flatteries my ready tongue would spray!"   126

Appresso ciò lo duca «Fa che pinghe»,

    mi disse, «il viso un poco più avante,

    sì che la faccia ben con l'occhio attinghe   129

di quella sozza e scapigliata fante

    che là si graffia con l'unghie merdose,

    e or s'accoscia e ora è in piedi stante.   132

Taïde è, la puttana che rispuose

    al drudo suo quando disse "Ho io grazie

    grandi apo te?": "Anzi maravigliose!".   135

E quinci sian le nostre viste sazie».

And my leader said: "Now let your vision trace

    a path a little way ahead, then drop

    your eyes till they can clearly see the face   129

of that vile disheveled slut who cannot stop

    scratching herself with her shitty nails as she

    stands up now, and now squats down in the slop.   132

That is Thaïs, the whore. 'Are you greatly pleased with me?'

    her paramour once asked her, and she stated:

    'Just "greatly"? Why, you please me marvelously!'   135

With that sight, we will let our eyes be sated."

Notes

line 2   "Malebolge" ("Evilditches") is a word coined by Dante, combining the terms for "evil" (*male*) and "ditch" or "pouch" (*bolgia*).

lines 28–34   In February 1300, Pope Boniface VIII proclaimed that year to be one of Jubilee (the first such in the Church's history), during which indulgences would be granted to those who visited the basilicas of Saints Peter and Paul. The heavy traffic on the Ponte Angelo over the Tiber (it is estimated that as many as 200,000 people visited Rome that year) was controlled in the manner described here: one file of pilgrims crossing the bridge with the Castel Sant'Angelo directly in view, on their way to Saint Peter's, and the other file crossing toward Monte Giordano and Saint Paul's.

line 50   Venedico Caccianemico (born c. 1228) was for many years a leader of the Bolognese Guelphs. Although Dante apparently believes that he was dead by 1300, documents indicate that he survived until 1302 or early 1303.

lines 55–57   Venedico was rumored to have procured his sister, "the lovely" Ghisola, for Obizzo II, the marchese d'Este (see note to Canto XII, line 111), either for a bribe or in order to win favor.

line 60   *Sipa* is old Bolognese dialect for "yes." The Sàvena and Reno rivers mark the western and eastern boundaries of the city.

lines 86–96   Jason, leader of the Argonauts, was promised the throne of Iolcus if he could return with the golden fleece belonging to King Aeëtes of Colchis. On the way, he stopped at the island of Lemnos, where the women had massacred all the men. Hypsipyle, the daughter of King

Thoas, had deceived the other women by hiding her father and pretending to have killed him. Jason won the fleece with the aid of Aeëtes' daughter Medea, whom he brought back with him and married. He later deserted her for Glauce, daughter of King Creon of Corinth. On their wedding day, Medea killed the bride and her own two children by Jason.

line 117　Under ordinary circumstances, a priest's tonsure would distinguish him from a layman.

line 122　The Interminei (or Interminelli) family were prominent members of the White party in Lucca. Little is known of Alessio.

line 133　Thaïs is a flattering courtesan in *Eunuchus,* a comedy by Terence (Publius Terentius Afer, c. 195–159 B.C.E.).

Canto XIX

O Simon mago, o miseri seguaci
    che le cose di Dio, che di bontate
    deon essere spose, e voi rapaci   3
per oro e per argento avolterate,
    or convien che per voi suoni la tromba,
    però che ne la terza bolgia state.   6
Già eravamo, a la seguente tomba,
    montati de lo scoglio in quella parte
    ch'a punto sovra mezzo 'l fosso piomba.   9
O somma sapïenza, quanta è l'arte
    che mostri in cielo, in terra e nel mal mondo,
    e quanto giusto tua virtù comparte!   12
Io vidi per le coste e per lo fondo
    piena la pietra livida di fóri,
    d'un largo tutti e ciascun era tondo.   15
Non mi parean men ampi né maggiori
    che que' che son nel mio bel San Giovanni,
    fatti per loco d'i battezzatori;   18
l'un de li quali, ancor non è molt' anni,
    rupp' io per un che dentro v'annegava:
    e questo sia suggel ch'ogn' omo sganni.   21
Fuor de la bocca a ciascun soperchiava
    d'un peccator li piedi e de le gambe
    infino al grosso, e l'altro dentro stava.   24
Le piante erano a tutti accese intrambe;
    per che sì forte guizzavan le giunte,
    che spezzate averien ritorte e strambe.   27

Canto XIX

O Simon Magus! and many more besides,
    his wretched followers, who have whored and sold
    the things of God, which ought to be the brides   3
of righteousness, for silver and for gold,
    now must the trumpet sound for you, I say,
    because the third pouch has you in its hold.   6
We had climbed the reef and reached the part that lay
    directly above the middle of the ditch
    containing the next tomb along the way.   9
O highest wisdom, how great your art, with which
    the heavens, the earth, and the evil world resound,
    and how justly does your power deal with each!   12
Along the bottom and the sides I found
    in the livid stone a multiplicity
    of identical holes that were all completely round.   15
By their dimensions they reminded me
    of my San Giovanni. They all were the same size
    as the fonts in that beautiful baptistery,   18
one of which I had to break once, otherwise
    someone would have drowned inside it—and here let
    this be the seal to open all men's eyes.   21
Protruding from each hole there was a set
    of feet, with legs up to the calves in view.
    All the rest was in the hole, pressed into it.   24
The soles of their feet were burning, and their legs flew
    so hard in convulsive thrashings that their throes
    could have broken withes or even ropes in two.   27

Qual suole il fiammeggiar de le cose unte
    muoversi pur su per la strema buccia,
    tal era lì dai calcagni a le punte.   30
«Chi è colui, maestro, che si cruccia
    guizzando più che li altri suoi consorti»,
    diss' io, «e cui più roggia fiamma succia?».   33
Ed elli a me: «Se tu vuo' ch'i' ti porti
    là giù per quella ripa che più giace,
    da lui saprai di sé e de' suoi torti».   36
E io: «Tanto m'è bel, quanto a te piace:
    tu se' segnore, e sai ch'i' non mi parto
    dal tuo volere, e sai quel che si tace».   39
Allor venimmo in su l'argine quarto;
    volgemmo e discendemmo a mano stanca
    là giù nel fondo foracchiato e arto.   42
Lo buon maestro ancor de la sua anca
    non mi dipuose, sì mi giunse al rotto
    di quel che si piangeva con la zanca.   45
«O qual che se' che 'l di sù tien di sotto,
    anima trista come pal commessa»,
    comincia' io a dir, «se puoi, fa motto».   48
Io stava come 'l frate che confessa
    lo perfido assessin, che, poi ch'è fitto,
    richiama lui per che la morte cessa.   51
Ed el gridò: «Se' tu già costì ritto,
    se' tu già costì ritto, Bonifazio?
    Di parecchi anni mi mentì lo scritto.   54
Se' tu sì tosto di quell' aver sazio
    per lo qual non temesti tòrre a 'nganno
    la bella donna, e poi di farne strazio?».   57
Tal mi fec' io, quai son color che stanno,
    per non intender ciò ch'è lor risposto,
    quasi scornati, e risponder non sanno.   60

On any oily substance fire flows
    along the surface, and here it was the same
    as the flames licked at their feet from heels to toes.   30
"Master," I said, "I would like to know his name
    who is twitching more than any other one
    and whose feet are leeched by a much redder flame."   33
And he: "If you wish, I will carry you down upon
    that sloping bank so you can hear him tell
    who he is and of the evil he has done."   36
And I: "Your pleasure pleases me as well.
    You are my lord, you know that I embrace
    your will, and you know every syllable   39
of what is unsaid." So we approached the place
    where the fourth bank is, moving leftward as we went
    toward the ditch's narrow, perforated base.   42
He held me to his hip in our descent,
    and soon we were standing right before that man
    whose legs were flailing in a fierce lament.   45
"Whoever you are, sad spirit," I began,
    "stuck in like a pole, with the upper part interred
    where the lower end should go, speak if you can."   48
I stood there like a friar who has heard
    the confession of a killer who, placed inside,
    calls him back so his death may be a bit deferred.   51
"Are you standing up there, Boniface," he cried,
    "are you standing there already? What was stated
    was wrong by several years, and the writ has lied.   54
Have all of your spoils left you so quickly sated?
    When you coveted them, you dared use guile to win
    the lovely lady that you lacerated."   57
I stood like those who think they may have been
    made fools of, not understanding the response
    they have heard, not knowing how they should begin   60

Allor Virgilio disse: «Dilli tosto:
    "Non son colui, non son colui che credi"»;
    e io rispuosi come a me fu imposto.   63
Per che lo spirto tutti storse i piedi;
    poi, sospirando e con voce di pianto,
    mi disse: «Dunque che a me richiedi?   66
Se di saper ch'i' sia ti cal cotanto,
    che tu abbi però la ripa corsa,
    sappi ch'i' fui vestito del gran manto;   69
e veramente fui figliuol de l'orsa,
    cupido sì per avanzar li orsatti,
    che sù l'avere e qui me misi in borsa.   72
Di sotto al capo mio son li altri tratti
    che precedetter me simoneggiando,
    per le fessure de la pietra piatti.   75
Là giù cascherò io altresì quando
    verrà colui ch'i' credea che tu fossi,
    allor ch'i' feci 'l sùbito dimando.   78
Ma più è 'l tempo già che i piè mi cossi
    e ch'i' son stato così sottosopra,
    ch'el non starà piantato coi piè rossi: 81
ché dopo lui verrà di più laida opra,
    di ver' ponente, un pastor sanza legge,
    tal che convien che lui e me ricuopra.   84
Nuovo Iasón sarà, di cui si legge
    ne' Maccabei; e come a quel fu molle
    suo re, così fia lui chi Francia regge».   87
Io non so s'i' mi fui qui troppo folle,
    ch'i' pur rispuosi lui a questo metro:
    «Deh, or mi dì: quanto tesoro volle   90
Nostro Segnore in prima da san Pietro
    ch'ei ponesse le chiavi in sua balìa?
    Certo non chiese se non "Viemmi retro".   93

to answer. Virgil said: "You must say at once:
    'I am not who you think I am, I am not he,'"
    and I responded with obedience.   63
At that the spirit's feet thrashed furiously,
    and then he sighed, and in a tearful tone
    he said: "What is it that you want from me?   66
If it means so much to you that for this alone
    you have come down here, to hear what I have to tell,
    then know that the great mantle was my own.   69
But I was a son of the she-bear, and strove so well
    to advance the cubs that on earth I pocketed
    my spoils, and now I pocket myself in hell.   72
My predecessors are pressed below my head,
    simoniacs all, and all of them flattened through
    the fissures hollowed in the rock's deep bed.   75
When my turn comes I will be flattened too,
    pressed down when he arrives, that other soul
    that I took you for when I started to question you.   78
I have spent more time already in this hole
    with cooked feet, upside down, than he will pass
    stuck here with *his* feet glowing like lumps of coal.   81
A lawless shepherd, his crimes more odious,
    will come from the west, and he will prove indeed
    a proper cover for the two of us,   84
a new Jason, like the one of whom we read
    in Maccabees, whose king showed him deference,
    as to this one France's ruler will pay heed."   87
I do not know whether in my vehemence
    I grew too bold in the thoughts that I expressed
    in this measure: "Tell me, on what recompense,   90
on how much treasure did our Lord insist
    before he placed the keys in Peter's hand?
    'Follow me,' I'm certain, was his sole request.   93

Né Pier né li altri tolsero a Matia
    oro od argento, quando fu sortito
    al loco che perdé l'anima ria.   96
Però ti sta, ché tu se' ben punito;
    e guarda ben la mal tolta moneta
    ch'esser ti fece contra Carlo ardito.   99
E se non fosse ch'ancor lo mi vieta
    la reverenza de le somme chiavi
    che tu tenesti ne la vita lieta,   102
io userei parole ancor più gravi;
    ché la vostra avarizia il mondo attrista,
    calcando i buoni e sollevando i pravi.   105
Di voi pastor s'accorse il Vangelista,
    quando colei che siede sopra l'acque
    puttaneggiar coi regi a lui fu vista;   108
quella che con le sette teste nacque,
    e da le diece corna ebbe argomento,
    fin che virtute al suo marito piacque.   111
Fatto v'avete dio d'oro e d'argento;
    e che altro è da voi a l'idolatre,
    se non ch'elli uno, e voi ne orate cento?   114
Ahi, Costantin, di quanto mal fu matre,
    non la tua conversion, ma quella dote
    che da te prese il primo ricco patre!».   117
E mentr' io li cantava cotai note,
    o ira o coscïenza che 'l mordesse,
    forte spingava con ambo le piote.   120
I' credo ben ch'al mio duca piacesse,
    con sì contenta labbia sempre attese
    lo suon de le parole vere espresse.   123
Però con ambo le braccia mi prese;
    e poi che tutto su mi s'ebbe al petto,
    rimontò per la via onde discese.   126

Nor did Peter or the other ones demand
    gold or silver from Matthias when it befell
    that he took the bad soul's place in their holy band.   96
So stay here in your fitting spot in hell.
    As for those ill-gotten gains that made you bold
    toward Charles, be certain that you guard them well.   99
And if this intensity were not controlled
    by my deep reverence for the sacred keys
    that in the happy life you used to hold,   102
I would speak in even stronger words than these,
    for your greed, grinding down the good, giving glory to
    the wicked, afflicts the world with its disease.   105
And when the Evangelist had that beast in view
    who sits on the waters whoring wantonly
    with kings, he was thinking of shepherds just like you.   108
She had seven heads when she was born, and she
    drew her strength from the ten horns, but it was gone
    when her spouse lost his delight in purity.   111
With your gold and silver god, what you have done
    differs from the idolators in this alone:
    you worship a hundred, they worship only one.   114
Ah, Constantine, how much evil seed was sown,
    not with your conversion, but your dowry, which
    the first rich father had from you as his own."   117
Perhaps it was his rage that made him twitch
    or his conscience, but his two feet kicked like mad
    as I sang these notes to him with a rising pitch.   120
I am sure this pleased my guide, because he had
    a look of satisfaction on his face
    as he listened to the truthful words I said.   123
Thereupon he swept me up in his embrace
    and held me to his breast, and once again
    walked the incline that had brought us to that place.   126

Né si stancò d'avermi a sé distretto,
    sì men portò sovra 'l colmo de l'arco
    che dal quarto al quinto argine è tragetto.   129
Quivi soavemente spuose il carco,
    soave per lo scoglio sconcio ed erto
    che sarebbe a le capre duro varco.   132
Indi un altro vallon mi fu scoperto.

Nor did he tire of holding me. Only when
    we stood upon the arch that spanned the fosse
    between the fourth and fifth walls, only then   129
did he gently put me down. He was gentle because
    the reef was steep and rugged, so much so
    that goats would find it difficult to cross.   132
And I saw another valley stretched below.

Notes

line 1   In Acts 8.9–24, Simon the magician was converted to Christianity by the preaching of Philip. When he saw Peter and John summon the holy spirit, he offered them money to acquire this power for himself, and was sternly rebuked. From his name comes the word "simony," which signifies a trafficking in holy things, especially the buying and selling of ecclesiastical offices.

lines 15–21   There is no documentation of the incident that Dante describes here. Some have argued the unlikelihood of his gratuitously interpolating a self-defense against a charge of sacrilege, and have instead suggested that the last clause has larger thematic and theological implications. For one such interpretation, see Mark Musa, *Dante Alighieri's Divine Comedy. Inferno: Commentary* (Indiana, 1996), pp. 257–59.

line 50   In the Middle Ages, an assassin would be executed by being placed upside down in a ditch and buried alive.

lines 52–57   Pope Boniface VIII (Benedetto Caetani, 1235–1303) is the subject of numerous gibes in the course of the poem. The speaker mistakes Dante for Boniface, who is not due to arrive for another three and a half years. The lovely lady that he tore to pieces by his corrupt practices is, of course, the Church; "guile" alludes to the common belief that Boniface had persuaded his predecessor, Celestine V (see note to Canto III, lines 59–60), to resign, and then won the support of King Charles II of Naples in his effort to become pope himself.

line 69   The speaker is Giovanni Gaetano degli Orsini (whose surname means "little bears"), Pope Nicholas III (1277–1280).

lines 79–87   Nicholas has been dead for nearly twenty years, and must wait another three for his replacement, Boniface, whose own feet will be exposed and aflame for only eleven years until he is pushed along by the arrival of the even more corrupt Clement V in 1314. Clement, born Bertrand de

Got in Gascony, intrigued with King Philip IV of France to win the papacy, offering him a share of the Church's revenues. Upon his accession, Clement moved the papal see to Avignon (where it remained until 1377) and created nine new French cardinals. In 2 Maccabees 4–5, Jason becomes high priest of the Jews by bribing King Antiochus of Syria and proceeds to introduce corrupt practices. He is soon displaced, however, by Menelaus, who offers the king an even greater bribe.

line 95   In Acts 1.13–26, Matthias is selected by lot to take Judas's place among the Apostles.

lines 98–99   This is probably a reference to the now discredited assumption that Nicholas III was bribed to support Giovanni da Procida, a force behind the bloody uprising known as the Sicilian Vespers (1282), which liberated Sicily from the rule of Charles I of Anjou.

lines 106–11   In Revelations 17, John gives his vision of pagan Rome, which Dante applies to the corrupt papacy. The seven heads are here understood to be the sacraments, and the ten horns are the commandments, whose power waned when the Church's husband, the pope, turned away from virtue.

lines 115–17   Constantine I (c. 274–337), known as the Great, was Roman emperor from 306 to 337. Dante alludes to the Donation of Constantine, a document forged in the papal curia and believed genuine for seven hundred years until its fraudulence was demonstrated in the fifteenth century. It claims that, in return for Constantine's being cured of leprosy by Pope Sylvester I (see note to Canto XXVII, lines 94–95), this "first rich father" and all succeeding popes were granted temporal sovereignty over the western part of the empire, including Italy.

Canto XX

Di nova pena mi conven far versi
    e dar matera al ventesimo canto
    de la prima canzon, ch'è d'i sommersi.   3
Io era già disposto tutto quanto
    a riguardar ne lo scoperto fondo,
    che si bagnava d'angoscioso pianto;   6
e vidi gente per lo vallon tondo
    venir, tacendo e lagrimando, al passo
    che fanno le letane in questo mondo.   9
Come 'l viso mi scese in lor più basso,
    mirabilmente apparve esser travolto
    ciascun tra 'l mento e 'l principio del casso,   12
ché da le reni era tornato 'l volto,
    e in dietro venir li convenia,
    perché 'l veder dinanzi era lor tolto.   15
Forse per forza già di parlasia
    si travolse così alcun del tutto;
    ma io nol vidi, né credo che sia.   18
Se Dio ti lasci, lettor, prender frutto
    di tua lezione, or pensa per te stesso
    com' io potea tener lo viso asciutto,   21
quando la nostra imagine di presso
    vidi sì torta, che 'l pianto de li occhi
    le natiche bagnava per lo fesso.   24
Certo io piangea, poggiato a un de' rocchi
    del duro scoglio, sì che la mia scorta
    mi disse: «Ancor se' tu de li altri sciocchi?   27

Canto XX

In this, the twentieth canto of the first
    canzone, describing souls submerged by sin,
      the new punishment I saw must now be versed.   3
I was leaning forward, ready to look within
    the depth of the ditch that lay visible to me,
      whose floor was awash with anguished tears, wherein   6
I saw a line of spirits silently
    weeping as they approached us, keeping the slow
      pace of the living praying a litany.   9
And as my line of vision dropped below
    their heads, I saw they were horribly distorted
      between the chin and where the chest should go.   12
Each head was turned to the rear, and thus contorted
    they all were walking backward, bit by bit,
      for their power to look before them had been thwarted.   15
Such distortion may have happened in a fit
    of palsy sometime, but never to my eye,
      and I put no faith in the likelihood of it.   18
So may God bestow the fruits of your reading, try
    to imagine yourself, reader, in my state,
      and ask how I could keep my own cheeks dry   21
when confronted close at hand with such a fate,
    our form so twisted that their tears rolled down
      to the cleft where the two buttocks separate.   24
I leaned my face upon the projecting stone
    and let my tears flow down, till my guide said:
      "I see the fools still claim you for their own!   27

Qui vive la pietà quand' è ben morta;
    chi è più scellerato che colui
    che al giudicio divin passion comporta?   30
Drizza la testa, drizza, e vedi a cui
    s'aperse a li occhi d'i Teban la terra;
    per ch'ei gridavan tutti: "Dove rui,   33
Anfïarao? perché lasci la guerra?".
    E non restò di ruinare a valle
    fino a Minòs che ciascheduno afferra.   36
Mira c'ha fatto petto de le spalle;
    perché volse veder troppo davante,
    di retro guarda e fa retroso calle.   39
Vedi Tiresia, che mutò sembiante
    quando di maschio femmina divenne,
    cangiandosi le membra tutte quante;   42
e prima, poi, ribatter li convenne
    li duo serpenti avvolti, con la verga,
    che rïavesse le maschili penne.   45
Aronta è quel ch'al ventre li s'atterga,
    che ne' monti di Luni, dove ronca
    lo Carrarese che di sotto alberga,   48
ebbe tra ' bianchi marmi la spelonca
    per sua dimora; onde a guardar le stelle
    e 'l mar non li era la veduta tronca.   51
E quella che ricuopre le mammelle,
    che tu non vedi, con le trecce sciolte,
    e ha di là ogne pilosa pelle,   54
Manto fu, che cercò per terre molte;
    poscia si puose là dove nacqu' io;
    onde un poco mi piace che m'ascolte.   57
Poscia che 'l padre suo di vita uscìo
    e venne serva la città di Baco,
    questa gran tempo per lo mondo gio.   60

Here piety lives when pity is truly dead.

    What is more wicked than spurning God's command

    to heed the promptings of one's heart instead?   30

Look up and see the one for whom the land

    opened up when all the Thebans raised the call:

    'Amphiaraus, where are you running? Stand   33

and fight the battle with us!' But his fall

    continued till he landed among the shades

    at the feet of Minos, who seizes one and all.   36

He who wished to see too far forward now parades

    backward and looks behind him in damnation,

    making a new chest of his shoulder blades.   39

See Tiresias, who made an alteration

    of his looks from masculine to feminine,

    and whose members made a similar transformation.   42

When he came upon the coupling snakes, he then

    had to strike them with his staff anew, to obtain

    the plumage of his manhood once again.   45

Backed up to that one's belly in the chain

    is Aruns. Up in the Luni hills worked by

    the peasants who dwell upon Carrara's plain,   48

he lived in a cave in the marble cliffs, his eye

    delighted by the unobstructed view

    of the sea below and the stars up in the sky.   51

And she whose breasts are turned away from you

    and covered by the long tresses that she wore,

    with all of her hairy parts on that side too,   54

was Manto, who searched through many lands before

    she came to my birthplace. And I wish to say

    some words on this subject for a moment more.   57

After her father the prophet passed away

    and the city of Bacchus fell into slavery,

    she roamed the earth's domains for many a day.   60

Suso in Italia bella giace un laco,
     a piè de l'Alpe che serra Lamagna
     sovra Tiralli, c'ha nome Benaco.   63
Per mille fonti, credo, e più si bagna
     tra Garda e Val Camonica e Pennino
     de l'acqua che nel detto laco stagna.   66
Loco è nel mezzo là dove 'l trentino
     pastore e quel di Brescia e 'l veronese
     segnar poria, s'e' fesse quel cammino.   69
Siede Peschiera, bello e forte arnese
     da fronteggiar Bresciani e Bergamaschi,
     ove la riva 'ntorno più discese.   72
Ivi convien che tutto quanto caschi
     ciò che 'n grembo a Benaco star non può,
     e fassi fiume giù per verdi paschi.   75
Tosto che l'acqua a correr mette co,
     non più Benaco, ma Mencio si chiama
     fino a Governol, dove cade in Po.   78
Non molto ha corso, ch'el trova una lama,
     ne la qual si distende e la 'mpaluda;
     e suol di state talor essere grama.   81
Quindi passando la vergine cruda
     vide terra, nel mezzo del pantano,
     sanza coltura e d'abitanti nuda.   84
Lì, per fuggire ogne consorzio umano,
     ristette con suoi servi a far sue arti,
     e visse, e vi lasciò suo corpo vano.   87
Li uomini poi che 'ntorno erano sparti
     s'accolsero a quel loco, ch'era forte
     per lo pantan ch'avea da tutte parti.   90
Fer la città sovra quell' ossa morte;
     e per colei che 'l loco prima elesse,
     Mantüa l'appellar sanz' altra sorte.   93

Below Tiralli, in lovely Italy
    lies a lake known as Benaco, at the base
    of the Alps that form the border of Germany.   63

The water of a thousand springs that race
    through Val Camonica and Pennino flows
    to Garda, and it gathers in that place.   66

An island sits in the middle. Three bishops, those
    of Brescia, Trent, and Verona, would have the right
    to give the blessing there if they so chose.   69

The low point of the lakeshore is the site
    of striking, strong Peschiera, built to restrain
    the spread of Bergamese and Brescian might.   72

The water Benaco's bosom cannot contain
    is collected at that point and begins to flow
    in a river running down through the green plain.   75

No longer Benaco now, but Mincio
    once the current starts to run, it travels then
    to Govèrnolo, where it drops into the Po,   78

and soon it spreads into a marsh, and when
    the summer's heat afflicts that level ground
    it is turned into a miserable fen.   81

In passing there, the untamed virgin found
    a stretch of dry land in the marshes where
    no one had farmed and no one was around.   84

She settled with her servants in that bare
    forbidding spot, shunned people while she plied
    her arts, then left her empty body there.   87

The people of those parts, when she had died,
    came together on that ground secure from foes,
    defended by the marsh on every side.   90

There, over those dead bones, the city rose.
    For her who came there first, with no divination
    Mantua was the name the people chose.   93

Già fuor le genti sue dentro più spesse,
   prima che la mattia da Casalodi
   da Pinamonte inganno ricevesse.   96

Però t'assenno che, se tu mai odi
   originar la mia terra altrimenti,
   la verità nulla menzogna frodi».   99

E io: «Maestro, i tuoi ragionamenti
   mi son sì certi e prendon sì mia fede,
   che li altri mi sarien carboni spenti.   102

Ma dimmi, de la gente che procede,
   se tu ne vedi alcun degno di nota;
   ché solo a ciò la mia mente rifiede».   105

Allor mi disse: «Quel che da la gota
   porge la barba in su le spalle brune,
   fu—quando Grecia fu di maschi vòta,   108

sì ch'a pena rimaser per le cune—
   augure, e diede 'l punto con Calcanta
   in Aulide a tagliar la prima fune.   111

Euripilo ebbe nome, e così 'l canta
   l'alta mia tragedìa in alcun loco:
   ben lo sai tu che la sai tutta quanta.   114

Quell' altro che ne' fianchi è così poco,
   Michele Scotto fu, che veramente
   de le magiche frode seppe 'l gioco.   117

Vedi Guido Bonatti; vedi Asdente,
   ch'avere inteso al cuoio e a lo spago
   ora vorrebbe, ma tardi si pente.   120

Vedi le triste che lasciaron l'ago,
   la spuola e 'l fuso, e fecersi 'ndivine;
   fecer malie con erbe e con imago.   123

Ma vienne omai, ché già tiene 'l confine
   d'amendue li emisperi e tocca l'onda
   sotto Sobilia Caino e le spine;   126

At one time it had a larger population,
> till idiot Casalodi fell victim to
>> the cunning Pinamonte's calculation.   96

Therefore, should another story come to you
> concerning my city and its establishment,
>> do not let lies devalue what is true."   99

"Master," I said, "I feel so confident
> in the sureness of your account that, should they try,
>> their words would be like coals that have been spent.   102

But speak to me about those who are passing by,
> if any have stories worthy to be heard,
>> for my mind goes back to them." And his reply: 105

"Then look upon that one there, with the spreading beard
> from his cheeks to his brown shoulders, for he was
>> augur when all the Greek males disappeared,   108

leaving even the cradles empty in the cause.
> He decided with Calchas when the time should be
>> to cut the first cable at Aulis. Eurypylus   111

was his name, and in my lofty tragedy
> I sing of him, as you are well aware,
>> who know the whole of it so thoroughly.   114

This other one, with thighs so thin and spare,
> was Michael Scot. In the tricks of magic fraud
>> he was a practitioner beyond compare.   117

See Guido Bonatti. Asdente, who if he could
> would stick to his last and practice his devotions,
>> but repentance comes too late to do him good.   120

See the sad hags who left their threads and notions
> for the false divining of the divine will,
>> who cast their spells with poppets and with potions.   123

But let us move along. While we stand still,
> Cain, carrying his thornbush, casts his light
>> where hemispheres meet, on the wave below Seville.   126

e già iernotte fu la luna tonda:

    ben ten de' ricordar, ché non ti nocque

    alcuna volta per la selva fonda».   129

Sì mi parlava, e andavamo introcque.

The moon was already round and full last night,
    as you must recall, for you came to no harm then
    in the deepest wood, when she was shining bright."   129
So he spoke to me, and we walked on again.

Notes

line 33	The seer Amphiaraus was one of the seven against Thebes (see note to Canto XIV, line 46). As he had foreseen, he died in battle during the siege, when the earth opened to swallow him as he was retreating.
line 40	The Theban Tiresias was turned into a woman when he struck a pair of copulating snakes. After seven years, he struck them again and was returned to his male form. When summoned to settle a dispute between Zeus and Hera over whether males or females enjoyed lovemaking more, he agreed with Zeus, stating that women experienced ten times as much sexual pleasure. For this, Hera struck him blind, and Zeus compensated him with the gift of prophecy. His story is told in Book III of Ovid's *Metamorphoses.* He appears most famously in Sophocles' *Oedipus the King* and T. S. Eliot's *The Waste Land,* as well as in the *Odyssey* (as a shade) and several plays by Euripides.
line 47	Aruns was an Etruscan soothsayer who, in Lucan's *Pharsalia,* foresaw but did not fully communicate the consequences of the war between Caesar and Pompey. According to Lucan, he lived in the ruins of Luni and divined by, among other things, examining entrails. It is Dante who situates him in a nearby cave and makes him, by implication, an astrologer.
line 55	Manto was the daughter of Tiresias. In Book X of the *Aeneid,* Manto is described as coming to Italy after her father's death and the fall of Thebes, and giving birth to Ocnus after mating with the river god Tiber.
lines 61–78	Benaco was the Latin name for Lake Garda, at the foot of the Tyrolean Alps. The city of Garda is on its eastern shore. Valcamonica is a valley west of the lake. The term "Pennino" alludes to the Alpine range (although precisely which part of it is alluded to is a matter of some dispute). The boundaries of the dioceses of Brescia, Trent, and Verona meet at a point in the middle of Lake Garda, at the southern end of which stand the fortress and town of Peschiera. The town of Governolo is some twelve miles from Mantua.
line 92	By some accounts, it was customary in the ancient world to determine the names of cities through the casting of lots.

lines 95–96   Alberto da Casalodi, a Guelph count from Brescia, was ruler of Mantua in 1272 and much resented by the native population. The Ghibelline Pinamonte Bonacolsi duped him into thinking that he could hold on to power only by exiling the city's noble families, which he did to such an extent that he deprived himself of his own supporters. Pinamonte led a revolt that resulted in the exile of Casalodi and the murders of the remaining nobles.

lines 97–99   This statement of Virgil's has occasioned much comment, especially since his account here contradicts the one in the *Aeneid* (see note to line 55). The matter is further complicated by the mention of "the daughter of Tiresias" as one of the souls in Limbo (*Purgatorio*, Canto XXII), in contrast to Virgil's identification of her here among the soothsayers.

lines 106–14   This passage presents additional difficulties. Eurypylus is indeed mentioned in the *Aeneid* (Book II), but the details there are very different from what Dante has Virgil claim. Calchas was the augur when the Greek fleet set sail from Aulis to lay siege to Troy. In the *Aeneid*, Eurypylus is a soldier sent to consult the oracle of Apollo to determine the most propitious time for the Greeks to sail home from Troy. (In fairness to Dante, it should be pointed out that Calchas does figure briefly in this incident also.)

line 116   Michael Scot (c. 1175–c. 1235), so called because of his national origin, was a philosopher and astrologer at the court of Frederick II (see note to Canto X, line 119) at Palermo. He wrote a number of works dealing with the occult sciences and translated Arabic versions of Aristotle into Latin.

line 118   The astrologer and soothsayer Guido Bonatti was a rooftiler from Forlì; he is believed to have been in the service of Guido da Montefeltro (see note to Canto XXVII, lines 28–30). Benvenuto, called Asdente ("toothless"), was a shoemaker from Parma who was said to possess magical powers.

lines 125–26   Cain with his thornbush, equivalent to the man in the moon, is above the point of demarcation between the northern hemisphere (land) and the southern (water). It is now about six in the morning.

Canto XXI

Così di ponte in ponte, altro parlando
  che la mia comedìa cantar non cura,
  venimmo; e tenavamo 'l colmo, quando   3
restammo per veder l'altra fessura
  di Malebolge e li altri pianti vani;
  e vidila mirabilmente oscura.   6
Quale ne l'arzanà de' Viniziani
  bolle l'inverno la tenace pece
  a rimpalmare i legni lor non sani,   9
ché navicar non ponno—in quella vece
  chi fa suo legno novo e chi ristoppa
  le coste a quel che più vïaggi fece;   12
chi ribatte da proda e chi da poppa;
  altri fa remi e altri volge sarte;
  chi terzeruolo e artimon rintoppa—:   15
tal, non per foco ma per divin' arte,
  bollia là giuso una pegola spessa,
  che 'nviscava la ripa d'ogne parte.   18
I' vedea lei, ma non vedëa in essa
  mai che le bolle che 'l bollor levava,
  e gonfiar tutta, e riseder compressa.   21
Mentr' io là giù fisamente mirava,
  lo duca mio, dicendo «Guarda, guarda!»,
  mi trasse a sé del loco dov' io stava.   24
Allor mi volsi come l'uom cui tarda
  di veder quel che li convien fuggire
  e cui paura sùbita sgagliarda,   27

Canto XXI

We went from bridge to bridge, exchanging talk
    of which my comedy does not wish to sing,
      and at the highest point we stopped our walk   3
to see the Malebolge's next opening
    and hear the vain cries of the miserable.
      An eerie darkness covered everything.   6
Just as when, flanked by boiling cauldrons full
    of sticky pitch, the worn-out vessels wait
      to be worked on at the Venice Arsenal,   9
since winter means they cannot navigate:
    some make their ships new, some recaulk the bow
      or the ribs of one that has carried many a freight,   12
some hammer at the stern or at the prow,
    and some carve oars, or twist lines, or repair
      the jibs and mainsails—so it was just now,   15
but for the fact there was no fire there.
    Through heavenly art the pitch boiled endlessly
      and spread its gluey coating everywhere.   18
I could see the pitch, but all that was clear to me
    inside it were the bubbles on its tide
      as it rose and fell in one great heaving sea.   21
"Look out, look out!" my leader quickly cried
    and suddenly reached out and pulled me near
      from where I was standing to peer down inside.   24
I turned like one who wants to have a clear
    look at the thing he has been warned to shun,
      who is taken by an overwhelming fear   27

che, per veder, non indugia 'l partire:
>e vidi dietro a noi un diavol nero
>correndo su per lo scoglio venire.   30
Ahi quant' elli era ne l'aspetto fero!
>e quanto mi parea ne l'atto acerbo,
>con l'ali aperte e sovra i piè leggero!   33
L'omero suo, ch'era aguto e superbo,
>carcava un peccator con ambo l'anche,
>e quei tenea de' piè ghermito 'l nerbo.   36
Del nostro ponte disse: «O Malebranche,
>ecco un de li anzïan di Santa Zita!
>Mettetel sotto, ch'i' torno per anche   39
a quella terra, che n'è ben fornita:
>ogn' uom v'è barattier, fuor che Bonturo;
>del no, per li denar, vi si fa *ita*».   42
Là giù 'l buttò, e per lo scoglio duro
>si volse; e mai non fu mastino sciolto
>con tanta fretta a seguitar lo furo.   45
Quel s'attuffò, e tornò sù convolto;
>ma i demon che del ponte avean coperchio,
>gridar: «Qui non ha loco il Santo Volto!   48
qui si nuota altrimenti che nel Serchio!
>Però, se tu non vuo' di nostri graffi,
>non far sopra la pegola soverchio».   51
Poi l'addentar con più di cento raffi,
>disser: «Coverto convien che qui balli,
>sì che, se puoi, nascosamente accaffi».   54
Non altrimenti i cuochi a' lor vassalli
>fanno attuffare in mezzo la caldaia
>la carne con li uncin, perché non galli.   57
Lo buon maestro «Acciò che non si paia
>che tu ci sia», mi disse, «giù t'acquatta
>dopo uno scheggio, ch'alcun schermo t'aia;   60

and flees, but looks while he keeps moving on,
> and then I saw a great black demon race
> up the crag behind us, coming at a run.   30

How savage were his bearing and his face!
> With wings spread, what ferocity he showed
> with every step, keeping up his rapid pace,   33

moving lightly on his feet! He bore the load,
> on his high, sharp shoulder, of a sinner's thighs,
> and he gripped the ankle tendons as he strode.   36

He called from our bridge: "Hey, Evilclaws, here's a prize,
> one of Saint Zita's Elders! Dunk him under,
> while I go back there for some fresh supplies.   39

That town is ripe for plucking, and no wonder.
> Except for our friend Bonturo, everyone
> is a grafter, changing *no* to *yes* for plunder."   42

He tossed the soul down, turned, and then was gone.
> Never did any hound that has been untied
> move faster after a burglar on the run.   45

The soul resurfaced, showing his backside,
> and the devils beneath the bridge began to crow.
> "This is no place for the Holy Face!" they cried.   48

"The swimming that you did in the Serchio
> is not the fashion here. If you don't care
> to be stuck with grappling hooks, then stay below."   51

With a hundred prongs they bit him everywhere.
> "Undercover dancing's what our minions do,"
> they said, "so, if you're able, graft down there."   54

And they did what cooks will set their scullions to
> when with forks they plunge the meat down in the pot
> to keep it under so it will cook through.   57

My master said: "It is better that you not
> be seen just now. Screen yourself behind a near
> outcrop of rock and crouch down on the spot.   60

e per nulla offension che mi sia fatta,

    non temer tu, ch'i' ho le cose conte,

    perch' altra volta fui a tal baratta».   63

Poscia passò di là dal co del ponte;

    e com' el giunse in su la ripa sesta,

    mestier li fu d'aver sicura fronte.   66

Con quel furore e con quella tempesta

    ch'escono i cani a dosso al poverello

    che di sùbito chiede ove s'arresta,   69

usciron quei di sotto al ponticello,

    e volser contra lui tutt' i runcigli;

    ma el gridò: «Nessun di voi sia fello!   72

Innanzi che l'uncin vostro mi pigli,

    traggasi avante l'un di voi che m'oda,

    e poi d'arruncigliarmi si consigli».   75

Tutti gridaron: «Vada Malacoda!»;

    per ch'un si mosse—e li altri stetter fermi—

    e venne a lui dicendo: «Che li approda?».   78

«Credi tu, Malacoda, qui vedermi

    esser venuto», disse 'l mio maestro,

    «sicuro già da tutti vostri schermi,   81

sanza voler divino e fato destro?

    Lascian' andar, ché nel cielo è voluto

    ch'i' mostri altrui questo cammin silvestro».   84

Allor li fu l'orgoglio sì caduto,

    ch'e' si lasciò cascar l'uncino a' piedi,

    e disse a li altri: «Omai non sia feruto».   87

E 'l duca mio a me: «O tu che siedi

    tra li scheggion del ponte quatto quatto,

    sicuramente omai a me ti riedi».   90

Per ch'io mi mossi e a lui venni ratto;

    e i diavoli si fecer tutti avanti,

    sì ch'io temetti ch'ei tenesser patto;   93

I know the way they do things. Never fear,
    no matter how outrageous their offense,
    for once before I tangled with them here."   63
He crossed the bridgehead and he passed at once
    to the sixth embankment, needing now to be
    steady in manner and in countenance.   66
With all the clamor and the savagery
    of mastiffs rushing a poor mendicant
    who freezes and starts begging instantly,   69
from beneath the little bridge, all at a sprint
    and pointing their hooks at him, came the whole crew,
    but he called out: "There's no need to be violent!   72
Before you grapple me, let one of you
    come forth and hear me out, and then you may
    decide if you still wish to run me through."   75
"Send Wickedtail!" I heard the demons say.
    Then one stepped forward, saying: "I wonder what
    he expects to gain by carrying on this way."   78
"Do you think that you would see me in this spot,"
    my master told the one called Wickedtail,
    "secure so far against each plan and plot,   81
without God's will and a fate that cannot fail?
    So let us pass, for it is heaven's command
    that I lead another on this savage trail."   84
The fiend was so crestfallen that his hand
    let go his grappling hook. "Now let him be,
    let no one strike at him," he told his band.   87
My leader called: "O you who fearfully
    crouch on the bridge, it is safe now to appear
    from the cover of your crag and come to me."   90
I rushed to him, and I began to fear
    whether the fiends would keep the pact they'd made,
    from the way they all pressed round and crowded near.   93

così vid' ïo già temer li fanti
    ch'uscivan patteggiati di Caprona,
    veggendo sé tra nemici cotanti.   96
I' m'accostai con tutta la persona
    lungo 'l mio duca, e non torceva li occhi
    da la sembianza lor ch'era non buona.   99
Ei chinavan li raffi e «Vuo' che 'l tocchi»,
    diceva l'un con l'altro, «in sul groppone?».
    E rispondien: «Sì, fa che gliel' accocchi».   102
Ma quel demonio che tenea sermone
    col duca mio, si volse tutto presto
    e disse: «Posa, posa, Scarmiglione!».   105
Poi disse a noi: «Più oltre andar per questo
    iscoglio non si può, però che giace
    tutto spezzato al fondo l'arco sesto.   108
E se l'andare avante pur vi piace,
    andatevene su per questa grotta;
    presso è un altro scoglio che via face.   111
Ier, più oltre cinqu' ore che quest' otta,
    mille dugento con sessanta sei
    anni compié che qui la via fu rotta.   114
Io mando verso là di questi miei
    a riguardar s'alcun se ne sciorina;
    gite con lor, che non saranno rei».   117
«Tra'ti avante, Alichino, e Calcabrina»,
    cominciò elli a dire, «e tu, Cagnazzo;
    e Barbariccia guidi la decina.   120
Libicocco vegn' oltre e Draghignazzo,
    Cirïatto sannuto e Graffiacane
    e Farfarello e Rubicante pazzo.   123
Cercate 'ntorno le boglienti pane;
    costor sian salvi infino a l'altro scheggio
    che tutto intero va sovra le tane».   126

Once I had seen a line of troops parade
　　out of Caprona amid their enemies.
　　　Despite the pledge of truce, they looked afraid.　　　96
I stood beside my leader and tried to squeeze
　　against him, keeping the fiends under close watch,
　　　for their looks were far from putting me at ease.　　　99
They aimed their hooks, and one said: "Should I scratch
　　his butt for him?" and another one replied:
　　　"Sure, why not stick it to him in the notch?"　　　102
But the demon speaking with my leader cried
　　aloud as he turned around to face them: "No!
　　　At ease there, Tangletop, put your hook aside."　　　105
Then he said to us: "It's impossible to go
　　along this crag, for the sixth arch is long gone.
　　　It's lying in pieces in the pit below.　　　108
But if it is still your pleasure to go on,
　　I know another way that you can take.
　　　Nearby is a spur that you can cross upon.　　　111
About five hours from now, it's going to make
　　twelve hundred and sixty-six years and one day
　　　since the road was broken by a mighty quake.　　　114
I was about to send a squad that way
　　to see if anyone's drying out in the air.
　　　You'll be safe with them." And then he turned to say:　　　117
"Step forward, Tramplefrost, and Droopwing there.
　　And Baddog, I want you to join the hunt.
　　　Let Spikebeard lead the ten. And let that pair　　　120
Lusthoney and Dragonsnout step to the front,
　　and Pigface with the tusks, and Scratchbitch too,
　　　and Littlehoof and crazy Rubicant.　　　123
Search round the edges of the boiling glue,
　　get these two safely to the next precipice
　　　that bridges all the ditches and runs clear through."　　　126

«Omè, maestro, che è quel ch'i' veggio?»,

    diss' io, «deh, sanza scorta andianci soli,

    se tu sa' ir; ch'i' per me non la cheggio.   129

Se tu se' sì accorto come suoli,

    non vedi tu ch'e' digrignan li denti

    e con le ciglia ne minaccian duoli?».   132

Ed elli a me: «Non vo' che tu paventi;

    lasciali digrignar pur a lor senno,

    ch'e' fanno ciò per li lessi dolenti».   135

Per l'argine sinistro volta dienno;

    ma prima avea ciascun la lingua stretta

    coi denti, verso lor duca, per cenno;   138

ed elli avea del cul fatto trombetta.

"Master," I said, "surely something is amiss.

    Let us go on, just the two of us alone,

    if you know the way. I don't like the looks of this.   129

Where is the caution that you've always shown?

    Do you not see their threatening brows and hear

    their grinding teeth, that may grind me to the bone?"   132

"I would not have you suffer needless fear,"

    he told me. "Let their teeth grind. That is what

    they do to scare the wretches stewing here."   135

They all turned round to face left on the spot,

    first pressing their tongues between their teeth en masse

    to signal their leader, who sounded the charge, but not   138

as you'd think—he made a trumpet of his ass.

Notes

line 38	Zita (d. 1270s) was a servant woman of Lucca, to whom miracles were attributed; she was known as Saint Zita, although she was not canonized until 1690. The Elders were the city's magistrates, ten in number, chosen for two-month terms. The dead soul (identified by an early commentator as Martino Bottaio, a Luccan politician who died the day on which this canto is set) is, like the others here, guilty of barratry, the buying and selling of public offices.
line 41	This line is highly ironic, since Bonturo Dati, who died in 1325, was reputed to be the most corrupt official in Lucca.
line 48	The "Holy Face" is an ancient crucifix in Lucca, carved from dark wood.
line 49	The Serchio is a river that flows near Lucca. According to the early commentaries, it was a popular site for swimming in summer.
line 95	Caprona, a castle about five miles from the city of Pisa, was surrendered to Tuscan Guelph forces (Florentines and Lucchese) in August 1289. Dante was a member of the invading army.
lines 112–14	See note to Canto XII, lines 37–45. It is now about seven o'clock on Saturday morning.

Canto XXII

Io vidi già cavalier muover campo,
    e cominciare stormo e far lor mostra,
    e talvolta partir per loro scampo;   3
corridor vidi per la terra vostra,
    o Aretini, e vidi gir gualdane,
    fedir torneamenti e correr giostra;   6
quando con trombe, e quando con campane,
    con tamburi e con cenni di castella,
    e con cose nostrali e con istrane;   9
né già con sì diversa cennamella
    cavalier vidi muover né pedoni,
    né nave a segno di terra o di stella.   12
Noi andavam con li diece demoni.
    Ahi fiera compagnia! ma ne la chiesa
    coi santi, e in taverna coi ghiottoni.   15
Pur a la pegola era la mia 'ntesa,
    per veder de la bolgia ogne contegno
    e de la gente ch'entro v'era incesa.   18
Come i dalfini, quando fanno segno
    a' marinar con l'arco de la schiena
    che s'argomentin di campar lor legno,   21
talor così, ad alleggiar la pena,
    mostrav' alcun de' peccatori 'l dosso
    e nascondea in men che non balena.   24
E come a l'orlo de l'acqua d'un fosso
    stanno i ranocchi pur col muso fuori,
    sì che celano i piedi e l'altro grosso,   27

Canto XXII

I have seen cavalry break camp and ride out,
    or make assaults or muster on command,
      or retreat to save themselves when put to rout,   3
I have seen coursers dash across your land,
    O Aretines, seen raiding parties there,
      watched tournaments and jousting near at hand,   6
signaled by ringing bells or trumpets' blare
    or drumbeats, castle signals near and far,
      our own and foreign, sound and sign and flare,   9
but never to a bagpipe so bizarre
    have I seen horsemen move, or infantry,
      or a ship set forth by landmark or by star.   12
We walked with the ten fiends. Savage company,
    but in the church with saints, as people say,
      in the tavern with the drunkards on a spree.   15
The sea of pitch was where my attention lay,
    to learn what the pit was like and to take note
      of the souls inside it as it boiled away.   18
Like dolphins swimming near a ship or boat
    whose arching backs make sailors realize
      that they have to act to keep their craft afloat,   21
from the pitch a sinner's back would sometimes rise
    to ease the pain, then plunge down into it
      faster than lightning streaks across the skies.   24
As frogs with only their muzzles showing sit
    at the water's edge inside a ditch and hide
      their feet and all their bulk, so in the pit   27

sì stavan d'ogne parte i peccatori;

    ma come s'appressava Barbariccia,

    così si ritraén sotto i bollori.   30

I' vidi, e anco il cor me n'accapriccia,

    uno aspettar così, com' elli 'ncontra

    ch'una rana rimane e l'altra spiccia;   33

e Graffiacan, che li era più di contra,

    li arruncigliò le 'mpegolate chiome

    e trassel sù, che mi parve una lontra.   36

I' sapea già di tutti quanti 'l nome,

    sì li notai quando fuorono eletti,

    e poi ch'e' si chiamaro, attesi come.   39

«O Rubicante, fa che tu li metti

    li unghioni a dosso, sì che tu lo scuoi!»,

    gridavan tutti insieme i maladetti.   42

E io: «Maestro mio, fa, se tu puoi,

    che tu sappi chi è lo sciagurato

    venuto a man de li avversari suoi».   45

Lo duca mio li s'accostò allato;

    domandollo ond' ei fosse, e quei rispuose:

    «I' fui del regno di Navarra nato.   48

Mia madre a servo d'un segnor mi puose,

    che m'avea generato d'un ribaldo,

    distruggitor di sé e di sue cose.   51

Poi fui famiglia del buon re Tebaldo;

    quivi mi misi a far baratteria,

    di ch'io rendo ragione in questo caldo».   54

E Cirïatto, a cui di bocca uscia

    d'ogne parte una sanna come a porco,

    li fé sentir come l'una sdruscia.   57

Tra male gatte era venuto 'l sorco;

    ma Barbariccia il chiuse con le braccia

    e disse: «State in là, mentr' io lo 'nforco».   60

I could see surfaced heads on every side,
 but when the souls saw Spikebeard come their way
 they plummeted below the boiling tide.   30
I saw—and my heart still shudders to this day—
 one head still up, as sometimes when you look
 one frog will dive and another one will stay.   33
And Scratchbitch, who was closest to him, took
 the soul by his pitch-soaked hair and hauled him high.
 To me he seemed like an otter on the hook.   36
I was familiar with their names, for I
 had watched them when they were chosen for this run
 and listened to what they called each other by.   39
The godforsaken gang cried out as one:
 "Hey, Rubicant, get out your claws and play,
 and flay his carcass till the skin is gone!"   42
"Master," I said, "I wonder if I may
 learn who he is, this luckless miscreant
 hanging helpless before his enemies this way.   45
Please speak to him." And so my leader went
 to the soul and asked about his origins.
 "I was born in the kingdom of Navarre, and sent   48
by my mother to serve a lord," he answered, "since
 she had had me by a wastrel, one who threw
 his property and his body to the winds.   51
Then I joined the good King Thibaut's retinue,
 where I became so skilled a barrator
 that in this heat I'm paying back what's due."   54
Then Pigface, who had tusks just like a boar
 that protruded from his snout on either side,
 let him feel the way that one of them ripped and tore.   57
Cruel cats had trapped the mouse. Now Spikebeard cried
 as he ringed his arms around the soul: "Look smart!
 Stand back while I enfork him!" Then to my guide   60

E al maestro mio volse la faccia;
    «Domanda», disse, «ancor, se più disii
    saper da lui, prima ch'altri 'l disfaccia».   63
Lo duca dunque: «Or dì: de li altri rii
    conosci tu alcun che sia latino
    sotto la pece?». E quelli: «I' mi partii,   66
poco è, da un che fu di là vicino.
    Così foss' io ancor con lui coperto,
    ch'i' non temerei unghia né uncino!».   69
E Libicocco «Troppo avem sofferto»,
    disse; e preseli 'l braccio col runciglio,
    sì che, stracciando, ne portò un lacerto.   72
Draghignazzo anco i volle dar di piglio
    giuso a le gambe; onde 'l decurio loro
    si volse intorno intorno con mal piglio.   75
Quand' elli un poco rappaciati fuoro,
    a lui, ch'ancor mirava sua ferita,
    domandò 'l duca mio sanza dimoro: 78
«Chi fu colui da cui mala partita
    di' che facesti per venire a proda?».
    Ed ei rispuose: «Fu frate Gomita,   81
quel di Gallura, vasel d'ogne froda,
    ch'ebbe i nemici di suo donno in mano,
    e fé sì lor, che ciascun se ne loda.   84
Danar si tolse e lasciolli di piano,
    sì com' e' dice; e ne li altri offici anche
    barattier fu non picciol, ma sovrano.   87
Usa con esso donno Michel Zanche
    di Logodoro; e a dir di Sardigna
    le lingue lor non si sentono stanche.   90
Omè, vedete l'altro che digrigna;
    i' direi anche, ma i' temo ch'ello
    non s'apparecchi a grattarmi la tigna».   93

he turned and said: "I think you'd better start
    asking now if there's anything else you want to know,
    before the others tear him all apart."   63

So my leader said: "Among the souls below,
    under the pitch, are there any Italians here?"
    And the soul replied: "Just a little while ago   66

I was with someone from there, or very near.
    I wish I were still hidden where he is,
    then there'd be no hooks or claws for me to fear."   69

Lusthoney yelled: "We've had enough of this!"
    And then he raked the sinner's arm and took
    a sinew out with that vicious hook of his.   72

Now Dragonsnout was gesturing with his hook
    at the sinner's legs, but turning toward his crew
    their captain faced them down with an evil look.   75

As they grew still, my leader turned back to
    the soul, who was staring at his mangled limb,
    and started in to question him anew: 78

"Who was it that you parted from to swim
    to so miserable an outcome on the banks?"
    "Fra Gomita of Gallura. I was with him,"   81

said the soul, "a receptacle of fraud who ranks
    at the head of the list, a first-class barrator.
    From his master's foes he garnered praise and thanks.   84

As he has said, he took their money for
    a smooth release when he had them in his hand.
    A silky trick, and he had a hundred more.   87

And there's one from Logodoro who's his friend,
    Don Michel Zanche. Once they start to jaw
    about Sardinia, there isn't any end.   90

How that demon grinds his teeth! They're like a saw!
    I want to go on, but I can't say a word,
    I'm afraid he'll scrub my mange and rub me raw!"   93

E 'l gran proposto, vòlto a Farfarello
    che stralunava li occhi per fedire,
        disse: «Fatti 'n costà, malvagio uccello!».   96

«Se voi volete vedere o udire»,
    ricominciò lo spaürato appresso,
        «Toschi o Lombardi, io ne farò venire;   99

ma stieno i Malebranche un poco in cesso,
    sì ch'ei non teman de le lor vendette;
        e io, seggendo in questo loco stesso,   102

per un ch'io son, ne farò venir sette
    quand' io suffolerò, com' è nostro uso
        di fare allor che fori alcun si mette».   105

Cagnazzo a cotal motto levò 'l muso,
    crollando 'l capo, e disse: «Odi malizia
        ch'elli ha pensata per gittarsi giuso!».   108

Ond' ei, ch'avea lacciuoli a gran divizia,
    rispuose: «Malizioso son io troppo,
        quand' io procuro a' mia maggior trestizia».   111

Alichin non si tenne e, di rintoppo
    a li altri, disse a lui: «Se tu ti cali,
        io non ti verrò dietro di gualoppo,   114

ma batterò sovra la pece l'ali.
    Lascisi 'l collo, e sia la ripa scudo,
        a veder se tu sol più di noi vali».   117

O tu che leggi, udirai nuovo ludo:
    ciascun da l'altra costa li occhi volse,
        quel prima, ch'a ciò fare era più crudo.   120

Lo Navarrese ben suo tempo colse;
    fermò le piante a terra, e in un punto
        saltò e dal proposto lor si sciolse.   123

Di che ciascun di colpa fu compunto,
    ma quei più che cagion fu del difetto;
        però si mosse e gridò: «Tu se' giunto!».   126

Littlehoof's eyes were rolling as he was spurred
      by a zeal to strike, but his provost suddenly
         wheeled round and barked: "Get back, you noxious bird!"   96
"If it's Lombards that you'd like to hear or see,
      or Tuscans," the frightened soul began to say,
         "then let me call for them, and here they'll be.   99
Let the Evilclaws drop back a little way,
      so the souls won't fear the things that they might do.
         Just one of me sitting here—and here I'll stay—   102
will make sure that seven souls come out for you
      when I whistle. That's the way we do it when
         any one of us gets free from the hot glue."   105
And Baddog lifted up his muzzle then,
      shook his head, and said: "Don't fall into the snare!
         It's a trick so he can jump back in again."   108
The spirit, who had trickery to spare,
      said: "I must be really tricky then, if I
         am procuring some new pains for my friends down there."   111
Droopwing, against the others, stood idly by
      no longer, but told the soul: "If you make a break,
         I won't come running after you, I'll fly,   114
beating my wings above the boiling lake.
      We'll go hide behind the bank. In any event,
         we'll see how much of a match for us you make."   117
Here, reader, is new sport. The whole complement
      looked off to the ridge, and the first to turn was he
         who had raised his voice the loudest in dissent.   120
The Navarrese had it measured perfectly.
      He planted his feet and broke from the embrace
         of the leader in one leap, and he was free.   123
They all were mortified at their disgrace,
      and most of all the one who had caused the error.
         "You're caught!" he called as he started to give chase,   126

Ma poco i valse: ché l'ali al sospetto
    non potero avanzar; quelli andò sotto,
    e quei drizzò volando suso il petto: 129
non altrimenti l'anitra di botto,
    quando 'l falcon s'appressa, giù s'attuffa,
    ed ei ritorna sù crucciato e rotto.   132
Irato Calcabrina de la buffa,
    volando dietro li tenne, invaghito
    che quei campasse per aver la zuffa;   135
e come 'l barattier fu disparito,
    così volse li artigli al suo compagno,
    e fu con lui sopra 'l fosso ghermito.   138
Ma l'altro fu bene sparvier grifagno
    ad artigliar ben lui, e amendue
    cadder nel mezzo del bogliente stagno.   141
Lo caldo sghermitor sùbito fue;
    ma però di levarsi era neente,
    sì avieno inviscate l'ali sue.   144
Barbariccia, con li altri suoi dolente,
    quattro ne fé volar da l'altra costa
    con tutt' i raffi, e assai prestamente   147
di qua, di là discesero a la posta;
    porser li uncini verso li 'mpaniati,
    ch'eran già cotti dentro da la crosta.   150
E noi lasciammo lor così 'mpacciati.

but his flapping wings could not outdistance terror.

      The one dove in and the other had to go

      looping swiftly upward as the pitch came nearer,   129

like the angry falcon left with nothing to show

      for his efforts when the wild duck he pursues

      eludes him with a rapid plunge below.   132

Tramplefrost, who was seething at the ruse,

      took wing, but hoped his quarry would abscond

      and provide him with a pretext he could use   135

to pick a fight. With the barrator beyond

      their reach, he turned and dug his claws into

      his fellow demon right above the pond.   138

But the other was a full-fledged hawk who knew

      how to give it back to him, and as they fought

      they dropped right down into the boiling glue.   141

There the heat shocked them apart, but when they sought

      to fly away, their wings were so besmeared,

      as if with lime, that they were truly caught.   144

Lamenting with his fellow fiends, Spikebeard

      sent four of them flying toward the other shore.

      Two landed on each side and quickly steered   147

their hooks above the lake to grapple for

      their limed companions, who'd already been

      baked in their crusts and cooked through to the core.   150

We left them to the mess they were stewing in.

Notes

line 5	According to a letter that has not survived, Dante was a cavalryman at the battle of Campaldino on June 11, 1289, in which the Aretine Ghibellines were defeated by the Florentine Guelphs.
lines 19–21	It was believed that the surfacing of dolphins near a vessel signified an approaching storm.
line 48	Once an independent kingdom, Navarre is now divided between north-

ern Spain and southwestern France. The speaker was named in early commentaries as one Ciampolo, but nothing is known of him.

line 52   Thibaut II, king of Navarre from 1253 to 1270, was highly regarded for his justice and generosity.

line 81   Around 1294, Fra Gomita was appointed chancellor by Nino Visconti (see note to Canto XXXIII, line 13), a Pisan who was the judge of Gallura, one of the four judicial districts of Sardinia. Visconti ignored all complaints against Gomita until he discovered that the friar had helped prisoners to escape, whereupon he had him hanged.

line 89   Don Michel Zanche was governor of Logudoro, another of the four judicial districts of Sardinia. He was murdered by his son-in-law, Branca d'Oria (see note to Canto XXXIII, line 137).

Canto XXIII

Taciti, soli, sanza compagnia
 n'andavam l'un dinanzi e l'altro dopo,
 come frati minor vanno per via.   3
Vòlt' era in su la favola d'Isopo
 lo mio pensier per la presente rissa,
 dov' el parlò de la rana e del topo;   6
ché più non si pareggia 'mo' e 'issa'
 che l'un con l'altro fa, se ben s'accoppia
 principio e fine con la mente fissa.   9
E come l'un pensier de l'altro scoppia,
 così nacque di quello un altro poi,
 che la prima paura mi fé doppia.   12
Io pensava così: 'Questi per noi
 sono scherniti con danno e con beffa
 sì fatta, ch'assai credo che lor nòi.   15
Se l'ira sovra 'l mal voler s'aggueffa,
 ei ne verranno dietro più crudeli
 che 'l cane a quella lievre ch'elli acceffa'.   18
Già mi sentia tutti arricciar li peli
 de la paura e stava in dietro intento,
 quand' io dissi: «Maestro, se non celi   21
te e me tostamente, i' ho pavento
 d'i Malebranche. Noi li avem già dietro;
 io li 'magino sì, che già li sento».   24
E quei: «S'i' fossi di piombato vetro,
 l'imagine di fuor tua non trarrei
 più tosto a me, che quella dentro 'mpetro.   27

Canto XXIII

We walked with no companions and no sounds,
    with one before and one behind, the way
    that Friars Minor do upon their rounds.   3
I was reminded by the demons' fray
    of Aesop's fables, the one in which we see
    the story of the frog and mouse. I say   6
that *now* is no closer to *immediately*
    than these two cases, if we scrutinize
    beginnings and conclusions carefully.   9
Out of one thought another one will rise,
    and that one bred another one that was
    making my fear grow twice its former size.   12
I thought: They have been tricked because of us,
    so hurt and humiliated that I swear
    by now they must be truly furious,   15
and if their spite is blended with a share
    of anger, they will follow where we've led
    more fiercely than a dog destroys a hare.   18
My scalp already tingled with cold dread
    and my senses fastened on what might appear
    behind us at any moment. "Master," I said,   21
"unless you conceal us now, I greatly fear
    the Evilclaws. I know they are in our wake.
    I fear them so, it sounds as if they're here."   24
He said: "Were I leaded glass, I could not take
    your outer form more quickly than I do
    the image that your inward motions make.   27

Pur mo venieno i tuo' pensier tra ' miei,
>   con simile atto e con simile faccia,
>   sì che d'intrambi un sol consiglio fei.   30
S'elli è che sì la destra costa giaccia,
>   che noi possiam ne l'altra bolgia scendere,
>   noi fuggirem l'imaginata caccia».   33
Già non compié di tal consiglio rendere,
>   ch'io li vidi venir con l'ali tese
>   non molto lungi, per volerne prendere.   36
Lo duca mio di sùbito mi prese,
>   come la madre ch'al romore è desta
>   e vede presso a sé le fiamme accese,   39
che prende il figlio e fugge e non s'arresta,
>   avendo più di lui che di sé cura,
>   tanto che solo una camiscia vesta;   42
e giù dal collo de la ripa dura
>   supin si diede a la pendente roccia,
>   che l'un de' lati a l'altra bolgia tura.   45
Non corse mai sì tosto acqua per doccia
>   a volger ruota di molin terragno,
>   quand' ella più verso le pale approccia,   48
come 'l maestro mio per quel vivagno,
>   portandosene me sovra 'l suo petto,
>   come suo figlio, non come compagno.   51
A pena fuoro i piè suoi giunti al letto
>   del fondo giù, ch'e' furon in sul colle
>   sovresso noi; ma non lì era sospetto: 54
ché l'alta provedenza che lor volle
>   porre ministri de la fossa quinta,
>   poder di partirs' indi a tutti tolle.   57
Là giù trovammo una gente dipinta
>   che giva intorno assai con lenti passi,
>   piangendo e nel sembiante stanca e vinta.   60

A moment ago, I felt these thoughts from you
  mingle with mine, the same movement and same face,
  so that I have drawn one counsel from the two.   30
If we follow the right slope down to its base
  we will reach the next ditch, in my expectation,
  and so escape from this imagined chase."   33
He had not finished with his explanation
  when I saw the demons with their wings outspread
  behind us, bent on our annihilation.   36
My leader drew me to him, and he sped
  like a mother wakened by the noise and seeing
  the rising flames as they crackle by her bed   39
and then picking up her child and quickly fleeing
  without stopping even to put on a shift,
  more concerned for his than for her own well-being.   42
Supine, he gave himself up to a swift
  slide on the hard ridge that slopes down below
  to form the outer wall of the next cleft.   45
Never did water make such a rapid flow
  to the bottom of the sluice where it ends its run
  by hitting the paddles to make the millwheel go   48
as my master sledded down the rock upon
  his back, and all the while he clasped me tight,
  not just as a companion, but as a son.   51
As we reached the base, I looked back to the height
  and saw the entire troop of fiends appear,
  but now there was no cause for further fright,   54
for that high providence that placed them here
  to rule the fifth ditch makes them powerless
  ever to pass beyond their proper sphere.   57
Below there were painted people in distress,
  weeping, and trudging slowly, with an air
  of great oppression and great weariness.   60

Elli avean cappe con cappucci bassi
dinanzi a li occhi, fatte de la taglia
che in Clugnì per li monaci fassi.   63

Di fuor dorate son, sì ch'elli abbaglia;
ma dentro tutte piombo, e gravi tanto,
che Federigo le mettea di paglia.   66

Oh in etterno faticoso manto!
Noi ci volgemmo ancor pur a man manca
con loro insieme, intenti al tristo pianto;   69

ma per lo peso quella gente stanca
venìa sì pian, che noi eravam nuovi
di compagnia ad ogne mover d'anca.   72

Per ch'io al duca mio: «Fa che tu trovi
alcun ch'al fatto o al nome si conosca,
e li occhi, sì andando, intorno movi».   75

E un che 'ntese la parola tosca,
di retro a noi gridò: «Tenete i piedi,
voi che correte sì per l'aura fosca!   78

Forse ch'avrai da me quel che tu chiedi».
Onde 'l duca si volse e disse: «Aspetta,
e poi secondo il suo passo procedi».   81

Ristetti, e vidi due mostrar gran fretta
de l'animo, col viso, d'esser meco;
ma tardavali 'l carco e la via stretta.   84

Quando fuor giunti, assai con l'occhio bieco
mi rimiraron sanza far parola;
poi si volsero in sé, e dicean seco: 87

«Costui par vivo a l'atto de la gola;
e s'e' son morti, per qual privilegio
vanno scoperti de la grave stola?».   90

Poi disser me: «O Tosco, ch'al collegio
de l'ipocriti tristi se' venuto,
dir chi tu se' non avere in dispregio».   93

Large cloaks were worn by all the sinners there,
> with cowls that hid their eyes, and cut like those
>> that are fashioned for the Cluny monks to wear.   63

Though the eye was dazzled by these gilded clothes,
> they were lead inside, and sat so heavily
>> they made the ones that Frederick would impose   66

seem straw. A weary cape for eternity!
> Turning left once more, we walked with that parade
>> and listened to their moans of misery.   69

The leaden capes with which they were arrayed
> so weighed them down and made their steps so slow,
>> we saw new faces with each stride we made.   72

I told my guide: "Please look round as we go,
> to see if there are people anywhere
>> of whom, by name or deed, I ought to know."   75

And hearing my Tuscan speech, one trudging there
> cried after us: "Don't go at such great speed,
>> you who are hurtling through the dusky air!   78

Perhaps I can provide you what you need."
> My leader said: "Till he overtakes you, stay,
>> then match your pace to his, and so proceed."   81

I stopped. There were two whose faces showed that they
> had minds that raced to join me, but they were balked
>> by their burden and by the narrowness of the way.   84

They looked at me askance when they had walked
> to where I was, and silently took note.
>> Then they turned to one another, and they talked: 87

"He seems alive, from the workings of his throat.
> And if they are dead, by what authority
>> are they exempted from the heavy coat?"   90

Then to me: "O Tuscan, who have come to see
> the college of sad hypocrites, we implore
>> that you not disdain to tell us who you might be."   93

E io a loro: «I' fui nato e cresciuto
    sovra 'l bel fiume d'Arno a la gran villa,
    e son col corpo ch'i' ho sempre avuto.   96
Ma voi chi siete, a cui tanto distilla
    quant' i' veggio dolor giù per le guance?
    e che pena è in voi che sì sfavilla?».   99
E l'un rispuose a me: «Le cappe rance
    son di piombo sì grosse, che li pesi
    fan così cigolar le lor bilance.   102
Frati godenti fummo, e bolognesi;
    io Catalano e questi Loderingo
    nomati, e da tua terra insieme presi   105
come suole esser tolto un uom solingo,
    per conservar sua pace; e fummo tali,
    ch'ancor si pare intorno dal Gardingo».   108
Io cominciai: «O frati, i vostri mali . . . »;
    ma più non dissi, ch'a l'occhio mi corse
    un, crucifisso in terra con tre pali.   111
Quando mi vide, tutto si distorse,
    soffiando ne la barba con sospiri;
    e 'l frate Catalan, ch'a ciò s'accorse,   114
mi disse: «Quel confitto che tu miri,
    consigliò i Farisei che convenia
    porre un uom per lo popolo a' martìri.   117
Attraversato è, nudo, ne la via,
    come tu vedi, ed è mestier ch'el senta
    qualunque passa, come pesa, pria.   120
E a tal modo il socero si stenta
    in questa fossa, e li altri dal concilio
    che fu per li Giudei mala sementa».   123
Allor vid' io maravigliar Virgilio
    sovra colui ch'era disteso in croce
    tanto vilmente ne l'etterno essilio.   126

And I: "The great city on fair Arno's shore
    is where I was born and where my youth was spent,
    and I wear the body that I always wore.   96
But who are you, whose misery has sent
    its distillations down along your cheek,
    and why do you wear this glittering punishment?"   99
Then one of the two souls began to speak:
    "The orange cape's thick lead weighs down our frame,
    which is its balance scale, and makes it creak.   102
We were Jolly Friars, and Bolognese. My name
    is Catalano and his is Loderingo.
    Chosen jointly by your city, we became   105
maintainers of the peace, a post for a single
    appointee in most times. How well we tried
    can still be seen in the region of the Gardingo."   108
"O friars, your wicked—" I started. The rest died
    in my throat as my eye was caught by someone nailed
    right into the ground with three stakes, crucified.   111
He began to writhe when he saw me, and exhaled
    great sighs in his beard. Catalano, carefully
    observing, said: "The one who is impaled   114
advised the Pharisees that it would be
    expedient that one man be made to die
    in order that the people might go free.   117
And just as you see before you, he must lie
    naked and stretched in the middle of the road
    under the weight of each one who passes by.   120
Transfixed with spikes and racked in the same mode,
    his father-in-law lies elsewhere in this fosse,
    and the others of that council, those who sowed   123
so much evil for the Jews." Seeming at a loss,
    Virgil was staring at the one who lay
    in such vile eternal exile, as on a cross.   126

Poscia drizzò al frate cotal voce:

    «Non vi dispiaccia, se vi lece, dirci

    s'a la man destra giace alcuna foce   129

onde noi amendue possiamo uscirci,

    sanza costrigner de li angeli neri

    che vegnan d'esto fondo a dipartirci».   132

Rispuose adunque: «Più che tu non speri

    s'appressa un sasso che da la gran cerchia

    si move e varca tutt' i vallon feri,   135

salvo che 'n questo è rotto e nol coperchia;

    montar potrete su per la ruina,

    che giace in costa e nel fondo soperchia».   138

Lo duca stette un poco a testa china;

    poi disse: «Mal contava la bisogna

    colui che i peccator di qua uncina».   141

E 'l frate: «Io udi' già dire a Bologna

    del diavol vizi assai, tra ' quali udi'

    ch'elli è bugiardo e padre di menzogna».   144

Appresso il duca a gran passi sen gì,

    turbato un poco d'ira nel sembiante;

    ond' io da li 'ncarcati mi parti'   147

dietro a le poste de le care piante.

Then he turned and spoke to the friar: "I hope it may
    not displease you, if the laws down here permit,
    to let us know if there is any way   129
on the right by which we two can leave this pit
    without our having to depend upon
    the black angels to deliver us from it."   132
"Much closer than you hope, making its run
    from the massive outer wall, there is a ridge
    linking all the savage valleys—except this one,   135
where it is broken and there is no bridge,"
    the friar replied, "but you may climb instead
    on the pile of the ruin up to the next ledge."   138
My leader stood for a moment with bowed head,
    then said: "The one who hooks sinners up on that rise
    gave a bad account of this." And the friar said: 141
"In Bologna once, I heard men philosophize
    on the devil's vices, and someone put the case
    that he is a liar, and even the father of lies."   144
A spot of anger darkened my guide's face
    as he strode away, and I no longer stayed
    among those weighted souls, but left that place   147
to follow in the steps his dear feet made.

Notes

line 3   The Friars Minor were the Franciscans. Following the example of their founder, St. Francis of Assisi, they cultivated poverty and humility. They made their begging rounds in pairs, the younger friar walking behind the elder.

lines 5–6   In most versions of this fable, a mouse asks a frog to carry him across a stream; before doing so, the frog ties the mouse to his leg, and during the crossing he tries to drown the mouse by submerging; the ensuing commotion attracts a hawk, who carries them off, eating the frog and freeing the mouse.

line 63   The abbey of Cluny in Burgundy was founded by the Benedictines in 910.

line 66   According to his enemies (although there is no confirmation), Emperor Frederick II punished treason by having the offender be boiled in a cauldron while wearing a lead cape; the cape, when it melted, peeled away the traitor's skin.

lines 103–8   The Knights of the Blessed Virgin Mary were a religious order whose charge was to reconcile factions and disputes and to protect the weak. They were known sarcastically as the Jolly Friars because of the laxity of their rules and their reputation for corruption. Among the founders of the order were Catalano di Guido di Ostia (c. 1210–1285), a Guelph, and Loderingo degli Andalò (c. 1210–1293), a Ghibelline, who served jointly as maintainers of public order in Bologna in 1265. Having arranged a truce between warring factions, they were appointed in 1266 to a similar function in Florence at the behest of Pope Clement IV, whose secret intent was to establish the Guelph party at the expense of the Ghibellines. In 1267, the Ghibellines were driven out of Florence, their property confiscated, and the houses of some of the more prominent familes destroyed, including those of the Uberti family in the Gardingo section of the city.

lines 114–24   Caiaphas, the high priest of the Jews, urged that Jesus be turned over to the Romans, ostensibly for the public good but secretly because Jesus' teachings posed a threat to the established leadership. In this he was abetted by his father-in-law, Annas, and other members of the Sanhedrin, the supreme council. From this betrayal, as Dante sees it, followed the destruction of Jerusalem and the diaspora.

CANTO XXIV

In quella parte del giovanetto anno
     che 'l sole i crin sotto l'Aquario tempra
     e già le notti al mezzo dì sen vanno,   3
quando la brina in su la terra assempra
     l'imagine di sua sorella bianca,
     ma poco dura a la sua penna tempra,   6
lo villanello a cui la roba manca,
     si leva, e guarda, e vede la campagna
     biancheggiar tutta; ond' ei si batte l'anca,   9
ritorna in casa, e qua e là si lagna,
     come 'l tapin che non sa che si faccia;
     poi riede, e la speranza ringavagna,   12
veggendo 'l mondo aver cangiata faccia
     in poco d'ora, e prende suo vincastro
     e fuor le pecorelle a pascer caccia.   15
Così mi fece sbigottir lo mastro
     quand' io li vidi sì turbar la fronte,
     e così tosto al mal giunse lo 'mpiastro;   18
ché, come noi venimmo al guasto ponte,
     lo duca a me si volse con quel piglio
     dolce ch'io vidi prima a piè del monte.   21
Le braccia aperse, dopo alcun consiglio
     eletto seco riguardando prima
     ben la ruina, e diedemi di piglio.   24
E come quei ch'adopera ed estima,
     che sempre par che 'nnanzi si proveggia,
     così, levando me sù ver' la cima   27

CANTO XXIV

In that part of the young year when the sun's rays
     are tempered beneath Aquarius, and when
     the nights grow shorter, equaling the days,   3
and when her white sister's image once again
     appears upon the ground as copied by
     the hoarfrost with her quickly dulling pen,   6
the peasant, with the loss of his supply
     of fodder, goes outside in anxiety
     to see the whitened fields, and smites his thigh   9
and mutters and starts to pace distractedly
     like a wretch whose mind can find no resting place,
     then grows hopeful, going out again, to see   12
how rapidly the world has changed its face,
     and taking staff in hand walks forth once more
     to lead his sheep to graze. Such was my case,   15
because the troubled look my master wore
     distressed me deeply, but he soothed my pain
     when he quickly put the plaster to the sore.   18
At the ruined bridge I saw his face regain,
     when he turned to me, the sweet look I first knew
     at the base of the mountain on the desert plain.   21
He looked carefully at the ruin, then he drew
     into himself in silent contemplation,
     and then took hold of me. Like someone who   24
while working keeps a constant calculation
     and thus is able to anticipate,
     he would look ahead and make an estimation   27

d'un ronchione, avvisava un'altra scheggia

    dicendo: «Sovra quella poi t'aggrappa;

    ma tenta pria s'è tal ch'ella ti reggia».   30

Non era via da vestito di cappa,

    ché noi a pena, ei lieve e io sospinto,

    potavam sù montar di chiappa in chiappa.   33

E se non fosse che da quel precinto

    più che da l'altro era la costa corta,

    non so di lui, ma io sarei ben vinto.   36

Ma perché Malebolge inver' la porta

    del bassissimo pozzo tutta pende,

    lo sito di ciascuna valle porta   39

che l'una costa surge e l'altra scende;

    noi pur venimmo al fine in su la punta

    onde l'ultima pietra si scoscende.   42

La lena m'era del polmon sì munta

    quand' io fui sù, ch'i' non potea più oltre,

    anzi m'assisi ne la prima giunta.   45

«Omai convien che tu così ti spoltre»,

    disse 'l maestro; «ché, seggendo in piuma,

    in fama non si vien, né sotto coltre;   48

sanza la qual chi sua vita consuma,

    cotal vestigio in terra di sé lascia,

    qual fummo in aere e in acqua la schiuma.   51

E però leva sù; vinci l'ambascia

    con l'animo che vince ogne battaglia,

    se col suo grave corpo non s'accascia.   54

Più lunga scala convien che si saglia;

    non basta da costoro esser partito.

    Se tu mi 'ntendi, or fa sì che ti vaglia».   57

Leva'mi allor, mostrandomi fornito

    meglio di lena ch'i' non mi sentia,

    e dissi: «Va, ch'i' son forte e ardito».   60

as he lifted me from rock to rock, and state:

>"Take hold of this one, but be sure to test
>
>beforehand whether it will bear your weight."   30

That was no road for anybody dressed

>in a lead cloak. Rock by rock we had to grope,
>
>he weightless and I half-carried, toward the crest.   33

And happily upon that side the slope

>was shorter than on the other, or else I—
>
>I cannot speak for him—would have had no hope.   36

All of the rungs of the Malebolge lie

>on an incline toward the deep well's mouth, and so
>
>one wall is always low and one is high   39

in each of the ten troughs along the row.

>But in the end we made our way to where
>
>the last rock had broken free and dropped below.   42

My aching lungs had been so milked of air,

>when I finally reached the top, that I had to sit,
>
>feeling unable to go on from there.   45

"Now you must rouse yourself, for never yet

>has anyone come to fame," my master cried,
>
>"sitting on cushions or under a coverlet.   48

He who consumes his life, when he has died

>without fame, leaves the world with the impress
>
>of smoke in the air or foam upon the tide.   51

Rise. Let your soul overcome your breathlessness,

>for, unless the heavy body lets it fail,
>
>the soul will always prove victorious.   54

There is still a longer ladder we must scale.

>It is not enough to have left the rest, and so
>
>act for your good, if you know what these words entail."   57

Then I stood up and said, with a greater show

>of breath than what I really felt within:
>
>"I am strong and I am ready. Let us go."   60

Su per lo scoglio prendemmo la via,
  ch'era ronchioso, stretto e malagevole,
  ed erto più assai che quel di pria.   63

Parlando andava per non parer fievole;
  onde una voce uscì de l'altro fosso,
  a parole formar disconvenevole.   66

Non so che disse, ancor che sovra 'l dosso
  fossi de l'arco già che varca quivi;
  ma chi parlava ad ire parea mosso.   69

Io era vòlto in giù, ma li occhi vivi
  non poteano ire al fondo per lo scuro;
  per ch'io: «Maestro, fa che tu arrivi   72

da l'altro cinghio e dismontiam lo muro;
  ché, com' i' odo quinci e non intendo,
  così giù veggio e neente affiguro».   75

«Altra risposta», disse, «non ti rendo
  se non lo far; ché la dimanda onesta
  si de' seguir con l'opera tacendo».   78

Noi discendemmo il ponte da la testa
  dove s'aggiugne con l'ottava ripa,
  e poi mi fu la bolgia manifesta: 81

e vidivi entro terribile stipa
  di serpenti, e di sì diversa mena
  che la memoria il sangue ancor mi scipa.   84

Più non si vanti Libia con sua rena;
  ché se chelidri, iaculi e faree
  produce, e cencri con anfisibena,   87

né tante pestilenzie né sì ree
  mostrò già mai con tutta l'Etïopia
  né con ciò che di sopra al Mar Rosso èe.   90

Tra questa cruda e tristissima copia
  corrëan genti nude e spaventate,
  sanza sperar pertugio o elitropia: 93

So we took up our journey once again.
        The ridge was narrow, difficult, and rough,
        much steeper than the previous one had been.   63
I was talking as I walked, to keep up the bluff
        of vigor, when a voice with little skill
        in forming words came from the nearby trough.   66
Although I had reached the high point of the hill
        made by the arch, I could not tell what was said
        and I sensed the speaker was not standing still.   69
Because of the darkness, even my riveted
        eyes could not see to the bottom of the ring,
        so I said: "Master, let us walk ahead   72
and descend the wall, for I am listening
        without understanding what I hear, and I
        am looking without seeing anything."   75
He said: "A right request should be followed by
        the deed itself without words' embellishment,
        and so the doing is my sole reply."   78
At the end of the bridge, we two made our descent
        to the eighth embankment, and from where we stood
        what was down there in the ditch was evident.   81
In it I saw a horrible multitude
        of serpents, of such weird variety
        that thinking about them now still chills my blood.   84
Let Libya boast no more of phareae
        and jaculi and chelydri in her sands,
        and cenchres with amphisbaena, because she,   87
with all Ethiopia or the Red Sea's lands,
        has never bred a pestilence of such scope
        or such malignancy. Here naked bands   90
of terrified souls were running, with no hope,
        amid this savage swarm, that they would find
        a crevice where they could hide, or a heliotrope.   93

con serpi le man dietro avean legate;
>quelle ficcavan per le ren la coda
>e 'l capo, ed eran dinanzi aggroppate.   96
Ed ecco a un ch'era da nostra proda,
>s'avventò un serpente che 'l trafisse
>là dove 'l collo a le spalle s'annoda.   99
Né O sì tosto mai né I si scrisse,
>com' el s'accese e arse, e cener tutto
>convenne che cascando divenisse;   102
e poi che fu a terra sì distrutto,
>la polver si raccolse per sé stessa
>e 'n quel medesmo ritornò di butto.   105
Così per li gran savi si confessa
>che la fenice more e poi rinasce,
>quando al cinquecentesimo anno appressa;   108
erba né biado in sua vita non pasce,
>ma sol d'incenso lagrime e d'amomo,
>e nardo e mirra son l'ultime fasce.   111
E qual è quel che cade, e non sa como,
>per forza di demon ch'a terra il tira,
>o d'altra oppilazion che lega l'omo,   114
quando si leva, che 'ntorno si mira
>tutto smarrito de la grande angoscia
>ch'elli ha sofferta, e guardando sospira: 117
tal era 'l peccator levato poscia.
>Oh potenza di Dio, quant' è severa,
>che cotai colpi per vendetta croscia!   120
Lo duca il domandò poi chi ello era;
>per ch'ei rispuose: «Io piovvi di Toscana,
>poco tempo è, in questa gola fiera.   123
Vita bestial mi piacque e non umana,
>sì come a mul ch'i' fui; son Vanni Fucci
>bestia, e Pistoia mi fu degna tana».   126

With serpents each one's hands were bound behind,
      and the ends poked through his loins and gathered tight
      in a knot at front, with head and tail entwined.   96

Not far from where we stood, I beheld the sight
      of a serpent darting at a sinner's nape,
      transfixing him where shoulders and neck unite.   99

Never did pen so quickly make the shape
      of an *o* or *i* as he flared and burned before
      he turned to ash and fell into a heap.   102

And when he lay destroyed on the ditch's floor,
      the loose dust gathered by itself and then
      quickly assumed its former shape once more.   105

In such fashion, as affirmed by learned men,
      when its five hundred years are near complete
      the phoenix dies and then is born again.   108

Tears of balsam and of incense are its meat,
      not grass or grain, and when it comes to die
      spikenard and myrrh are its final winding-sheet.   111

Just as when someone falls without knowing why,
      seized by a devil hidden from his eyes
      or a blockage that a man may be stricken by,   114

and looks around him as he starts to rise,
      stunned by the anguish that he undergoes,
      and in his great bewilderment he sighs,   117

such was the soul before us as he rose.
      O power of God, so rigorously applied,
      that in its vengeance showers down such blows!   120

My leader asked who he was, and he replied:
      "Not long ago I was rained from Tuscany
      down to this savage gullet. I enjoyed   123

a beast's, not a man's life, mule that I used to be.
      I am Vanni Fucci, beast. Pistoia was
      a proper den for an animal like me."   126

E ïo al duca: «Dilli che non mucci,
　　e domanda che colpa qua giù 'l pinse;
　　ch'io 'l vidi uomo di sangue e di crucci».　　　129
E 'l peccator, che 'ntese, non s'infinse,
　　ma drizzò verso me l'animo e 'l volto,
　　e di trista vergogna si dipinse;　　　132
poi disse: «Più mi duol che tu m'hai colto
　　ne la miseria dove tu mi vedi,
　　che quando fui de l'altra vita tolto.　　　135
Io non posso negar quel che tu chiedi;
　　in giù son messo tanto perch' io fui
　　ladro a la sagrestia d'i belli arredi,　　　138
e falsamente già fu apposto altrui.
　　Ma perché di tal vista tu non godi,
　　se mai sarai di fuor da' luoghi bui,　　　141
apri li orecchi al mio annunzio, e odi.
　　Pistoia in pria d'i Neri si dimagra;
　　poi Fiorenza rinova gente e modi.　　　144
Tragge Marte vapor di Val di Magra
　　ch'è di torbidi nuvoli involuto;
　　e con tempesta impetüosa e agra　　　147
sovra Campo Picen fia combattuto;
　　ond' ei repente spezzerà la nebbia,
　　sì ch'ogne Bianco ne sarà feruto.　　　150
E detto l'ho perché doler ti debbia!».

I said to my guide: "Tell him not to slip from us,
  and ask what sin has thrown him down here, since
  I knew him to be bloody and furious."   129
The soul had heard me, and with no pretense
  fastened on me with his face and with his mind,
  and said, as sad shame colored his countenance: 132
"It pains me more to be caught by you in the bind
  of this misery than it did a short while ago
  to be snatched away from the life I left behind. 135
I cannot deny the thing you wish to know.
  I am this far down because I was the one
  who stole the sacristy's ornaments, although 138
others were wrongly blamed for what I'd done.
  But lest this sight please you, if you ever do
  escape this land that never sees the sun, 141
open your ears and hear what I'm telling you.
  Pistoia puts out its Blacks, then Florence makes
  its population and its ways anew. 144
Mars goes to Val di Magra, where he takes
  a vapor wrapped in dense clouds, and the might
  of a violent and a bitter tempest breaks 147
on Campo Piceno, where there is a fight
  till the vapor rends the mist above the plain
  all of a sudden, striking every White. 150
And I have told you this to give you pain."

Notes

lines 1–3 The sun is in Aquarius between January 21 and February 21.
lines 85–88 Libya (the ancient term for northern Africa, exclusive of Egypt),
    Ethiopia (from Egypt south to Zanzibar), and Arabia ("the Red Sea's
    lands") were considered to be largely uninhabitable and filled with
    exotic creatures. All the species of serpents mentioned here are taken
    from Book IX of Lucan's *Pharsalia*.

line 125	Vanni Fucci was the illegitimate son ("mule") of Fuccio dei Lazzari and an extreme partisan of the Blacks in Pistoia. He was notorious for his rage and was known to have committed at least one murder (thus Dante's surprise, in lines 128–29, at finding him here and not among the violent).
lines 137–39	The theft of sacred objects from the sacristy of the chapel of San Jacopo caused a sensation in Pistoia in 1293. Fucci revealed his involvement in this crime in order to save the life of one Rampino di Francesco Foresi, who was about to be hanged for it.
lines 143–50	Fucci's prophecy alludes to the following events: In May 1301, the Pistoian Whites, with the aid of their Florentine counterparts, expelled the Blacks from their city. In November of that year, the Blacks began an uprising in Florence that led to their recapture of the city the following year and the banishment of the Whites, which would result in Dante's permanent exile from Florence (see note to Canto VI, lines 64–75). The vapor—or hot wind, which clashes with the cold, moist clouds to produce the storm—is generally understood to be Moroello Malaspina, from the region of Val di Magra, a highly effective military leader of the Blacks. Campo Piceno refers to a field near Pistoia, believed to be the site of Catiline's defeat in 63 B.C.E., and also the location of a raid by Malaspina against the Whites.

Canto XXV

Al fine de le sue parole il ladro
    le mani alzò con amendue le fiche,
    gridando: «Togli, Dio, ch'a te le squadro!».   3
Da indi in qua mi fuor le serpi amiche,
    perch' una li s'avvolse allora al collo,
    come dicesse 'Non vo' che più diche';   6
e un'altra a le braccia, e rilegollo,
    ribadendo sé stessa sì dinanzi,
    che non potea con esse dare un crollo.   9
Ahi Pistoia, Pistoia, ché non stanzi
    d'incenerarti sì che più non duri,
    poi che 'n mal fare il seme tuo avanzi?   12
Per tutt' i cerchi de lo 'nferno scuri
    non vidi spirto in Dio tanto superbo,
    non quel che cadde a Tebe giù da' muri.   15
El si fuggì che non parlò più verbo;
    e io vidi un centauro pien di rabbia
    venir chiamando: «Ov' è, ov' è l'acerbo?».   18
Maremma non cred' io che tante n'abbia,
    quante bisce elli avea su per la groppa
    infin ove comincia nostra labbia.   21
Sovra le spalle, dietro da la coppa,
    con l'ali aperte li giacea un draco;
    e quello affuoca qualunque s'intoppa.   24
Lo mio maestro disse: «Questi è Caco,
    che, sotto 'l sasso di monte Aventino,
    di sangue fece spesse volte laco.   27

CANTO XXV

When he had finished speaking, the thief threw
    his arms up, making figs with both his hands,
    and shouted: "Take these, God, they're aimed at you!"   3
From that moment on, the serpents were my friends,
    for one approached his neck and circled it,
    as if to tell him "Now your talking ends,"   6
and another retied him with so tight a fit,
    knotting itself in front, that he could not free
    his arms to even wriggle them a bit.   9
Pistoia, Pistoia, why do you not decree
    the flames of your own destruction and downfall,
    since you surpass your seed in villainy?   12
I saw no soul so proud toward God through all
    the murky rings of hell, not even the one
    who assaulted Thebes and fell from the high wall.   15
He fled without a word, and on the run
    came a raging centaur who was calling out:
    "Where is he, where's the unripe spirit gone?"   18
I believe not even Maremma has such a rout
    of snakes as I saw upon him, from the rear
    to the part where our human shape begins to sprout.   21
A dragon with its wings stretched out was here
    across his shoulders, crouched behind his head,
    spitting fire and burning anyone who was near.   24
"That centaur there is Cacus," my master said.
    "Below the rock of Mount Avetine, blood flowed
    because of him into frequent lakes of red.   27

Non va co' suoi fratei per un cammino,
 per lo furto che frodolente fece
  del grande armento ch'elli ebbe a vicino;   30
onde cessar le sue opere biece
 sotto la mazza d'Ercule, che forse
  gliene diè cento, e non sentì le diece».   33
Mentre che sì parlava, ed el trascorse,
 e tre spiriti venner sotto noi,
  de' quai né io né 'l duca mio s'accorse,   36
se non quando gridar: «Chi siete voi?»;
 per che nostra novella si ristette,
  e intendemmo pur ad essi poi.   39
Io non li conoscea; ma ei seguette,
 come suol seguitar per alcun caso,
  che l'un nomar un altro convenette,   42
dicendo: «Cianfa dove fia rimaso?»;
 per ch'io, acciò che 'l duca stesse attento,
  mi puosi 'l dito su dal mento al naso.   45
Se tu se' or, lettore, a creder lento
 ciò ch'io dirò, non sarà maraviglia,
  ché io che 'l vidi, a pena il mi consento.   48
Com' io tenea levate in lor le ciglia,
 e un serpente con sei piè si lancia
  dinanzi a l'uno, e tutto a lui s'appiglia.   51
Co' piè di mezzo li avvinse la pancia
 e con li anterïor le braccia prese;
  poi li addentò e l'una e l'altra guancia;   54
li diretani a le cosce distese,
 e miseli la coda tra 'mbedue
  e dietro per le ren sù la ritese.   57
Ellera abbarbicata mai non fue
 ad alber sì, come l'orribil fiera
  per l'altrui membra avviticchiò le sue.   60

And owing to the craftiness he showed
 when he stole the great herd grazing near his den,
 he and his brothers are not on the same road.   30
That brought the end of his crooked dealings when
 Hercules clubbed him down, although he may,
 of a hundred blows, have felt not even ten."   33
While he said these words, the centaur ran away
 and three souls came to stand below us two,
 although neither my guide nor I perceived that they   36
were there until they called out: "Who are you?"
 We stopped what we were saying, and we were
 attentive to them. I couldn't make out who   39
these three might be, but as it will occur
 by chance sometimes, at that moment it occurred
 that one of them had occasion to refer   42
to someone else—"Where's Cianfa?"—at which I stirred,
 and I placed a finger on my lips to show
 my leader we should watch without a word.   45
Reader, it is no wonder if you are slow
 to credit what comes next, for I was there
 and I hardly can believe that it was so.   48
As I fixed upon those three with a steady stare,
 all at once I saw a six-legged serpent race
 up to one and fasten on him everywhere.   51
Its front feet moved to pin his arms in place,
 its middle feet gripped his belly like a vise
 while it sank its fangs in both sides of his face,   54
and between his legs its tail began to rise
 and it curved up to secure him from behind
 after its rear feet spread apart his thighs.   57
Never did any strand of ivy bind
 its clinging roots more closely to a tree
 than the limbs of that disgusting beast entwined   60

Poi s'appiccar, come di calda cera
    fossero stati, e mischiar lor colore,
    né l'un né l'altro già parea quel ch'era: 63
come procede innanzi da l'ardore,
    per lo papiro suso, un color bruno
    che non è nero ancora e 'l bianco more.   66
Li altri due 'l riguardavano, e ciascuno
    gridava: «Omè, Agnel, come ti muti!
    Vedi che già non se' né due né uno».   69
Già eran li due capi un divenuti,
    quando n'apparver due figure miste
    in una faccia, ov' eran due perduti.   72
Fersi le braccia due di quattro liste;
    le cosce con le gambe e 'l ventre e 'l casso
    divenner membra che non fuor mai viste.   75
Ogne primaio aspetto ivi era casso:
    due e nessun l'imagine perversa
    parea; e tal sen gio con lento passo.   78
Come 'l ramarro sotto la gran fersa
    dei dì canicular, cangiando sepe,
    folgore par se la via attraversa,   81
sì pareva, venendo verso l'epe
    de li altri due, un serpentello acceso,
    livido e nero come gran di pepe;   84
e quella parte onde prima è preso
    nostro alimento, a l'un di lor trafisse;
    poi cadde giuso innanzi lui disteso.   87
Lo trafitto 'l mirò, ma nulla disse;
    anzi, co' piè fermati, sbadigliava
    pur come sonno o febbre l'assalisse.   90
Elli 'l serpente e quei lui riguardava;
    l'un per la piaga e l'altro per la bocca
    fummavan forte, e 'l fummo si scontrava.   93

round the soul's. The two seemed like hot wax to me
  as their colors mingled and they were stuck tight,
  and neither kept its own identity.   63
In the same way, when a paper is alight,
  ahead of the flame a dark hue starts to spread
  that is not yet black but already no longer white. 66
The other two were watching, and they said:
  "Alas, Agnello, how fast you are defaced,
  neither two nor one, but something else instead." 69
Where there had been two heads, they were replaced
  by a single one, and in the face it wore
  all the details of their own two were erased. 72
Now two arms sprouted where there had been four,
  and thighs, legs, chests, and bellies mixed and grew
  into members that were never seen before. 75
All of their features had disappeared into
  a perverse thing that was both and neither one,
  that with slow steps went trudging out of view. 78
As across the lane you may see a lizard run
  like a lightning flash as it darts from hedge to hedge
  when the dog days scourge the earth with a burning sun, 81
so I saw a little serpent in a rage,
  as fiery and as black as pepper, bound
  toward the bellies of the two beneath our ledge. 84
Lunging, it bit one where that part is found
  through which we all take in our earliest food,
  and then fell back, stretched out upon the ground. 87
The one it had bitten made no sound. He stood
  gazing and yawning, as if he had been hit
  with a sleepy or a feverish lassitude. 90
The serpent looked at him and he looked at it.
  Thick smoke poured from its mouth, and met and mixed
  with smoke from his belly, where the reptile bit. 93

Taccia Lucano ormai là dov' e' tocca
    del misero Sabello e di Nasidio,
    e attenda a udir quel ch'or si scocca.   96
Taccia di Cadmo e d'Aretusa Ovidio,
    ché se quello in serpente e quella in fonte
    converte poetando, io non lo 'nvidio;   99
ché due nature mai a fronte a fronte
    non trasmutò sì ch'amendue le forme
    a cambiar lor matera fosser pronte.   102
Insieme si rispuosero a tai norme,
    che 'l serpente la coda in forca fesse,
    e 'l feruto ristrinse insieme l'orme.   105
Le gambe con le cosce seco stesse
    s'appiccar sì, che 'n poco la giuntura
    non facea segno alcun che si paresse.   108
Togliea la coda fessa la figura
    che si perdeva là, e la sua pelle
    si facea molle, e quella di là dura.   111
Io vidi intrar le braccia per l'ascelle,
    e i due piè de la fiera, ch'eran corti,
    tanto allungar quanto accorciavan quelle.   114
Poscia li piè di rietro, insieme attorti,
    diventaron lo membro che l'uom cela,
    e 'l misero del suo n'avea due porti.   117
Mentre che 'l fummo l'uno e l'altro vela
    di color novo, e genera 'l pel suso
    per l'una parte e da l'altra il dipela,   120
l'un si levò e l'altro cadde giuso,
    non torcendo però le lucerne empie,
    sotto le quai ciascun cambiava muso.   123
Quel ch'era dritto, il trasse ver' le tempie,
    e di troppa matera ch'in là venne
    uscir li orecchi de le gote scempie;   126

Let Lucan be still, who tells us in his text
       of poor Sabellus and Nasidius,
       and let him wait to hear what is sent forth next.   96
Let Ovid be still. If he tells how Cadmus was
       made a snake, how Arethusa came to be
       a fountain, I do not envy him, because   99
in all his transmutations we never see
       two different natures facing one another
       whose forms exchange their substance instantly.   102
The two responded readily to each other,
       so that the serpent split its tail in two
       and the wounded spirit drew his feet together.   105
Then his legs, from thigh to ankle, also drew
       together, and they were joined so seamlessly
       that soon the juncture disappeared from view.   108
The cloven tail took on the anatomy
       the other abandoned, and the serpent's hide
       grew soft as the other's skin grew leathery.   111
I saw the spirit's arms drawn up inside
       at the armpits, while the serpent's short feet surged
       and correspondingly grew long and wide.   114
While its hind feet, which had twisted and converged,
       became the member man hides, from within
       the wretch's member two small feet emerged.   117
As the smoke began to envelop each one in
       a different color and to generate
       on the one the hair it stripped from the other's skin,   120
the one fell down and the other stood up straight.
       Neither turned his pitiless lamps aside, and so
       each watched the other's features modulate   123
to his own. The standing one made its muzzle go
       in toward its temples and made its cheeks express
       ears from the shifted matter's overflow.   126

ciò che non corse in dietro e si ritenne

di quel soverchio, fé naso a la faccia

e le labbra ingrossò quanto convenne.   129

Quel che giacëa, il muso innanzi caccia,

e li orecchi ritira per la testa

come face le corna la lumaccia;   132

e la lingua, ch'avëa unita e presta

prima a parlar, si fende, e la forcuta

ne l'altro si richiude; e 'l fummo resta.   135

L'anima ch'era fiera divenuta,

suffolando si fugge per la valle,

e l'altro dietro a lui parlando sputa.   138

Poscia li volse le novelle spalle,

e disse a l'altro: «I' vo' che Buoso corra,

com' ho fatt' io, carpon per questo calle».   141

Così vid' io la settima zavorra

mutare e trasmutare; e qui mi scusi

la novità se fior la penna abborra.   144

E avvegna che li occhi miei confusi

fossero alquanto e l'animo smagato,

non poter quei fuggirsi tanto chiusi,   147

ch'i' non scorgessi ben Puccio Sciancato;

ed era quel che sol, di tre compagni

che venner prima, non era mutato;   150

l'altr' era quel che tu, Gaville, piagni.

With what it still retained of that excess,
    in the middle of its face a man's nose grew
    and its lips plumped to a human fleshiness.   129
Meanwhile, the one who had fallen started to
    push out a snout and pull his ears inside,
    as a snail when it retracts its horns will do.   132
His tongue, which had been fit for speech and wide,
    now forked. The other's tongue, which had been split,
    became one. And I saw the smoke subside.   135
The new-formed beast went scampering through the pit,
    emitting hissing noises as it fled.
    The other one was spitting after it.   138
He turned his new shoulders toward the third and said:
    "Now I'll let Buoso have the degradation
    of running on six legs the way I did."   141
Thus the mutation and the transmutation
    in the seventh dump. Put it down to my surprise
    at the strangeness, if I err in my narration.   144
My mind had been bewildered and my eyes
    had been confused, but no matter how furtively
    they fled away, I could clearly recognize   147
Puccio Sciancato. Of the original three
    he was the only one to undergo
    no transformation. The other one was he   150
on whose account, Gaville, your tears still flow.

Notes

lines 10–12   The "seed" of Pistoia was presumed to be the remains of the defeated
    army of Catiline; see note to Canto XV, lines 61–78, for similar pre-
    sumptions regarding the origins of Florence.

lines 13–15   The reference is to Capaneus (see Canto XIV, lines 43–72).

line 19   The Maremma (see note to Canto XIII, line 8) was, in addition to its
    other harsh features, swampy and snake-infested.

line 25 Cacus, son of Vulcan and Medusa, was a fire-breathing monster who lived in a cave beneath Mount Avetine and preyed upon travelers. In Book VIII of the *Aeneid*, Virgil describes him as "half-human"; Dante has adapted these details to make him a centaur with a fire-breathing dragon on his back. Cacus stole some of the cattle that Hercules had taken from Geryon (see note to Canto XVII, line 1), for which he was slain by Hercules—strangled, according to Virgil; clubbed, according to Ovid. Other centaurs guard the violent who are punished in the river of blood (Canto XII), but Cacus, even though he has something of a guard's function here, is punished with the thieves.

line 43 Cianfa (died c. 1289) appears to have been a member of the Donati family of Florence. He is the serpent who comes running up at line 50.

line 68 Agnello was a member of the Brunelleschi family, Ghibellines of Florence. There is little historically reliable information about him.

lines 94–96 In Book IX of *Pharsalia*, Lucan tells of Sabellus, a soldier in Cato's army who was bitten by a snake in the Libyan desert and became a festering mass, and of Nasidius, another of Cato's soldiers, also bitten by a serpent, whose body became so swollen that it burst.

lines 97–99 Cadmus, son of King Agenor of Phoenicia, and his wife, Harmonia, were turned into serpents for killing a dragon sacred to Mars (*Metamorphoses*, Book IV), and the nymph Arethusa was transformed to a fountain to escape the river god Alpheus, who nonetheless mingled his waters with hers (Book V).

line 140 Variously identified, Buoso is believed to have been Buoso di Forese Donati (died c. 1285; not the Buoso Donati mentioned in Canto XXX, line 43).

line 148 Puccio Galigai, called Sciancato ("lame"), was a member of a Ghibelline family and appears to have had the reputation of a gentleman thief.

line 151 Francesco de' Cavalcanti, called Guercio ("squinting" or "cross-eyed"), was murdered by people from Gaville, a town near Florence. The Cavalcanti avenged his death by killing many of Gaville's inhabitants. There is no solid evidence that he was a thief.

Canto XXVI

Godi, Fiorenza, poi che se' sì grande
    che per mare e per terra batti l'ali,
    e per lo 'nferno tuo nome si spande! 3

Tra li ladron trovai cinque cotali
    tuoi cittadini onde mi ven vergogna,
    e tu in grande orranza non ne sali. 6

Ma se presso al mattin del ver si sogna,
    tu sentirai, di qua da picciol tempo,
    di quel che Prato, non ch'altri, t'agogna. 9

E se già fosse, non saria per tempo.
    Così foss' ei, da che pur esser dee!
    ché più mi graverà, com' più m'attempo. 12

Noi ci partimmo, e su per le scalee
    che n'avea fatto iborni a scender pria,
    rimontò 'l duca mio e trasse mee; 15

e proseguendo la solinga via,
    tra le schegge e tra ' rocchi de lo scoglio
    lo piè sanza la man non si spedia. 18

Allor mi dolsi, e ora mi ridoglio
    quando drizzo la mente a ciò ch'io vidi,
    e più lo 'ngegno affreno ch'i' non soglio, 21

perché non corra che virtù nol guidi;
    sì che, se stella bona o miglior cosa
    m'ha dato 'l ben, ch'io stessi nol m'invidi. 24

Quante 'l villan ch'al poggio si riposa,
    nel tempo che colui che 'l mondo schiara
    la faccia sua a noi tien meno ascosa, 27

Canto XXVI

Florence, rejoice at how great you have grown,
     beating your wings over land and sea, with fame
     that has spread through hell! I found five of your own   3
among the thieves, and such to inflict a shame
     that is clinging to me still, and I say to you
     that the fact adds no great honor to your name.   6
But if the things we dream toward dawn are true,
     then you will feel, in a time that is soon to come,
     what Prato craves for you, as others do.   9
It were not too soon had it already come.
     I could wish it had, since it must surely be,
     and will grieve me more the older I become.   12
We left that place, going up where previously
     we had descended on the crags we found.
     My leader mounted first, then lifted me.   15
We made our solitary way around
     the rocks and the projections as we went.
     Without the hand, the foot could gain no ground.   18
I lamented then, and once more I lament
     over what I saw, and here I have denied
     my genius its full freedom, to prevent   21
its wandering where virtue does not guide.
     If my good star or an even higher grace
     has given this gift, it should not be misapplied.   24
In the season when the light-giver turns his face
     the least from us, at the hour when flies yield
     to mosquitoes that have come to take their place,   27

come la mosca cede a la zanzara,
    vede lucciole giù per la vallea,
    forse colà dov' e' vendemmia e ara: 30
di tante fiamme tutta risplendea
    l'ottava bolgia, sì com' io m'accorsi
    tosto che fui là 've 'l fondo parea.   33
E qual colui che si vengiò con li orsi
    vide 'l carro d'Elia al dipartire,
    quando i cavalli al cielo erti levorsi,   36
che nol potea sì con li occhi seguire,
    ch'el vedesse altro che la fiamma sola,
    sì come nuvoletta, in sù salire: 39
tal si move ciascuna per la gola
    del fosso, ché nessuna mostra 'l furto,
    e ogne fiamma un peccatore invola.   42
Io stava sovra 'l ponte a veder surto,
    sì che s'io non avessi un ronchion preso,
    caduto sarei giù sanz' esser urto.   45
E 'l duca che mi vide tanto atteso,
    disse: «Dentro dai fuochi son li spirti;
    catun si fascia di quel ch'elli è inceso».   48
«Maestro mio», rispuos' io, «per udirti
    son io più certo; ma già m'era avviso
    che così fosse, e già voleva dirti: 51
chi è 'n quel foco che vien sì diviso
    di sopra, che par surger de la pira
    dov' Eteòcle col fratel fu miso?».   54
Rispuose a me: «Là dentro si martira
    Ulisse e Dïomede, e così insieme
    a la vendetta vanno come a l'ira;   57
e dentro da la lor fiamma si geme
    l'agguato del caval che fé la porta
    onde uscì de' Romani il gentil seme.   60

as many as are the fireflies revealed
>to the peasant as he rests upon the height,
>>looking down where he harvests grapes and tills the field,   30
with so many flames the eighth pouch was alight,
>as I could see upon arriving where
>>the bottom of the ditch came into sight.   33
As the one who was avenged by bears was there
>to see the chariot of Elijah rise
>>when the horses strode right up into the air,   36
but found he could not follow it with his eyes,
>seeing nothing but the fire in its glide
>>toward heaven like a cloudlet through the skies,   39
so it was here, where all the fires hide
>their theft, as through the gullet of the ditch
>>each steals away with a sinner hidden inside.   42
In my zeal to see, I had risen up on the bridge,
>and had I not grasped a rock, I have no doubt
>>that without a push I'd have fallen from the ledge.   45
My leader said, when he saw me leaning out:
>"Inside the fire the spirits are confined.
>>With a burning sheet each wraps himself about."   48
"Master, your words confirm what I was inclined
>to assume was so already," I replied,
>>"and already I had this question in my mind: 51
Who is in that flame whose top parts so divide
>that it seems to surge up from the funeral pyre
>>where Eteocles was laid at his brother's side?"   54
He answered: "Joined in torment in that fire
>Ulysses and Diomed endure the force
>>of vengeance, as they once were joined in ire.   57
There they bemoan the ambush of the horse
>which made the gate that the noble seed of Rome
>>passed through as it set forth upon its course,   60

Piangevisi entro l'arte per che, morta,
    Deïdamìa ancor si duol d'Achille,
    e del Palladio pena vi si porta».   63

«S'ei posson dentro da quelle faville
    parlar», diss' io, «maestro, assai ten priego
    e ripriego, che 'l priego vaglia mille,   66

che non mi facci de l'attender niego
    fin che la fiamma cornuta qua vegna;
    vedi che del disio ver' lei mi piego!».   69

Ed elli a me: «La tua preghiera è degna
    di molta loda, e io però l'accetto;
    ma fa che la tua lingua si sostegna.   72

Lascia parlare a me, ch'i' ho concetto
    ciò che tu vuoi; ch'ei sarebbero schivi,
    perch' e' fuor greci, forse del tuo detto».   75

Poi che la fiamma fu venuta quivi
    dove parve al mio duca tempo e loco,
    in questa forma lui parlare audivi: 78

«O voi che siete due dentro ad un foco,
    s'io meritai di voi mentre ch'io vissi,
    s'io meritai di voi assai o poco   81

quando nel mondo li alti versi scrissi,
    non vi movete; ma l'un di voi dica
    dove, per lui, perduto a morir gissi».   84

Lo maggior corno de la fiamma antica
    cominciò a crollarsi mormorando,
    pur come quella cui vento affatica;   87

indi la cima qua e là menando,
    come fosse la lingua che parlasse,
    gittò voce di fuori e disse: «Quando   90

mi diparti' da Circe, che sottrasse
    me più d'un anno là presso a Gaeta,
    prima che sì Enëa la nomasse,   93

and lament the deceit that took Achilles from
    Deidamía, who mourns him still, though dead.
    And there they pay for the Palladium."   63
"If they can speak within those sparks," I said,
    "Master, I pray you fervently, and I pray
    that you hear a thousand prayers in this one's stead,   66
that you not deny me my desire to stay
    till that two-pronged flame approaches. You can see
    how eagerly I am leaning out that way."   69
"Your prayer deserves much praise," he said to me,
    "and I accede to it. But you should restrain
    your tongue just now and listen quietly.   72
Leave speech to me. There is no need to explain
    what you wish to know. But since those two were Greek,
    any words from you might be greeted with disdain."   75
The fire came nearer, leaving him to seek
    the appropriate place and moment to pursue
    his purpose. Then I heard my leader speak: 78
"O you who are in one flame and yet are two,
    if I earned merit with you while I drew breath,
    if I earned merit great or small with you   81
when I wrote my lofty verses, then herewith
    remain, and let the one of you tell where
    he went, when he was lost, to find his death."   84
Humming, the greater of the horns that share
    that ancient fire fluttered like a flame
    struggling against a current in the air,   87
and its tip began to wriggle with the same
    undulations as a tongue engaged in speech,
    and a voice was flung from it, and these words came: 90
"When I was freed at last from Circe's reach,
    who had detained me for a year or more
    near Gaeta, as Aeneas would name that beach,   93

né dolcezza di figlio, né la pieta
    del vecchio padre, né 'l debito amore
    lo qual dovea Penelopè far lieta,   96
vincer potero dentro a me l'ardore
    ch'i' ebbi a divenir del mondo esperto
    e de li vizi umani e del valore;   99
ma misi me per l'alto mare aperto
    sol con un legno e con quella compagna
    picciola da la qual non fui diserto.   102
L'un lito e l'altro vidi infin la Spagna,
    fin nel Morrocco, e l'isola d'i Sardi,
    e l'altre che quel mare intorno bagna.   105
Io e ' compagni eravam vecchi e tardi
    quando venimmo a quella foce stretta
    dov' Ercule segnò li suoi riguardi   108
acciò che l'uom più oltre non si metta;
    da la man destra mi lasciai Sibilia,
    da l'altra già m'avea lasciata Setta.   111
"O frati", dissi "che per cento milia
    perigli siete giunti a l'occidente,
    a questa tanto picciola vigilia   114
d'i nostri sensi ch'è del rimanente
    non vogliate negar l'esperïenza,
    di retro al sol, del mondo sanza gente.   117
Considerate la vostra semenza:
    fatti non foste a viver come bruti,
    ma per seguir virtute e canoscenza".   120
Li miei compagni fec' io sì aguti,
    con questa orazion picciola, al cammino,
    che a pena poscia li avrei ritenuti;   123
e volta nostra poppa nel mattino,
    de' remi facemmo ali al folle volo,
    sempre acquistando dal lato mancino.   126

neither reverence for an aged father, nor
      a son's sweetness, nor the love I should profess
      to Penelope, which she would be happy for,   96
could overcome my ardor to possess
      experience of the world and humanity
      in all its worth and all its wickedness.   99
But I set forth upon the open sea
      with just one vessel from my fleet's remains
      and those few men who had not deserted me.   102
We sailed both shores, Morocco's coast and Spain's.
      As far as to Sardinia did we go,
      and the other islands which that sea contains.   105
My mariners and I were old and slow
      when at last we reached that narrow channel lined
      by Hercules with his marks so men would know   108
that they must not go beyond the bounds assigned.
      On the starboard side Seville now disappeared,
      on the other Ceuta already lay behind.   111
'Through a hundred thousand dangers we have steered,
      my brothers,' I said, 'to reach these western gates.
      Now has the brief vigil of our senses neared   114
its close, so let us not forswear our fates
      but embrace experience, tracing the sun's route
      to the uninhabited region that awaits.   117
Consider your origins. Living like a brute
      is not the destiny of men like you,
      but knowledge and virtue ever our pursuit.'   120
With these few words of mine, my shipmates grew
      so eager to go on that even I
      could not have stopped them had I wanted to.   123
Setting our stern against the morning sky,
      we turned our oars to wings in our mad flight,
      gaining always on the left as days flew by.   126

Tutte le stelle già de l'altro polo
     vedea la notte, e 'l nostro tanto basso,
     che non surgëa fuor del marin suolo.   129
Cinque volte racceso e tante casso
     lo lume era di sotto da la luna,
     poi che 'ntrati eravam ne l'alto passo,   132
quando n'apparve una montagna, bruna
     per la distanza, e parvemi alta tanto
     quanto veduta non avëa alcuna.   135
Noi ci allegrammo, e tosto tornò in pianto;
     ché de la nova terra un turbo nacque
     e percosse del legno il primo canto.   138
Tre volte il fé girar con tutte l'acque;
     a la quarta levar la poppa in suso
     e la prora ire in giù, com' altrui piacque,   141
infin che 'l mar fu sovra noi richiuso».

The other pole and all its stars showed night
    their faces now, and so near was our own
    to the ocean's floor that it barely was in sight.   129
Five times already had the light that shone
    below the moon been lit and then quenched once more
    since we had sailed into the vast unknown,   132
when in the distance on the course we bore
    a huge dark mountain loomed, that seemed to be
    taller than any I had seen before.   135
Our joy was quickly turned to misery
    as a whirlwind rose from the land where we were bound
    and rammed the prow of our vessel violently.   138
With the churning sea it spun the ship around
    three times, and on the fourth time the stern rose,
    as it pleased another, and the prow was downed,   141
and over us we saw the waters close."

Notes

line 4	The five thieves were all members of upper-class families.
line 7	There was a common belief that morning dreams are prophetic in nature.
line 9	The reference may be either to Cardinal Niccolò da Prato, who excommunicated the city's inhabitants in 1304 after failing to reconcile its rival factions, or to the town of Prato, eleven miles northwest of the city, which expelled its Black Guelphs in 1309.
lines 19–24	See note to Canto IV, lines 100–102.
lines 34–39	When the prophet Elisha cursed forty-two young boys who had mocked his baldness, two bears came from the forest and tore them to pieces (2 Kings 2.23–24). Elisha also beheld the prophet Elijah borne to heaven in a whirlwind by fiery horses and a fiery chariot (2 Kings 2.7–14).
line 54	In the siege of Thebes (see note to Canto XIV, line 46), the warring sons of Oedipus, Eteocles and Polynices, killed one another. The dividing of the flame of their mutual pyre communicated their undying hatred.

lines 56–63   The condemnation of the Greek heroes Ulysses (Odysseus) and Diomedes among the fraudulent is based on three incidents, the first and third of which are drawn from Book II of the *Aeneid*, the second from the unfinished *Achilleid* of Statius: (1) They devised the Trojan horse, whose role in the fall of Troy made it the portal through which the surviving Trojans passed to become the founders of Rome. (2) They went to Scyros to lure the beardless Achilles out of hiding among the women—where his mother, the goddess Thetis, had placed him—because he would be needed for success against the Trojans; the news of his death in Troy would cause Deidamia, the mother of his son, to die of grief. (3) They sneaked into Troy by night to steal the statue of Pallas Athena, upon which the city's safety was believed to depend.

lines 91–142   Ulysses' speech was the primary inspiration for Tennyson's great monologue "Ulysses." It is fascinating to observe how the same material is made to yield opposite conclusions: where Dante presents Ulysses' final journey as a failure of familial responsibilities and a hubristic flouting of divinely imposed limitations, Tennyson celebrates the spirit of quest and daring without which there would be no human progress.

lines 91–93   Dante would have known the story of Ulysses' entanglement with the enchantress Circe from Ovid's *Metamorphoses*, Book XIV. Gaeta, a town on the southeastern coast of Italy, was named by Aeneas for his nurse, Caieta, who died there (*Aeneid*, Book VII).

lines 107–11   The narrow channel is the Strait of Gibraltar. The Pillars of Hercules are Calpe in Spain and Abyla on the African promontory. In legend, they were originally one mountain, which was torn apart by Hercules, marking the point beyond which no one may sail and survive. Seville here connotes southern Spain, near Gibraltar. Ceuta is on the north coast of Morocco opposite Gibraltar.

line 126   They are sailing southwest, toward the point on the globe that is exactly opposite Jerusalem, where Dante locates Mount Purgatory (line 134).

lines 127–29   The ship has now crossed the equator into the Southern Hemisphere.

Canto XXVII

Già era dritta in sù la fiamma e queta
    per non dir più, e già da noi sen gia
    con la licenza del dolce poeta,   3
quand' un'altra, che dietro a lei venìa,
    ne fece volger li occhi a la sua cima
    per un confuso suon che fuor n'uscia.   6
Come 'l bue cicilian che mugghiò prima
    col pianto di colui, e ciò fu dritto,
    che l'avea temperato con sua lima,   9
mugghiava con la voce de l'afflitto,
    sì che, con tutto che fosse di rame,
    pur el pareva dal dolor trafitto;   12
così, per non aver via né forame
    dal principio nel foco, in suo linguaggio
    si convertïan le parole grame.   15
Ma poscia ch'ebber colto lor vïaggio
    su per la punta, dandole quel guizzo
    che dato avea la lingua in lor passaggio,   18
udimmo dire: «O tu a cu' io drizzo
    la voce e che parlavi mo lombardo,
    dicendo "Istra ten va, più non t'adizzo", 21
perch' io sia giunto forse alquanto tardo,
    non t'incresca restare a parlar meco;
    vedi che non incresce a me, e ardo!   24
Se tu pur mo in questo mondo cieco
    caduto se' di quella dolce terra
    latina ond' io mia colpa tutta reco,   27

CANTO XXVII

Its speaking done, the flame stood straight and still,
    and then it went away when allowed to take
    its leave of us through the gentle poet's will.   3
Another one came following in its wake.
    We looked to its tip because of the sputtering
    and garbled noises that we heard it make.   6
And as the Sicilian bull (whose bellowing
    began with the cries—and this was justified—
    of the artisan whose file had shaped the thing),   9
although it was fashioned out of brass, still cried
    as if transfixed with pain, with a voice that came
    from the victim who was sealed in its inside,   12
with these miserable words it was much the same.
    When at first they found no path or outlet, they
    were translated to the language of the flame.   15
But when at last the sounds had pushed their way
    to the tip of the fire and then forced it through
    the movements the tongue had made, we heard it say: 18
"O you at whom I aim my voice, and who
    just now spoke Lombard, for I could discern
    the words 'Now go, I ask no more of you,'   21
perhaps I have come late, but before you turn
    may it not displease you to converse with me.
    It does not displease me, even though I burn!   24
If you have just now left sweet Italy,
    out of which I bring my guilt, and are dropped below
    to this blind world, tell me what there is to see   27

dimmi se Romagnuoli han pace o guerra;
    ch'io fui d'i monti là intra Orbino
    e 'l giogo di che Tever si diserra».   30

Io era in giuso ancora attento e chino,
    quando il mio duca mi tentò di costa,
    dicendo: «Parla tu; questi è latino».   33

E io, ch'avea già pronta la risposta,
    sanza indugio a parlare incominciai:
    «O anima che se' là giù nascosta,   36

Romagna tua non è, e non fu mai,
    sanza guerra ne' cuor de' suoi tiranni;
    ma 'n palese nessuna or vi lasciai.   39

Ravenna sta come stata è molt' anni:
    l'aguglia da Polenta la si cova,
    sì che Cervia ricuopre co' suoi vanni.   42

La terra che fé già la lunga prova
    e di Franceschi sanguinoso mucchio,
    sotto le branche verdi si ritrova.   45

E 'l mastin vecchio e 'l nuovo da Verrucchio,
    che fecer di Montagna il mal governo,
    là dove soglion fan d'i denti succhio.   48

Le città di Lamone e di Santerno
    conduce il lïoncel dal nido bianco,
    che muta parte da la state al verno.   51

E quella cu' il Savio bagna il fianco,
    così com' ella sie' tra 'l piano e 'l monte,
    tra tirannia si vive e stato franco.   54

Ora chi se', ti priego che ne conte;
    non esser duro più ch'altri sia stato,
    se 'l nome tuo nel mondo tegna fronte».   57

Poscia che 'l foco alquanto ebbe rugghiato
    al modo suo, l'aguta punta mosse
    di qua, di là, e poi diè cotal fiato: 60

in Romagna: peace or war? I wish to know
  for I come from the mountains between Urbino and
  the chain in which the Tiber starts its flow." 30
And then my leader, when he saw me stand
  intently forward, touched me on the side
  and said: "You speak to him. He is of your land." 33
I did not delay, but readily replied
  with an answer there was no need to prepare.
  "O spirit down below whom the fires hide, 36
today in your Romagna war is where
  it has always been, in her tyrants' hearts," I said,
  "but when I left, there was no fighting there. 39
Polenta's eagle sits brooding overhead
  at Ravenna, where things are still as they have been,
  and as far as Cervia his wings are spread. 42
The city that piled up Frenchmen's corpses when
  it resisted the long siege it suffered through
  finds itself beneath the green paws once again. 45
The mastiffs of Verrucchio, old and new,
  who sank their teeth into Montagna's throat,
  still ply those fangs as they are wont to do. 48
The white-laired lionet has the towns on both
  the Lamone and the Santerno beneath his sway.
  As summer turns to winter, he turns his coat. 51
And the city on the Savio lies today
  between tyranny and freedom, as it lies
  between the plain and mountain. Now I pray 54
to know who you are. Be as free in your replies
  as another has been with you, so may your name
  remain forever vivid in men's eyes." 57
After the fire had bellowed in the same
  way as before, its pointed tip went through
  its movements once again, and these words came: 60

«S'i' credesse che mia risposta fosse
    a persona che mai tornasse al mondo,
    questa fiamma staria sanza più scosse;   63
ma però che già mai di questo fondo
    non tornò vivo alcun, s'i' odo il vero,
    sanza tema d'infamia ti rispondo.   66
Io fui uom d'arme, e poi fui cordigliero,
    credendomi, sì cinto, fare ammenda;
    e certo il creder mio venìa intero,   69
se non fosse il gran prete, a cui mal prenda!,
    che mi rimise ne le prime colpe;
    e come e *quare*, voglio che m'intenda.   72
Mentre ch'io forma fui d'ossa e di polpe
    che la madre mi diè, l'opere mie
    non furon leonine, ma di volpe.   75
Li accorgimenti e le coperte vie
    io seppi tutte, e sì menai lor arte,
    ch'al fine de la terra il suono uscie.   78
Quando mi vidi giunto in quella parte
    di mia etade ove ciascun dovrebbe
    calar le vele e raccoglier le sarte,   81
ciò che pria mi piacëa, allor m'increbbe,
    e pentuto e confesso mi rendei;
    ahi miser lasso! e giovato sarebbe.   84
Lo principe d'i novi Farisei,
    avendo guerra presso a Laterano,
    e non con Saracin né con Giudei,   87
ché ciascun suo nimico era cristiano,
    e nessun era stato a vincer Acri
    né mercatante in terra di Soldano,   90
né sommo officio né ordini sacri
    guardò in sé, né in me quel capestro
    che solea fare i suoi cinti più macri.   93

"If I thought my answer were to someone who
    might see the world again, then there would be
    no more stirrings of this flame. Since it is true   63
that no one leaves these depths of misery
    alive, from all that I have heard reported,
    I answer you without fear of infamy.   66
I was a man of arms, and then a corded
    friar, to make amends, and all seemed well
    and would have been, but that my hopes were thwarted   69
by the high priest—may his spirit rot in hell—
    who pulled me back to those first sins I had known,
    the how and the *why* of which I wish to tell.   72
While I still had the form of flesh and bone
    that my mother gave to me, it was the style
    of the fox, not the lion, that I made my own.   75
All covert ways and every kind of wile
    I mastered, and did such fine things in that art
    that reports went round the earth of my great guile.   78
When I saw myself arriving at that part
    of the life of every man when it is best
    to strike the sails and coil the ropes, my heart   81
was pained by what had pleased it. I confessed,
    repented, and turned friar, and all of these,
    alas, would have secured my interest.   84
Ah, but the prince of the new Pharisees
    was waging war hard by the Lateran.
    Neither Jews nor Saracens were his enemies.   87
His foes were Christians, every single one,
    and none had gone to conquer Acre or
    been a merchant where the sultan's will is done.   90
He heeded neither the great keys that he bore
    nor his holy orders, nor my friar's cord,
    which had made its wearers thin in times before.   93

Ma come Costantin chiese Silvestro
    d'entro Siratti a guerir de la lebbre,
    così mi chiese questi per maestro   96
a guerir de la sua superba febbre;
    domandommi consiglio, e io tacetti
    perché le sue parole parver ebbre.   99
E' poi ridisse: "Tuo cuor non sospetti;
    finor t'assolvo, e tu m'insegna fare
    sì come Penestrino in terra getti.   102
Lo ciel poss' io serrare e diserrare,
    come tu sai; però son due le chiavi
    che 'l mio antecessor non ebbe care".   105
Allor mi pinser li argomenti gravi
    là 've 'l tacer mi fu avviso 'l peggio,
    e dissi: "Padre, da che tu mi lavi   108
di quel peccato ov' io mo cader deggio,
    lunga promessa con l'attender corto
    ti farà trïunfar ne l'alto seggio".   111
Francesco venne poi, com' io fu' morto,
    per me; ma un d'i neri cherubini
    li disse: "Non portar; non mi far torto.   114
Venir se ne dee giù tra ' miei meschini
    perché diede 'l consiglio frodolente,
    dal quale in qua stato li sono a' crini;   117
ch'assolver non si può chi non si pente,
    né pentere e volere insieme puossi
    per la contradizion che nol consente".   120
Oh me dolente! come mi riscossi
    quando mi prese dicendomi: "Forse
    tu non pensavi ch'io löico fossi!".   123
A Minòs mi portò; e quelli attorse
    otto volte la coda al dosso duro;
    e poi che per gran rabbia la si morse,   126

As Constantine sent to Soracte and implored
    Sylvester to cure his leprosy, so I
    had been sent for to be doctor to this lord,   96

for the fever of his pride was burning high.
    He solicited advice from his physician,
    but his words seemed drunken, so I did not reply.   99

Then he said: 'Your heart need harbor no suspicion.
    I absolve you on the spot, so you must state
    how I may cause Penestrino's demolition.   102

For I can lock and unlock heaven's gate,
    as you know, with these two keys that I display,
    which my predecessor failed to venerate.'   105

These weighty reasons convinced me that to stay
    silent would be the worst response of all,
    so I said: 'Father, since you wash away   108

the sin in which I am about to fall,
    you will hold your throne in triumph if you provide
    long promise, but make the keeping short and small.'   111

Saint Francis came to get me when I died,
    but one of the black cherubim came along,
    saying: 'Leave him! He's mine! Justice will be denied   114

if he does not join my miserable throng
    because of the fraudulent counsel he presented.
    I've been at his hair since the instant of that wrong,   117

for no one can be absolved who has not repented,
    and repent what he still wills, no one can do.
    The inherent contradiction must prevent it.'   120

O wretched me! how I shivered when he threw
    his hands upon me, saying: 'Did you fail
    to realize that I know logic too?'   123

He dragged me down to Minos, who wrapped his tail
    eight times round his hard back, and in an excess
    of rage he bit it and began to rail: 126

disse: "Questi è d'i rei del foco furo";

    per ch'io là dove vedi son perduto,

    e sì vestito, andando, mi rancuro».   129

Quand' elli ebbe 'l suo dir così compiuto,

    la fiamma dolorando si partio,

    torcendo e dibattendo 'l corno aguto.   132

Noi passamm' oltre, e io e 'l duca mio,

    su per lo scoglio infino in su l'altr' arco

    che cuopre 'l fosso in che si paga il fio   135

a quei che scommettendo acquistan carco.

'This sinner goes to the thieving flames!' And thus
    have I come to perdition, robed in the array
    you see before you, going in bitterness."   129
When he had finished what he had to say,
    with its pointed tip still twisting to and fro
    the grieving fire slowly went away.   132
My guide and I walked on from there, to go
    as far as the bridge the next pouch stretches under.
    The souls sent here to pay the debt they owe   135
take their burden on by putting things asunder.

Notes

line 7   Several classical sources tell of Phalaris, tyrant of Agrigentum in the sixth century B.C.E., who had the Athenian Perillus fashion a bronze bull in which victims would be roasted alive, with their muffled cries passing through pipes that made them sound like the bellowing of a bull. Phalaris tested the device with Perillus himself as subject.

lines 28–30   Romagna is a district in northeastern Italy stretching from the Po south to the eastern Apennines, the range that includes Mount Coronaro, where the Tiber originates. The speaker, who is never identified by name, is Guido da Montefeltro (c. 1220–1298), perhaps the greatest of the Ghibelline commanders, who kept Romagna under Ghibelline rule when most of Italy, including the papacy, was Guelph-dominated. The bane of several popes, he was excommunicated in 1289, but was later reconciled to the Church and joined the Franciscan order (the "corded friars" of lines 67–68) in 1296.

lines 40–42   Guido da Polenta, whose coat of arms displayed an eagle, had ruled Ravenna since 1275. Cervia is a town on the Adriatic, southeast of Ravenna. Guido was the father of Francesca da Rimini (see note to Canto V, line 97) and the grandfather of Guido Novello, who was Dante's host in Ravenna in 1321.

lines 43–45   Forlì, the central city of Romagna, held off a yearlong siege by a Guelph army, of French and Italian troops, sent by Pope Martin IV. The successful defense of the city was directed by Guido da Montefeltro, whom Dante does not yet realize he is addressing. "Green paws" alludes to the escutcheon of the Ordelaffi family, who despotically ruled Forlì at the end of the thirteenth century.

lines 46–48   In 1295, when the Ghibellines of Rimini were defeated by Malatesta da Verrucchio, the Ghibelline leader, Montagna de' Parcitati, was captured and then killed by Malatesta's son Malatestino. Malatesta ruled until his death in 1312, at the age of 100, when he was succeeded by Malatestino, who was succeeded in 1317 by his brother Pandolfo. Malatesta's other sons were Gianciotto, the husband of Francesca da Rimini, and Paolo, her lover.

lines 49–51   Faenza is on the Lamone River, Imola on the Santerno. In 1300, they were under the control of Maghinardo de' Pagani da Susinana, here called the lionet because of his coat of arms. He was known for his political inconsistency.

lines 52–54   Cesena was ruled by the relatively benign Galasso da Montefeltro, Guido's cousin.

lines 61–66   These lines, untranslated and unidentified, were used by T. S. Eliot as the epigraph to "The Love Song of J. Alfred Prufrock."

line 70   The corrupt pope alluded to here is Boniface VIII.

lines 85–90   There was endless strife, erupting into armed conflict in 1297, between Boniface and the powerful Colonna family, whose residences were not far from his own, the Lateran Palace. The Colonna refused to accept the abdication of Celestine V (see note to Canto III, lines 59–60) and thus denied the legitimacy of Boniface's papacy. Here Boniface is attacked for launching a crusade against his fellow Christians, while doing nothing to oppose the Saracens who had in 1291 conquered Acre, the last Christian stronghold in the Holy Land, or to punish those who defied the order, imposed by Pope Nicholas IV after the fall of Acre, forbidding all commerce with Muslim lands.

line 93   The cord worn by the Franciscan friars made its wearers thin through their adherence to the vows of poverty and abstinence; "in times before" is an attack on the corruption of the contemporary Church.

lines 94–95   It was widely believed during the Middle Ages that Constantine, afflicted with leprosy for his persecution of Christians, sent for Pope Sylvester I, who was hiding in a cave on Mount Soracte; Constantine was cured instantly upon being baptized by Sylvester and, according to the fraudulent Donation of Constantine, gave the Church temporal power in the western part of the empire (see note to Canto XIX, lines 115–17).

line 102   Palestrina (Praeneste in ancient times) is a city some twenty miles east of Rome, where the Colonna resisted Boniface's siege until September 1298, when they surrendered under promise of amnesty. Supposedly, although their lives were spared, the Colonna were ruined and the city was destroyed.

lines 110–11   It is not clear whether Guido actually gave Boniface such advice, since later chroniclers may have had Dante as their only source for the story.

line 112   According to Singleton, "The transition is the more effective for being so abrupt. Guido in fact did die in September 1298, the month in which Boniface tricked the Colonna."

Canto XXVIII

Chi poria mai pur con parole sciolte
    dicer del sangue e de le piaghe a pieno
    ch'i' ora vidi, per narrar più volte?   3
Ogne lingua per certo verria meno
    per lo nostro sermone e per la mente
    c'hanno a tanto comprender poco seno.   6
S'el s'aunasse ancor tutta la gente
    che già, in su la fortunata terra
    di Puglia, fu del suo sangue dolente   9
per li Troiani e per la lunga guerra
    che de l'anella fé sì alte spoglie,
    come Livïo scrive, che non erra,   12
con quella che sentio di colpi doglie
    per contastare a Ruberto Guiscardo;
    e l'altra il cui ossame ancor s'accoglie   15
a Ceperan, là dove fu bugiardo
    ciascun Pugliese, e là da Tagliacozzo,
    dove sanz' arme vinse il vecchio Alardo;   18
e qual forato suo membro e qual mozzo
    mostrasse, d'aequar sarebbe nulla
    il modo de la nona bolgia sozzo.   21
Già veggia, per mezzul perdere o lulla,
    com' io vidi un, così non si pertugia,
    rotto dal mento infin dove si trulla.   24
Tra le gambe pendevan le minugia;
    la corata pareva e 'l tristo sacco
    che merda fa di quel che si trangugia.   27

Canto XXVIII

Even in words not bounded by rhyme's law,
    through many repetitions of the tale,
    how could the blood and wounds that I now saw   3
be fully told? Every tongue would surely fail,
    because our powers of speech and memory
    are not meant to comprehend on such a scale.   6
If all of Apulia's battle dead could be
    assembled, those of that battered country who
    bewailed blood spilled by Trojan infantry,   9
and those in the long war who fell victim to
    the immense spoils of the rings (so does Livy say
    in his history, where what he tells is true),   12
and those who felt the heavy blows when they
    resisted Robert Guiscard's steady press,
    and those whose bones are still piled up today   15
at Ceprano, failed by Apulian faithlessness,
    and there near Tagliacozzo where the old
    Alardo won the victory weaponless,   18
and one showed his pierced limb and one made bold
    to display his stumps, it all would not begin
    to approach the loathsomeness of the ninth hold.   21
A cask, when its midboard or its cant has been
    removed, is not so open as one I saw
    whose body was split apart right from the chin   24
to the farthole. Down between his legs his raw
    entrails spilled out, with his vitals visible
    and the sorry sack where what goes through the maw   27

Mentre che tutto in lui veder m'attacco,
    guardommi e con le man s'aperse il petto,
    dicendo: «Or vedi com' io mi dilacco!   30
vedi come storpiato è Mäometto!
    Dinanzi a me sen va piangendo Alì,
    fesso nel volto dal mento al ciuffetto.   33
E tutti li altri che tu vedi qui,
    seminator di scandalo e di scisma
    fuor vivi, e però son fessi così.   36
Un diavolo è qua dietro che n'accisma
    sì crudelmente, al taglio de la spada
    rimettendo ciascun di questa risma,   39
quand' avem volta la dolente strada;
    però che le ferite son richiuse
    prima ch'altri dinanzi li rivada.   42
Ma tu chi se' che 'n su lo scoglio muse,
    forse per indugiar d'ire a la pena
    ch'è giudicata in su le tue accuse?».   45
«Né morte 'l giunse ancor, né colpa 'l mena»,
    rispuose 'l mio maestro, «a tormentarlo;
    ma per dar lui esperïenza piena,   48
a me, che morto son, convien menarlo
    per lo 'nferno qua giù di giro in giro;
    e quest' è ver così com' io ti parlo».   51
Più fuor di cento che, quando l'udiro,
    s'arrestaron nel fosso a riguardarmi
    per maraviglia, oblïando il martiro.   54
«Or dì a fra Dolcin dunque che s'armi,
    tu che forse vedra' il sole in breve,
    s'ello non vuol qui tosto seguitarmi,   57
sì di vivanda, che stretta di neve
    non rechi la vittoria al Noarese,
    ch'altrimenti acquistar non saria leve».   60

is turned to shit. I was looking at him, full
  of awe and wonder, when he saw me stare
  and spread his breast open, saying: "Watch me pull,   30
see mangled Mohammed tear himself! And there
  walking before me and weeping is Alì,
  with his face split from his chin right to his hair.   33
And since all of these other sinners that you see
  sowed scandal and schism in their lives, now they
  are ripped apart in reciprocity.   36
Back there a devil waits to hack and flay
  each one of us with the sharp edge of his blade,
  cleaving anew, each time we pass his way,   39
every member of this miserable parade,
  for by the time we have circled the whole pit
  we are healed of the cuts he has already made.   42
But who are you? Are you putting off for a bit,
  by musing upon the bridge, the punishments
  pronounced on you for the sins you must admit?"   45
"Death has not found him," my guide said. "No offense
  brings him here for torment, but in order to
  provide him with a full experience,   48
it is fitting that I, who am dead, conduct him through
  ring after ring of hell, and every word
  is as true as that I am speaking them to you."   51
More than a hundred in the ditch were stirred
  to gape at me, forgetting their agony
  as they stood amazed at what they had just heard.   54
"Tell Fra Dolcino, since you may shortly see
  the sun again, that if he still wants to live
  before joining me, he should fill his armory   57
with provisions, lest the grip of snow should give
  to the Novarese a victory that they
  might otherwise find difficult to achieve."   60

Poi che l'un piè per girsene sospese,
  Mäometto mi disse esta parola;
  indi a partirsi in terra lo distese.   63
Un altro, che forata avea la gola
  e tronco 'l naso infin sotto le ciglia,
  e non avea mai ch'una orecchia sola,   66
ristato a riguardar per maraviglia
  con li altri, innanzi a li altri aprì la canna,
  ch'era di fuor d'ogne parte vermiglia,   69
e disse: «O tu cui colpa non condanna
  e cu' io vidi su in terra latina,
  se troppa simiglianza non m'inganna,   72
rimembriti di Pier da Medicina,
  se mai torni a veder lo dolce piano
  che da Vercelli a Marcabò dichina.   75
E fa saper a' due miglior da Fano,
  a messer Guido e anco ad Angiolello,
  che, se l'antiveder qui non è vano,   78
gittati saran fuor di lor vasello
  e mazzerati presso a la Cattolica
  per tradimento d'un tiranno fello.   81
Tra l'isola di Cipri e di Maiolica
  non vide mai sì gran fallo Nettuno,
  non da pirate, non da gente argolica.   84
Quel traditor che vede pur con l'uno,
  e tien la terra che tale qui meco
  vorrebbe di vedere esser digiuno,   87
farà venirli a parlamento seco;
  poi farà sì, ch'al vento di Focara
  non sarà lor mestier voto né preco».   90
E io a lui: «Dimostrami e dichiara,
  se vuo' ch'i' porti sù di te novella,
  chi è colui da la veduta amara».   93

Before Mohammed had turned to me to say
    these words, he had raised his foot into the air,
    and now he put it down and went away.   63
A soul with his throat pierced through was standing there.
    His nose had been cut off to the brows, his head
    had only one ear left. He had stopped to stare,   66
amazed with the rest at what my guide had said.
    Before the others, he stuck his fingers in
    and pulled apart his throat, which was all red,   69
and spoke: "O you who are not condemned by sin,
    and whom I sometimes saw in Italy
    unless there is someone who could be your twin,   72
you know the sweet plain sloping tenderly
    from Vercelli to Marcabò. If you see it again,
    keep Pier da Medicina in memory.   75
Tell Guido and Angiolello, Fano's best men,
    that if our foresight here is in accord
    with what will be, the time is coming when   78
they'll be bound with weights and then thrown overboard
    near La Cattolica, sunk without a trace
    through the machinations of an evil lord.   81
Neptune has never seen a crime so base
    from Cyprus to the isles that lie near Spain,
    neither by pirates nor the Argive race.   84
That one-eyed traitor, who holds as his domain
    the city from whose sight one at my side
    could wish he had been able to abstain,   87
will call them there to parley, but provide
    such treatment that they will need no vow or prayer
    that Focara's perilous wind be pacified."   90
I said: "Tell me who he is, and show me where,
    who found the city bitter to his eye,
    if you wish me to carry news of you up there."   93

Allor puose la mano a la mascella
    d'un suo compagno e la bocca li aperse,
    gridando: «Questi è desso, e non favella.   96
Questi, scacciato, il dubitar sommerse
    in Cesare, affermando che 'l fornito
    sempre con danno l'attender sofferse».   99
Oh quanto mi pareva sbigottito
    con la lingua tagliata ne la strozza
    Curïo, ch'a dir fu così ardito!   102
E un ch'avea l'una e l'altra man mozza,
    levando i moncherin per l'aura fosca,
    sì che 'l sangue facea la faccia sozza,   105
gridò: «Ricordera'ti anche del Mosca,
    che disse, lasso!, "Capo ha cosa fatta",
    che fu mal seme per la gente tosca».   108
E io li aggiunsi: «E morte di tua schiatta»;
    per ch'elli, accumulando duol con duolo,
    sen gio come persona trista e matta.   111
Ma io rimasi a riguardar lo stuolo,
    e vidi cosa ch'io avrei paura,
    sanza più prova, di contarla solo;   114
se non che coscïenza m'assicura,
    la buona compagnia che l'uom francheggia
    sotto l'asbergo del sentirsi pura.   117
Io vidi certo, e ancor par ch'io 'l veggia,
    un busto sanza capo andar sì come
    andavan li altri de la trista greggia;   120
e 'l capo tronco tenea per le chiome,
    pesol con mano a guisa di lanterna:
    e quel mirava noi e dicea: «Oh me!».   123
Di sé facea a sé stesso lucerna,
    ed eran due in uno e uno in due;
    com' esser può, quei sa che sì governa.   126

Then he grabbed the jaw of one who stood nearby
    and pulled it so the mouth came open, stating:
      "Here he is, and he doesn't talk. He was forced to fly   96
from Rome, and when he saw Caesar hesitating,
    he extinguished Caesar's doubts. 'A man prepared,'
      he said, 'can only hurt himself by waiting.' "   99
I was shocked to see him looking lost and scared,
    his tongue hacked out right down to his throat's base,
      this Curio whose speech had always dared.   102
And one with both hands lopped began to raise
    his stumps in the dusky air imploringly
      so that they spattered blood upon his face.   105
He cried: "And Mosca too! Remember me
    who said 'What's done is finished,' the seed that had
      such ill effects for all of Tuscany—"   108
"—and that killed off your whole line," I was quick to add,
    at which, piling pain on pain, he turned to go
      like a man that misery has driven mad.   111
I stayed to watch the multitude below
    and saw a sight that I would not have revealed
      without more proof that it was really so,   114
but, knowing that I saw it, I am steeled
    by conscience, a just man's support and stay
      whose sense of right protects him like a shield.   117
Truly I saw, as I can see today,
    a headless body with the others there,
      trudging like them along the dismal way.   120
It held its severed head up by the hair,
    swinging it like a lantern in the night
      as it cried "Oh me!" and caught us with its stare.   123
Out of itself it had made for itself a light.
    They were two in one and one in two. How this
      could be is known to him who in his might   126

Quando diritto al piè del ponte fue,

 levò 'l braccio alto con tutta la testa

 per appressarne le parole sue,   129

che fuoro: «Or vedi la pena molesta,

 tu che, spirando, vai veggendo i morti:

 vedi s'alcuna è grande come questa.   132

E perché tu di me novella porti,

 sappi ch'i' son Bertram dal Bornio, quelli

 che diedi al re giovane i ma' conforti.   135

Io feci il padre e 'l figlio in sé ribelli;

 Achitofèl non fé più d'Absalone

 e di Davìd coi malvagi punzelli.   138

Perch' io parti' così giunte persone,

 partito porto il mio cerebro, lasso!,

 dal suo principio ch'è in questo troncone. 141

Così s'osserva in me lo contrapasso».

ordains it. When he stood right under us,

    beneath the bridge, he held his arm up straight

    to bring us closer so we would not miss   129

these words: "Behold my miserable fate.

    Live man among the dead, in your journeying

    try to find another punishment so great.   132

Know I am Bertran de Born, so you may bring

    news of me back with you. I am the one

    who counseled wickedness to the young king.   135

Because of me, the father fought the son.

    Ahithophel did no worse when he instigated

    wickedly with King David and Absalon.   138

Two who were one, by me were separated.

    I carry my brain separated from its source

    inside this trunk. In me is demonstrated   141

how the law of retribution takes its course."

Notes

lines 7–9   Puglia is the southeastern corner of Italy, the heel of the boot. Dante uses the term, as was common in his time, to denote the entire southern portion of the peninsula. He alludes to several battles, ancient and modern, that were fought there, beginning with the invasion by Aeneas and his forces.

lines 10–12   According to Livy (Titus Livius, 59 B.C.E.–17 C.E.) in his monumental history of Rome, *Ab urbe condita*, Hannibal had his soldiers remove the rings of Roman officers they had killed at the battle of Cannae (216 B.C.E.), an Apulian village, and sent them to the Carthaginian senate to demonstrate the magnitude of his victory. The "long war" was the second Punic War (218–201 B.C.E.).

lines 13–14   Robert Guiscard (1015–1085), brother of the duke of Normandy, was made ruler of Apulia and Calabria by Pope Nicholas II. He spent twenty years battling the Greeks and Saracens in southern Italy, and is cited in Canto XVIII of the *Paradiso* among warriors for the faith.

lines 15–16   The forces of King Manfred of Sicily met the invading army of Charles of Anjou near Benevento (not Ceprano) on February 26, 1266. When his Apulian allies fled the field, Manfred chose to die in battle rather than flee. Because he had been excommunicated, he was buried in unconsecrated ground and subsequently disinterred (according to some, on the orders of Pope Clement IV). In Canto III of the *Purgatorio*, Manfred is the first penitent soul Dante encounters as he begins his ascent of the mountain.

lines 17–18   In 1268, Charles of Anjou fought Conradin, nephew of Manfred and grandson of Frederick II, near Tagliacozzo. Charles was advised by the chevalier Érard de Valéry (c. 1200–c. 1277) to hold back his reserves as long as possible, which strategy turned the tide of battle in his favor.

line 31   Ronald L. Martinez and Robert M. Durling state: "In the Christian polemics that were Dante's sources of information, Mohammed was said to have been a Nestorian Christian (the Nestorians denied that Christ's divine and human natures were united) before founding Islam; thus he was thought both a heretic and a schismatic, having drawn one third of the world's believers away from the true faith" (*The Divine Comedy of Dante Alighieri. Volume I: Inferno*, Oxford, 1996). According to Mark Musa, Dante's treatment of Mohammed "reflects the medieval belief that Mohammed was responsible not only for a schism but the invasion of Palestine and the dismantling of Christian power and influence in the Middle East. Opinion in Dante's day ignored the fact that Mohammed was a monotheist in a pagan culture and that his split from Christianity followed the development of its trinitarian dogma."

line 32   Ali (c. 592–661) was Mohammed's cousin and son-in-law. Controversy over his assumption of the caliphate in 656 led to the splitting of Islam into the Sunni and Shiite sects.

lines 55–60   Dolcino Tornielli of Novara was known as Fra Dolcino because of his association with the Apostolic Brethren, who sought to bring the Church back to the simplicity of its earliest times, the days of the Apostles. After the death of the group's founder, Gherardo Segarelli, Dolcino took command of the Brethren. He was accused of holding heretical views, and in 1305 Pope Clement V preached against the sect. Dolcino and a large group of his followers, including his companion and presumed mistress, Margaret of Trent, held out for some time in the hills between Novara and Vercelli, but were driven out by hunger and repeated attacks. Dolcino and Margaret were captured in June 1307 and burned at the stake.

lines 73–75   The plain is the entire Po valley. Medicina is a town between Bologna and Imola. Pier has not been positively identified.

lines 76–90   Guido del Cassero and Angiolello di Carignano were leaders of opposing political parties in Fano. La Cattolica is midway between Fano and

Rimini on the Adriatic coast. The references to Cyprus and Majorca signify the entire extent of the Mediterranean; the Argives are the people of Argos—broadly speaking, the Greeks. The "one-eyed traitor" is Malatestino, ruler of Rimini (see note to Canto XXVII, lines 46–48). The incident in question, for which there is no definite historical authority, is believed to have occurred around 1312.

lines 96–102   Gaius Scribonius Curio the Younger was a follower of Pompey, then went over to Julius Caesar, and in the ensuing civil war led the campaign that drove Cato's army out of Sicily. Dante follows Lucan in claiming that it was on the advice of Curio that Caesar decided to cross the Rubicon at Rimini, which action marked the beginning of the civil war.

lines 106–9   In 1215, Buondelmonte de' Buondelmonti, a Florentine noble, broke his engagement to a daughter of the Amidei for what he considered a better offer. When allies of the Amidei discussed how best to avenge the shame, Mosca dei Lamberti spoke the words signifying that the matter should be resolved with finality, by the death of Buondelmonte, and himself took part in the murder. Although there had previously been tension between the Guelphs and Ghibellines, this killing crystallized the hostility that was to plague the city thereafter. Dante's taunt in line 109 refers to the expulsion of the Lamberti from Florence in 1258, after which they no longer figured in the affairs of the city. In Canto VI, line 80, Dante had asked Ciacco about Mosca's posthumous whereabouts.

lines 133–36   Bertran de Born (c. 1140–c. 1215) was one of the greatest of the Provençal troubadours. Ezra Pound adapted or loosely translated several of his poems, including the "Planh for the Young English King," Bertran's elegy for Prince Henry (1155–1183), second and oldest surviving son of King Henry II and called "the young king" because he was twice crowned during his father's lifetime. Encouraged by his mother, Eleanor of Aquitaine, and King Louis VII of France, Prince Henry rebelled against his father, demanding that he be given a substantial portion of his patrimony. The ensuing conflict lasted until "the young king" died of a fever; unlike his younger brothers, Richard and John, he never attained the throne.

lines 137–38   In 2 Samuel 15–17, Ahithophel counseled Absalom to rebel against his father, King David, a course of action that led to Absalom's death and Ahithophel's suicide.

line 142   This line is the poem's only direct mention of the *contrapasso*, the principle of fitting the punishment to the nature of the offense.

Canto XXIX

La molta gente e le diverse piaghe
   avean le luci mie sì inebrïate,
   che de lo stare a piangere eran vaghe.   3

Ma Virgilio mi disse: «Che pur guate?
   perché la vista tua pur si soffolge
   là giù tra l'ombre triste smozzicate?   6

Tu non hai fatto sì a l'altre bolge;
   pensa, se tu annoverar le credi,
   che miglia ventidue la valle volge.   9

E già la luna è sotto i nostri piedi;
   lo tempo è poco omai che n'è concesso,
   e altro è da veder che tu non vedi».   12

«Se tu avessi», rispuos' io appresso,
   «atteso a la cagion per ch'io guardava,
   forse m'avresti ancor lo star dimesso».   15

Parte sen giva, e io retro li andava,
   lo duca, già faccendo la risposta,
   e soggiugnendo: «Dentro a quella cava   18

dov' io tenea or li occhi sì a posta,
   credo ch'un spirto del mio sangue pianga
   la colpa che là giù cotanto costa».   21

Allor disse 'l maestro: «Non si franga
   lo tuo pensier da qui innanzi sovr' ello.
   Attendi ad altro, ed ei là si rimanga;   24

ch'io vidi lui a piè del ponticello
   mostrarti e minacciar forte col dito,
   e udi' 'l nominar Geri del Bello.   27

Canto XXIX

So many souls with wounds so red and raw
  made my besotted eyes desire to stay
  and weep for the mutilation that they saw.   3
"What are you staring at?" I heard Virgil say.
  "Why do you keep your sight so riveted
  on those maimed and miserable shades this way?   6
You have not done that with all the other dead.
  This ring is twenty-two miles around, and so
  keep that in mind if you mean to count each head.   9
The moon is beneath our feet, and we must go.
  Our allotted time grows short, and you will find
  there is more to see than what you see below."   12
"If you had realized why I was so inclined
  to stand and look down there," I told him then,
  "perhaps you would have agreed to stay behind."   15
He had taken up the journey once again,
  and I followed in his footsteps while I made
  my answer, adding: "There, where I have been   18
staring so hard, I believe I saw the shade
  of one of my kinsmen in the crowd that cry
  the guilt for which they have so dearly paid."   21
My master said: "Your attention should not lie
  in that direction. Let him stay there, and switch
  your thoughts to other things as we pass by.   24
He was pointing at you as he stood beneath the bridge,
  thrusting his finger threateningly, the one
  called Geri del Bello by others in the ditch.   27

Tu eri allor sì del tutto impedito
     sovra colui che già tenne Altaforte,
     che non guardasti in là, sì fu partito».   30
«O duca mio, la vïolenta morte
     che non li è vendicata ancor», diss' io,
     «per alcun che de l'onta sia consorte,   33
fece lui disdegnoso; ond' el sen gio
     sanza parlarmi, sì com' ïo estimo:
     e in ciò m'ha el fatto a sé più pio».   36
Così parlammo infino al loco primo
     che de lo scoglio l'altra valle mostra,
     se più lume vi fosse, tutto ad imo.   39
Quando noi fummo sor l'ultima chiostra
     di Malebolge, sì che i suoi conversi
     potean parere a la veduta nostra,   42
lamenti saettaron me diversi,
     che di pietà ferrati avean li strali;
     ond' io li orecchi con le man copersi.   45
Qual dolor fora, se de li spedali
     di Valdichiana tra 'l luglio e 'l settembre
     e di Maremma e di Sardigna i mali   48
fossero in una fossa tutti 'nsembre,
     tal era quivi, e tal puzzo n'usciva
     qual suol venir de le marcite membre.   51
Noi discendemmo in su l'ultima riva
     del lungo scoglio, pur da man sinistra;
     e allor fu la mia vista più viva   54
giù ver' lo fondo, là 've la ministra
     de l'alto Sire infallibil giustizia
     punisce i falsador che qui registra.   57
Non credo ch'a veder maggior tristizia
     fosse in Egina il popol tutto infermo,
     quando fu l'aere sì pien di malizia,   60

At that moment you were all intent upon
    the soul that once held Hautefort. When you came
    to look where he'd been standing, he was gone."   30
"My leader," I said, "his violent death, whose claim
    for vengeance is not yet satisfied by those
    who have been implicated in the shame,   33
made him indignant: I think that is why he chose
    to go away without any word to me,
    and that is why my pity for him grows."   36
We spoke these words as we moved gradually
    to the crag overlooking where the next valley lies,
    right to the bottom, were there light to see.   39
And now, from where we stood upon the rise,
    Malebolge's final cloister was unveiled,
    with its lay brothers visible to our eyes.   42
Weird lamentations, barbed with pity, assailed
    my ears so horribly that my hands flew
    to cover them against the souls that wailed.   45
Such pain as there would be all summer through
    if the sick from Maremma's hospitals, as well
    as those from Sardinia's and Valdichiana's too,   48
were piled into a single ditch to dwell,
    such pain was here, and all the air was rank
    with putrefaction's flesh-decaying smell.   51
Still turning left, we moved along the flank.
    I saw the depths more clearly as we wound
    our way down to the long reef's final bank.   54
Infallible Justice, God's minister, is found
    meting punishment to the falsifiers there
    whose sins she has recorded above ground.   57
I do not believe that it was worse to bear
    the sight of Aegina when all its people fell
    victim to such contagion in the air   60

che li animali, infino al picciol vermo,

 cascaron tutti, e poi le genti antiche,

 secondo che i poeti hanno per fermo,   63

si ristorar di seme di formiche;

 ch'era a veder per quella oscura valle

 languir li spirti per diverse biche.   66

Qual sovra 'l ventre e qual sovra le spalle

 l'un de l'altro giacea, e qual carpone

 si trasmutava per lo tristo calle.   69

Passo passo andavam sanza sermone,

 guardando e ascoltando li ammalati,

 che non potean levar le lor persone.   72

Io vidi due sedere a sé poggiati,

 com' a scaldar si poggia tegghia a tegghia,

 dal capo al piè di schianze macolati;   75

e non vidi già mai menare stregghia

 a ragazzo aspettato dal segnorso,

 né a colui che mal volontier vegghia,   78

come ciascun menava spesso il morso

 de l'unghie sopra sé per la gran rabbia

 del pizzicor, che non ha più soccorso;   81

e sì traevan giù l'unghie la scabbia,

 come coltel di scardova le scaglie

 o d'altro pesce che più larghe l'abbia.   84

«O tu che con le dita ti dismaglie»,

 cominciò 'l duca mio a l'un di loro,

 «e che fai d'esse talvolta tanaglie,   87

dinne s'alcun Latino è tra costoro

 che son quinc' entro, se l'unghia ti basti

 etternalmente a cotesto lavoro».   90

«Latin siam noi, che tu vedi sì guasti

 qui ambedue», rispuose l'un piangendo;

 «ma tu chi se' che di noi dimandasti?».   93

that along with every other animal
    even the worm succumbed (but the ancient men,
      as the poets who believe the story tell,   63
from the seed of ants sprang into life again)
    than to see these spirits heaped in disarray
      like sheaves as they languished there in that dark den.   66
One lay on another's belly, and one lay
    across another's shoulders, and one went
      crawling on all fours down the dismal way.   69
With slow steps, without speaking, all intent,
    we watched and heard the sick, who could not put
      themselves upright. Two who were sitting leant   72
against each other, looking, as I thought,
    like two pots set to keep warm side by side,
      and both were marked with scabs from head to foot.   75
I have never seen a currycomb being plied
    by a groom who against his will is still awake
      or a stableboy whose master waits to ride   78
so fiercely as I saw these sinners rake
    their own flesh, because nothing else avails
      against the burning itch. The scabs would flake   81
when they were dragged by the sinners' fingernails,
    the way a knife will scrape a carp or do
      the same to a fish with even larger scales.   84
My leader spoke to one of them: "O you
    whose fingers undo your chain mail bit by bit
      and now and then turn into pincers too,   87
tell us if any Italian sinners sit
    among you, so may your nails be vigorous
      and for the work at hand prove ever fit."   90
"We that you see disfigured, both of us
    are Italian," said the soul, who now began
      to weep. "And you, who are so curious?"   93

E 'l duca disse: «I' son un che discendo
    con questo vivo giù di balzo in balzo,
    e di mostrar lo 'nferno a lui intendo».   96

Allor si ruppe lo comun rincalzo;
    e tremando ciascuno a me si volse
    con altri che l'udiron di rimbalzo.   99

Lo buon maestro a me tutto s'accolse,
    dicendo: «Dì a lor ciò che tu vuoli»;
    e io incominciai, poscia ch'ei volse: 102

«Se la vostra memoria non s'imboli
    nel primo mondo da l'umane menti,
    ma s'ella viva sotto molti soli,   105

ditemi chi voi siete e di che genti;
    la vostra sconcia e fastidiosa pena
    di palesarvi a me non vi spaventi».   108

«Io fui d'Arezzo, e Albero da Siena»,
    rispuose l'un, «mi fé mettere al foco;
    ma quel per ch'io mori' qui non mi mena.   111

Vero è ch'i' dissi lui, parlando a gioco:
    "I' mi saprei levar per l'aere a volo";
    e quei, ch'avea vaghezza e senno poco,   114

volle ch'i' li mostrassi l'arte; e solo
    perch' io nol feci Dedalo, mi fece
    ardere a tal che l'avea per figliuolo.   117

Ma ne l'ultima bolgia de le diece
    me per l'alchìmia che nel mondo usai
    dannò Minòs, a cui fallar non lece».   120

E io dissi al poeta: «Or fu già mai
    gente sì vana come la sanese?
    Certo non la francesca sì d'assai!».   123

Onde l'altro lebbroso, che m'intese,
    rispuose al detto mio: «Tra'mene Stricca
    che seppe far le temperate spese,   126

Said my leader: "I conduct this living man
    ever deeper through the regions of the dead.
    To show him all hell's levels is my plan."   96
They broke their shared support and each turned his head,
    trembling, to look at me. Among the rest
    who had heard the echo of what Virgil said,   99
many did likewise. My good master pressed
    close to me, saying: "Say what you would say,"
    and I began, in accord with his request: 102
"So may the thought of you not fade away,
    up in the first world, from man's memory
    but live instead for many and many a day,   105
tell me who you are and of what ancestry.
    Do not let your hideous penalty and its shame
    keep you from speaking." And one said to me: 108
"Born in Arezzo, I was put to the flame
    at Albero of Siena's will, although
    why I died is not the reason why I came   111
to this. I told him: 'I can fly, you know,'
    thinking to have myself a bit of fun,
    and he, who was eager but whose wits were slow,   114
demanded that I show him how it was done.
    Because I could not make him Dedalus,
    he had me burned by one who called him son.   117
What brought me to this tenth and last pit was
    alchemy. Minos damned me to this place,
    whose judgment cannot be erroneous."   120
To the poet I said: "Has there ever been a race
    so empty-headed as the Sienese?
    They're far worse than the French, in any case."   123
The other leper, listening to these
    remarks of mine, responded: "Even so,
    you must make an exception for Stricca, if you please,   126

e Niccolò che la costuma ricca
 del garofano prima discoverse
 ne l'orto dove tal seme s'appicca;   129

e tra'ne la brigata in che disperse
 Caccia d'Ascian la vigna e la gran fonda,
 e l'Abbagliato suo senno proferse.   132

Ma perché sappi chi sì ti seconda
 contra i Sanesi, aguzza ver' me l'occhio,
 sì che la faccia mia ben ti risponda: 135

sì vedrai ch'io son l'ombra di Capocchio,
 che falsai li metalli con l'alchìmia;
 e te dee ricordar, se ben t'adocchio,   138

com' io fui di natura buona scimia».

that moderate spender, and for Niccolò,
> who showed how clove and costliness could sit
>> together in the garden where such seeds grow,   129
and that club where Caccia d'Asciano once saw fit
> to squander his vineyard and his woodland too
>> and Meo the pixilated showed his wit.   132
But let your eye grow sharp to show you who
> seconds you on Sienese stupidity,
>> so that my face may also answer you.   135
I am Capocchio's shade. Through alchemy
> I gave the metals a deceptive shape.
>> And you, if I have eyed you properly,   138
will recall how skilled I was as nature's ape."

Notes

line 27   Geri del Bello degli Alighieri was a first cousin of Dante's father. According to Dante's son Pietro, he was murdered by Brodaio dei Sacchetti, a murder that was not avenged until many years later, in 1310. Peace between the feuding families was not arranged until 1342. Vengeance for the murders of one's kinsmen was sanctioned by both law and custom.

line 29   Hautefort was the castle of Bertran de Born.

lines 47–48   Like the island of Sardinia, the Tuscan areas of the Maremma (see notes to Canto XIII, line 8, and Canto XXV, line 19) and the Valdichiana are swampy, and in medieval times all were breeding grounds for malaria in the summer.

lines 58–64   As the story is told in Book VII of the *Metamorphoses*, Aeacus was the son of Jupiter (Zeus) and the nymph Aegina, and ruler of the island that bore his mother's name. After Juno (Hera) devastated the island with a plague, Zeus repopulated it by turning its ants into men (hence the name Myrmidons for the inhabitants, from the Greek for "ant"). Aeacus was the father of Peleus and the grandfather of Achilles.

lines 109–10   Early commentators identify the Aretine as one Griffolino, who was burned at the stake for heresy around 1272. The credulous Albero was the protégé and perhaps the actual son of the bishop of Siena.

lines 126–32   Stricca, about whom nothing is known for certain, has been tentatively identified with Stricca di Giovanni de' Salimbeni, whose brother Niccolò was a member of the *brigata spendereccia* ("spendthrifts' club"), a group of young Sienese nobles who dedicated themselves to squandering their wealth as lavishly as possible, and were believed to have run through their entire fortunes in less than two years. Some claim that Niccolò introduced cloves, then extremely expensive, to the "garden" of Siena. Other spendthrifts in good standing were Caccia d'Asciano and Bartolommeo dei Folcacchieri, called Abbagliato, or "bedazzled." Meo was fined in 1278 for drinking in a tavern.

line 136   Capocchio was burned alive at Siena in 1293. Some early commentators claim that he and Dante knew one another as students.

Canto XXX

Nel tempo che Iunone era crucciata
    per Semelè contra 'l sangue tebano,
    come mostrò una e altra fïata,   3
Atamante divenne tanto insano,
    che veggendo la moglie con due figli
    andar carcata da ciascuna mano,   6
gridò: «Tendiam le reti, sì ch'io pigli
    la leonessa e ' leoncini al varco»;
    e poi distese i dispietati artigli,   9
prendendo l'un ch'avea nome Learco,
    e rotollo e percosselo ad un sasso;
    e quella s'annegò con l'altro carco.   12
E quando la fortuna volse in basso
    l'altezza de' Troian che tutto ardiva,
    sì che 'nsieme col regno il re fu casso,   15
Ecuba trista, misera e cattiva,
    poscia che vide Polissena morta,
    e del suo Polidoro in su la riva   18
del mar si fu la dolorosa accorta,
    forsennata latrò sì come cane;
    tanto il dolor le fé la mente torta.   21
Ma né di Tebe furie né troiane
    si vider mäi in alcun tanto crude,
    non punger bestie, nonché membra umane, 24
quant' io vidi in due ombre smorte e nude,
    che mordendo correvan di quel modo
    che 'l porco quando del porcil si schiude. 27

Canto XXX

In days when Juno burned with indignation
    at the Theban blood because of Semelè,
      showing her wrath on more than one occasion,   3
Athamas suffered such insanity
    that when he saw his wife, who was holding one
      of their sons in each arm, he cried violently: 6
"See the lioness and her cubs! Before they run
    to the pass, spread out the nets along the ground!"
      And then with ruthless claws he seized his son   9
Learchus and began to whirl him round
    and smashed him on a rock. She, horrified,
      leaped in the sea with her other charge and drowned.   12
When Fortune leveled the all-daring pride
    of the Trojans by inflicting the long war
      in which the king and all his kingdom died,   15
Hecuba, lost, enslaved, her heart made sore
    to see Polyxena dead and then to find
      her Polydorus stretched upon the shore,   18
was driven to such madness that she declined
    to howling and barking like a dog because
      the weight of the great grief had so wrenched her mind.   21
But frenzy never showed so furious
    a face in Thebes or Troy, inciting men
      or beasts with such ferocity as was   24
shown by two souls that came running up just then,
    naked and pale, biting everything around
      like pigs that have been turned out of the pen.   27

L'una giunse a Capocchio, e in sul nodo
    del collo l'assannò, sì che, tirando,
    grattar li fece il ventre al fondo sodo.   30
E l'Aretin che rimase, tremando
    mi disse: «Quel folletto è Gianni Schicchi,
    e va rabbioso altrui così conciando».   33
«Oh», diss' io lui, «se l'altro non ti ficchi
    li denti a dosso, non ti sia fatica
    a dir chi è, pria che di qui si spicchi».   36
Ed elli a me: «Quell' è l'anima antica
    di Mirra scellerata, che divenne
    al padre, fuor del dritto amore, amica.   39
Questa a peccar con esso così venne,
    falsificando sé in altrui forma,
    come l'altro che là sen va, sostenne,   42
per guadagnar la donna de la torma,
    falsificare in sé Buoso Donati,
    testando e dando al testamento norma».   45
E poi che i due rabbiosi fuor passati
    sovra cu' io avea l'occhio tenuto,
    rivolsilo a guardar li altri mal nati.   48
Io vidi un, fatto a guisa di lëuto,
    pur ch'elli avesse avuta l'anguinaia
    tronca da l'altro che l'uomo ha forcuto.   51
La grave idropesì, che sì dispaia
    le membra con l'omor che mal converte,
    che 'l viso non risponde a la ventraia,   54
faceva lui tener le labbra aperte
    come l'etico fa, che per la sete
    l'un verso 'l mento e l'altro in sù rinverte.   57
«O voi che sanz' alcuna pena siete,
    e non so io perché, nel mondo gramo»,
    diss' elli a noi, «guardate e attendete   60

Sinking its tusks into his nape, one downed
    Capocchio and dragged him on ahead
      so that his belly scraped the solid ground.   30
"That lunatic is Gianni Schicchi," said
    the Aretine, who was shivering with fear.
      "Like a rabid dog he rips the other dead."   33
"So may its fangs not find you, please make clear,"
    I said to him, "who the other one may be
      before it turns and runs away from here."   36
"That is the ancient shade," he answered me,
    "of wicked Myrrha, who came to love her father
      beyond the bounds of all propriety.   39
She counterfeited the image of another
    so she might dare to lie with him in sin,
      much like the demon running off, that other   42
who counterfeited Buoso Donati to win
    the lady of the herd, and even made
      a will with the proper language all put in."   45
When those rabid two on whom my eyes had stayed
    were gone at last, I turned round to survey
      the ranks of many a misbegotten shade.   48
There was one shaped like a lute, so I would say,
    if the part below the groin where man is split,
      forking in two, had here been cut away.   51
Because of the dropsy, in which the humors sit
    so ill-mixed that the members are badly blended,
      with face and belly disproportionate,   54
his lips spread like a hectic's when distended
    by racking thirst, with both of them thrusting out,
      one curling up while the other one descended.   57
"O you who are here in this horrid world without
    any punishment," he said, "though I cannot see
      just why that is, behold me and take note   60

a la miseria del maestro Adamo;
    io ebbi, vivo, assai di quel ch'i' volli,
    e ora, lasso!, un gocciol d'acqua bramo.   63
Li ruscelletti che d'i verdi colli
    del Casentin discendon giuso in Arno,
    faccendo i lor canali freddi e molli,   66
sempre mi stanno innanzi, e non indarno,
    ché l'imagine lor vie più m'asciuga
    che 'l male ond' io nel volto mi discarno.   69
La rigida giustizia che mi fruga
    tragge cagion del loco ov' io peccai
    a metter più li miei sospiri in fuga.   72
Ivi è Romena, là dov' io falsai
    la lega suggellata del Batista;
    per ch'io il corpo sù arso lasciai.   75
Ma s'io vedessi qui l'anima trista
    di Guido o d'Alessandro o di lor frate,
    per Fonte Branda non darei la vista.   78
Dentro c'è l'una già, se l'arrabbiate
    ombre che vanno intorno dicon vero;
    ma che mi val, c'ho le membra legate?   81
S'io fossi pur di tanto ancor leggero
    ch'i' potessi in cent' anni andare un'oncia,
    io sarei messo già per lo sentiero,   84
cercando lui tra questa gente sconcia,
    con tutto ch'ella volge undici miglia,
    e men d'un mezzo di traverso non ci ha.   87
Io son per lor tra sì fatta famiglia;
    e' m'indussero a batter li fiorini
    ch'avevan tre carati di mondiglia».   90
E io a lui: «Chi son li due tapini
    che fumman come man bagnate 'l verno,
    giacendo stretti a' tuoi destri confini?».   93

of Master Adam in his misery.

    Alive I had everything I wished, and here

    one drop of water would be all to me.   63

The streams of Casentino, cool and clear,

    flowing softly from the green hills as they race

    down to the Arno, constantly appear   66

before me, and not vainly, in this place.

    The image of them parches me much more

    than this disease that wastes away my face.   69

The rigid justice prodding at my core

    uses the place where I misused my wit

    and makes my sighs fly faster than before.   72

Romena is there, where I learned to counterfeit

    the coins stamped with the Baptist, and was thrown

    on the flames and burnt alive because of it.   75

I would rather see one of those brothers moan—

    Alessandro, Guido, the other one—at my side

    than have the Fonte Branda for my own.   78

If the rabid souls who run around have not lied,

    one of the three is already here below.

    What good is that to me, whose limbs are tied?   81

Were I still light enough that I could go,

    every hundred years, one inch along the ground,

    I would have set out already, even though   84

this circle is eleven miles around

    and half a mile across, to find that man

    down here where the disfigured ones abound.   87

Because of them I am numbered in this clan.

    The striking of the florins with the three

    carats of alloy—it was all their plan."   90

I said: "And who might these two wretches be,

    steaming like wet hands in the winter chill,

    lying close by your western boundary?"   93

«Qui li trovai—e poi volta non dierno—»,
    rispuose, «quando piovvi in questo greppo,
    e non credo che dieno in sempiterno.   96
L'una è la falsa ch'accusò Gioseppo;
    l'altr' è 'l falso Sinon greco di Troia:
    per febbre aguta gittan tanto leppo».   99
E l'un di lor, che si recò a noia
    forse d'esser nomato sì oscuro,
    col pugno li percosse l'epa croia.   102
Quella sonò come fosse un tamburo;
    e mastro Adamo li percosse il volto
    col braccio suo, che non parve men duro,   105
dicendo a lui: «Ancor che mi sia tolto
    lo muover per le membra che son gravi,
    ho io il braccio a tal mestiere sciolto».   108
Ond' ei rispuose: «Quando tu andavi
    al fuoco, non l'avei tu così presto;
    ma sì e più l'avei quando coniavi».   111
E l'idropico: «Tu di' ver di questo:
    ma tu non fosti sì ver testimonio
    là 've del ver fosti a Troia richesto».   114
«S'io dissi falso, e tu falsasti il conio»,
    disse Sinon; «e son qui per un fallo,
    e tu per più ch'alcun altro demonio!».   117
«Ricorditi, spergiuro, del cavallo»,
    rispuose quel ch'avëa infiata l'epa;
    «e sieti reo che tutto il mondo sallo!».   120
«E te sia rea la sete onde ti crepa»,
    disse 'l Greco, «la lingua, e l'acqua marcia
    che 'l ventre innanzi a li occhi sì t'assiepa!».   123
Allora il monetier: «Così si squarcia
    la bocca tua per tuo mal come suole;
    ché, s'i' ho sete e omor mi rinfarcia,   126

And he: "I found them there, completely still,
    when I was first rained down into this trench.
    They have never moved, and I think they never will.   96
Joseph's accuser is that lying wench,
    and this is Sinon, Troy's false Greek. The drought
    of fever makes them give off such a stench."   99
And perhaps annoyed at being talked about
    with such dark insinuation, one of them
    punched him right where his solid paunch puffed out.   102
It sounded like the beating of a drum.
    Then Master Adam smacked him in the face
    with an arm that was just as hard, and said to him: 105
"My limbs may keep me fastened to this place
    because they are so heavy, but at my side
    I have a free arm fit for such a case."   108
"When you were burned," the other one replied,
    "there wasn't very much that arm could do,
    but it worked just fine for the coins you falsified."   111
And the dropsical: "What you're saying now is true,
    but you didn't give such truthful testimony
    the day the Trojan leaders questioned you."   114
"My words were false. You falsified the money,"
    said Sinon. "One sin brought me here. Yours were
    a multitude. What demon did so many?"   117
And the paunch: "Recall the horse, you perjurer.
    May it stretch you on the rack to realize
    the whole world knows you for a lying cur."   120
"May you be racked by the thirst that cracks and dries
    your tongue," the Greek said, "and the rancid fen
    that makes your gut a hedge before your eyes."   123
"Your sickness spreads your big mouth, which has been
    your bane before," said the coiner. "I am sick
    with thirst, and humors make me swell, but then   126

tu hai l'arsura e 'l capo che ti duole,

 e per leccar lo specchio di Narcisso,

 non vorresti a 'nvitar molte parole».   129

Ad ascoltarli er' io del tutto fisso,

 quando 'l maestro mi disse: «Or pur mira,

 che per poco che teco non mi risso!».   132

Quand' io 'l senti' a me parlar con ira,

 volsimi verso lui con tal vergogna,

 ch'ancor per la memoria mi si gira.   135

Qual è colui che suo dannaggio sogna,

 che sognando desidera sognare,

 sì che quel ch'è, come non fosse, agogna,   138

tal mi fec' io, non possendo parlare,

 che disïava scusarmi, e scusava

 me tuttavia, e nol mi credea fare.   141

«Maggior difetto men vergogna lava»,

 disse 'l maestro, «che 'l tuo non è stato;

 però d'ogne trestizia ti disgrava.   141

E fa ragion ch'io ti sia sempre allato,

 se più avvien che fortuna t'accoglia

 dove sien genti in simigliante piato: 147

ché voler ciò udire è bassa voglia».

your head aches and your limbs burn. You'd be quick
    to give, without much need for an invitation,
    the mirror of Narcissus a good lick."   129
I was following this with all my concentration
    when my master told me: "Watch some more, I say,
    and then you will answer to my indignation."   132
And when I heard him speak to me that way
    in anger, I turned to face him hurriedly
    with a shame that shakes me to this very day.   135
As one who dreams he is in jeopardy
    and, dreaming, wishes it were a dream, and thus
    wants what is real as if it were fantasy,   138
so I became, all speechless there, because
    I wanted to seek pardon, and I did
    seek pardon without knowing that I was.   141
"Less shame would wash away," my master said,
    "a greater fault than yours, so do not fear,
    and let your sadness dissipate. Instead,   144
remember that I always will be near
    if it ever should befall that fortune brings
    such arguments as this one to your ear,   147
for it is low to want to hear such things."

Notes

lines 1–12   Semele was the daughter of Cadmus, founder of Thebes, and one of the many loves of Zeus. After Semele was accidentally killed by lightning when Zeus manifested himself to her in his godly form, their unborn child was saved, placed in Zeus's thigh and ultimately born there, and then given to Semele's sister, Ino. Her wrath unabated, Hera maddened Athamas, Ino's husband, making him kill their son Learchus; Ino then leaped into the sea with their other son, Melicertes (*Metamorphoses*, Book IV).

lines 13–21   Hecuba, widow of King Priam of Troy, and her daughter Polyxena were enslaved by the conquering Greeks. Hecuba was driven mad by the sacrifice of Polyxena on the tomb of Achilles and her discovery of the body of her murdered son Polydorus, which had washed up on the shore.

line 31   According to early commentators, after Buoso Donati died intestate, his nephew Simone enlisted Gianni Schicchi (died c. 1280), of the Cavalcanti family, to impersonate the dead man and dictate a will in Simone's favor. During the impersonation, Schicchi proceeded to make lavish bequests to himself of Donati's property. The story is the basis of Giacomo Puccini's one-act opera, one of the components of his *Trittico*.

line 38   For her refusal to honor the goddess Aphrodite, Myrrha was afflicted with an incestuous passion for her father, King Cinyras of Cyprus. After she seduced him by impersonating her mother, he threatened to kill her. She fled, and was turned into a myrtle (or myrrh) tree, from whose trunk Adonis was born (*Metamorphoses*, Book X).

lines 58–90   A Master Adam, an Englishman, was identified in a 1277 document as a member of the household of the Conti Guidi of Romena, a village in the region of the Casentino, east of Florence. In 1281, someone in their employ was burned alive for coining florins with twenty-one carats of gold instead of twenty-four; the first gold florin had been coined in 1252, and soon became the standard gold coin throughout Europe. The Guidi were four brothers in all; the two not named in line 77 were Aghinolfo and Ildebrandino. The reference in line 80 must be to Guido, who also died in 1281; the other three were still alive in 1300. There is a Fonte Branda in Romena and a more famous one in Siena; it is not clear which one is meant.

line 97   The wife of Potiphar, an officer of Pharaoh, made repeated attempts to seduce Joseph, who was her husband's overseer. Spurned by him, she made the false accusation that he had tried to assault her sexually, and he was imprisoned (Genesis 39.6–20).

line 98   Sinon allowed himself to be captured by the Trojans, claiming falsely that he had escaped his fate as an intended sacrifice by the Greeks and that the Trojan horse was meant as an atonement to Athena for the theft of the Palladium (see note to Canto XXVI, lines 56–63). On the basis of his lies, the Trojans took the horse into the city.

line 129   The reference is to a surface of water, like that of the fountain in which the beautiful youth Narcissus became enamored of his own image, ultimately dying of despair over his inability to possess it.

Canto XXXI

Una medesma lingua pria mi morse,
    sì che mi tinse l'una e l'altra guancia,
    e poi la medicina mi riporse; 3
così od' io che solea far la lancia
    d'Achille e del suo padre esser cagione
    prima di trista e poi di buona mancia. 6
Noi demmo il dosso al misero vallone
    su per la ripa che 'l cinge dintorno,
    attraversando sanza alcun sermone. 9
Quiv' era men che notte e men che giorno,
    sì che 'l viso m'andava innanzi poco;
    ma io senti' sonare un alto corno, 12
tanto ch'avrebbe ogne tuon fatto fioco,
    che, contra sé la sua via seguitando,
    dirizzò li occhi miei tutti ad un loco. 15
Dopo la dolorosa rotta, quando
    Carlo Magno perdé la santa gesta,
    non sonò sì terribilmente Orlando. 18
Poco portäi in là volta la testa,
    che me parve veder molte alte torri;
    ond' io: «Maestro, dì, che terra è questa?». 21
Ed elli a me: «Però che tu trascorri
    per le tenebre troppo da la lungi,
    avvien che poi nel maginare abborri. 24
Tu vedrai ben, se tu là ti congiungi,
    quanto 'l senso s'inganna di lontano;
    però alquanto più te stesso pungi». 27

Canto XXXI

I had been pricked by one and the same tongue,
 making my two cheeks tingle and turn red,
 which then supplied the balm where it had stung.   3
In much the same way, I have heard it said,
 where the spear of Achilles and his father hit
 came a sad gift, then a good one in its stead.   6
We turned our backs upon the dreadful pit
 and then without a word we climbed the height
 of the embankment that surrounded it.   9
Here it was less than day and less than night.
 I could hardly see ahead as we went on,
 but then I heard a horn blast with such might   12
that thunder is quiet in comparison.
 My eyes were drawn to one spot as I traced
 the sound right back to where it had begun.   15
Not even Roland blew so fiercely, faced
 with the dolorous rout of Charlemagne's brigade
 when the ranks of the holy guardsmen were laid waste.   18
And shortly after I had turned my head
 to look that way, I saw what seemed to be
 a host of enormous towers, so I said: 21
"Master, what is that city there?" And he:
 "You pierce the darkness from too far, and stray
 in your imaginings of what you see.   24
When you are near, your vision will display
 how distance makes the sense misunderstand,
 so spur your footsteps on along the way."   27

Poi caramente mi prese per mano
    e disse: «Pria che noi siam più avanti,
    acciò che 'l fatto men ti paia strano,   30
sappi che non son torri, ma giganti,
    e son nel pozzo intorno da la ripa
    da l'umbilico in giuso tutti quanti».   33
Come quando la nebbia si dissipa,
    lo sguardo a poco a poco raffigura
    ciò che cela 'l vapor che l'aere stipa,   36
così forando l'aura grossa e scura,
    più e più appressando ver' la sponda,
    fuggiemi errore e cresciemi paura;   39
però che, come su la cerchia tonda
    Montereggion di torri si corona,
    così la proda che 'l pozzo circonda   42
torreggiavan di mezza la persona
    li orribili giganti, cui minaccia
    Giove del cielo ancora quando tuona.   45
E io scorgeva già d'alcun la faccia,
    le spalle e 'l petto e del ventre gran parte,
    e per le coste giù ambo le braccia.   48
Natura certo, quando lasciò l'arte
    di sì fatti animali, assai fé bene
    per tòrre tali essecutori a Marte.   51
E s'ella d'elefanti e di balene
    non si pente, chi guarda sottilmente,
    più giusta e più discreta la ne tene;   54
ché dove l'argomento de la mente
    s'aggiugne al mal volere e a la possa,
    nessun riparo vi può far la gente.   57
La faccia sua mi parea lunga e grossa
    come la pina di San Pietro a Roma,
    e a sua proporzione eran l'altre ossa;   60

Then, as he took me lovingly by the hand:

    "Lest the strangeness overwhelm you, you should know

    before we cross the intervening land   30

that those are giants, not towers, where we must go,

    and from the waist down they are standing where

    the bank surrounds them, in the pit below."   33

As when a mist whose vapor packs the air

    begins to dissipate, and bit by bit

    the eye makes out more clearly what is there,   36

as I came nearer and nearer to the pit,

    cutting the dark and thick air with my sight,

    my error fled and fear succeeded it.   39

For just as Montereggione crowns the height

    of its long round wall with towers in the sky,

    so here the horrible giants, whom Jove's might   42

still threatens when he thunders from on high,

    betowered with half themselves the bank that drew

    a circle round the pit. Already I   45

saw the face of one of them come into view,

    his dangling arms, his shoulders and his chest,

    and the upper portion of his belly too.   48

Nature, when she decided to desist

    from making them, and took such instruments

    away from Mars, was acting for the best.   51

Although she does not repent of elephants

    and whales, those who consider it will find

    that she demonstrates more justice and good sense,   54

for if she added faculty of mind

    to power and malevolence, our race

    would be helpless against creatures of such kind.   57

His face was as big as the pinecone Rome displays

    before Saint Peter's on the holy ground,

    and his bones were in proportion to his face.   60

sì che la ripa, ch'era perizoma

    dal mezzo in giù, ne mostrava ben tanto

    di sovra, che di giugnere a la chioma   63

tre Frison s'averien dato mal vanto;

    però ch'i' ne vedea trenta gran palmi

    dal loco in giù dov' omo affibbia 'l manto.   66

«*Raphèl maì amècche zabì almi*»,

    cominciò a gridar la fiera bocca,

    cui non si convenia più dolci salmi.   69

E 'l duca mio ver' lui: «Anima sciocca,

    tienti col corno, e con quel ti disfoga

    quand' ira o altra passïon ti tocca!   72

Cércati al collo, e troverai la soga

    che 'l tien legato, o anima confusa,

    e vedi lui che 'l gran petto ti doga».   75

Poi disse a me: «Elli stessi s'accusa;

    questi è Nembrotto per lo cui mal coto

    pur un linguaggio nel mondo non s'usa.   78

Lasciànlo stare e non parliamo a vòto;

    ché così è a lui ciascun linguaggio

    come 'l suo ad altrui, ch'a nullo è noto».   81

Facemmo adunque più lungo vïaggio,

    vòlti a sinistra; e al trar d'un balestro

    trovammo l'altro assai più fero e maggio.   84

A cigner lui qual che fosse 'l maestro,

    non so io dir, ma el tenea soccinto

    dinanzi l'altro e dietro il braccio destro   87

d'una catena che 'l tenea avvinto

    dal collo in giù, sì che 'n su lo scoperto

    si ravvolgëa infino al giro quinto.   90

«Questo superbo volle esser esperto

    di sua potenza contra 'l sommo Giove»,

    disse 'l mio duca, «ond' elli ha cotal merto. 93

The bank, which was an apron all around

    his lower parts, revealed his upper shape

    and length, so that three Frieslanders would sound   63

an empty boast if they thought to reach his nape,

    for I noted thirty spans of him, or more,

    downward from where a man will tie his cape.   66

"*Raphèl maì amècche zabì almi!*" tore

    from his raw throat, and that fierce cry seemed to be

    the sweetest psalm his mouth was fitted for.   69

And then my leader: "Mass of stupidity,

    keep to your horn for venting your frustration

    when these rages come upon you suddenly!   72

Tower of confusion, make an examination

    of your own neck till you find the strap you wear

    that holds it on your huge chest like a decoration."   75

Then he said to me: "That self-accuser there

    is Nimrod. Through his evil thought alone

    there is not one common language everywhere.   78

Let us not waste breath, but leave him on his own.

    All languages will sound to him as will

    his tongue to us, which is totally unknown."   81

Then, turning to the left, we walked until

    we had gone as far as a crossbow shot and found

    the next one, far more fierce and huger still.   84

Just who the master was who had him bound

    I cannot say, but he was shackled tight

    by a chain that ringed his neck and wrapped around   87

to pin his left arm before him and his right

    behind his back, then coiled five times before

    it wound below his waist and out of sight.   90

"This proud one tried his strength by making war

    upon almighty Jove," said my leader then,

    "and here you see the fruit his efforts bore.   93

Fïalte ha nome, e fece le gran prove
    quando i giganti fer paura a' dèi;
    le braccia ch'el menò, già mai non move».   96

E io a lui: «S'esser puote, io vorrei
    che de lo smisurato Brïareo
    esperïenza avesser li occhi mei».   99

Ond' ei rispuose: «Tu vedrai Anteo
    presso di qui che parla ed è disciolto,
    che ne porrà nel fondo d'ogne reo.   102

Quel che tu vuo' veder, più là è molto
    ed è legato e fatto come questo,
    salvo che più feroce par nel volto».   105

Non fu tremoto già tanto rubesto,
    che scotesse una torre così forte,
    come Fïalte a scuotersi fu presto.   108

Allor temett' io più che mai la morte,
    e non v'era mestier più che la dotta,
    s'io non avessi viste le ritorte.   111

Noi procedemmo più avante allotta,
    e venimmo ad Anteo, che ben cinque alle,
    sanza la testa, uscia fuor de la grotta.   114

«O tu che ne la fortunata valle
    che fece Scipïon di gloria reda,
    quand' Anibàl co' suoi diede le spalle,   117

recasti già mille leon per preda,
    e che, se fossi stato a l'alta guerra
    de' tuoi fratelli, ancor par che si creda   120

ch'avrebber vinto i figli de la terra:
    mettine giù, e non ten vegna schifo,
    dove Cocito la freddura serra.   123

Non ci fare ire a Tizio né a Tifo:
    questi può dar di quel che qui si brama;
    però ti china e non torcer lo grifo.   126

He, Ephialtes, struck the great blows when
    giants made gods afraid. Then they swung free,
    those arms of his, but they did not move again."   96
And then I said to him: "If it could be,
    these eyes of mine would wish to gaze upon
    Briareus in his immensity."   99
"You will see Antaeus not much further on,
    who can speak and who is also unrestrained.
    He will set us down where the guiltiest have gone.   102
The one you want is far off," he explained.
    "Though his face is more ferocious, his limbs take
    the shape of this one's, and he too is chained."   105
Never did nature cause the earth to quake
    and make a tower tremble with such might
    as when Ephialtes now began to shake.   108
Now more than ever, death filled me with fright,
    and the fear alone would have furnished the event
    had I not seen the chains that held him tight.   111
Then we came upon Antaeus as we went.
    He rose a full five ells above the ground,
    with his head not counted in the measurement.   114
"O you who, in the fateful vale that crowned
    Scipio heir of glory on the day
    when Hannibal and his army turned around,   117
once took a thousand lions as your prey,
    through whom, had you joined your brothers in the field
    in their high war, there are many who still say   120
that the sons of earth would have forced the gods to yield,
    now lower us, not disdaining to do so,
    to the cold in which Cocytus has been sealed.   123
Do not curl your lip, but bend. Do not make us go
    to Tityus or Typhon. Be assured
    this man can give what is longed for here below.   126

Ancor ti può nel mondo render fama,
 ch'el vive, e lunga vita ancor aspetta
 se 'nnanzi tempo grazia a sé nol chiama». 129
Così disse 'l maestro; e quelli in fretta
 le man distese, e prese 'l duca mio,
 ond' Ercule sentì già grande stretta. 132
Virgilio, quando prender si sentio,
 disse a me: «Fatti qua, sì ch'io ti prenda»;
 poi fece sì ch'un fascio era elli e io. 135
Qual pare a riguardar la Carisenda
 sotto 'l chinato, quando un nuvol vada
 sovr' essa sì, ched ella incontro penda: 138
tal parve Antëo a me che stava a bada
 di vederlo chinare, e fu tal ora
 ch'i' avrei voluto ir per altra strada. 141
Ma lievemente al fondo che divora
 Lucifero con Giuda, ci sposò;
 né, sì chinato, lì fece dimora, 144
e come albero in nave si levò.

Through him your earthly fame may be restored,
> for he lives, and expects a long life, unless graced
> by an early summons to his last reward."   129

So spoke my master. The other one in haste
> held out the huge hands in whose vigorous
> clutches had Hercules once been embraced.   132

When Virgil felt their grip, he called me thus:
> "Come here to me, so I may gather you,"
> and made one bundle of the two of us.   135

As the Garisenda seems to someone who
> stands under it when a cloud comes overhead
> athwart the way the tower leans, so too   138

Antaeus seemed as he stooped with his hands spread
> to pick me up. Just then I wished we were
> descending by another road instead.   141

Where the bottom swallows Judas and Lucifer
> he set us down, and waited not at all,
> but as soon as we were clear began to stir   144

and like a ship's mast rose up straight and tall.

Notes

line 5   The spear of Achilles had the power to heal the wounds that it inflicted. Homer asserts that the spear had previously belonged to Achilles' father, Peleus. But Dante, who did not know Greek, seems, like other medieval poets, to have made this association through a misreading of Ovid, mistaking a reference to Mount Pelion for an allusion to Peleus.

line 16   As recounted in the *Chanson de Roland*, Ganelon, the stepfather of Roland, betrayed the rear guard of Charlemagne's army to the Saracens at Roncesvalles in 778. Roland blew his horn to summon the main force to their rescue, but Ganelon dissuaded Charlemagne from responding, and Roland and all his companions were killed.

line 40   Montereggione was a heavily fortified castle outside Siena. Fourteen towers, each over sixty feet tall, were added to its walls after the battle of Montaperti (see note to Canto X, line 32).

lines 42–43   Jove still thunders because of the giants' assault on Mount Olympus (see Canto XIV, lines 52–60, and note to line 58).

lines 58–59   The bronze pinecone, now located in the Belvedere Gardens of the papal palace, is about thirteen feet high.

line 63   Frieslanders, or Frisians, inhabitants of the Frisian Islands in the North Sea, were known for their great height.

line 65   A span is the width of an outstretched hand, roughly nine inches.

line 67   A number of attempts have been made to decipher Nimrod's words, despite the clear indication in lines 80–81 that they are unintelligible.

line 77   Nimrod, king of Babylon, is described in Genesis 10.9 as "a mighty hunter before the Lord," which may account for his horn. According to tradition, it was he who built the tower of Babel.

line 94   In an attempt to scale the heavens during the assault on the gods, Ephialtes and his brother Otus tried to pile Ossa on Olympus and Pelion on Ossa, but were killed by Zeus.

lines 97–105   Briareus is another of the giants who made war on Olympus. In the *Aeneid*, he is described as fifty-headed and hundred-handed. By deflecting Dante from viewing him and by characterizing him as normally shaped, Virgil seems to implicitly acknowledge the absurdity of that depiction.

line 100   Antaeus was the son of Neptune and Gaea (Earth), who retained his great strength by maintaining contact with his mother. He wrestled Hercules (lines 131–32), who lifted him off the ground and crushed him to death. His unfettered state may be a result of his not participating in the assault on Olympus, which took place before he was born.

lines 115–17   Scipio defeated Hannibal at Zama in North Africa in 202 B.C.E., resolving the second Punic War in favor of Rome.

line 123   Cocytus is the frozen lake of the ninth circle of hell; in Cocytus are embedded the worst of all sinners.

line 125   Tityus was a giant killed by Apollo and Artemis when he attempted to rape their mother, Leto. Typhon, who had a hundred fire-breathing serpent heads, was killed by the thunderbolts of Zeus.

lines 136–38   The Garisenda, built c. 1110, is the smaller of two leaning towers in Bologna.

S'ïo avessi le rime aspre e chiocce,
    come si converrebbe al tristo buco
    sovra 'l qual pontan tutte l'altre rocce,   3
io premerei di mio concetto il suco
    più pienamente; ma perch' io non l'abbo,
    non sanza tema a dicer mi conduco;   6
ché non è impresa da pigliare a gabbo
    discriver fondo a tutto l'universo,
    né da lingua che chiami mamma o babbo.   9
Ma quelle donne aiutino il mio verso
    ch'aiutaro Anfïone a chiuder Tebe,
    sì che dal fatto il dir non sia diverso.   12
Oh sovra tutte mal creata plebe
    che stai nel loco onde parlare è duro,
    mei foste state qui pecore o zebe!   15
Come noi fummo giù nel pozzo scuro
    sotto i piè del gigante assai più bassi,
    e io mirava ancora a l'alto muro,   18
dicere udi'mi: «Guarda come passi:
    va sì, che tu non calchi con le piante
    le teste de' fratei miseri lassi».   21
Per ch'io mi volsi, e vidimi davante
    e sotto i piedi un lago che per gelo
    avea di vetro e non d'acqua sembiante.   24
Non fece al corso suo sì grosso velo
    di verno la Danoia in Osterlicchi,
    né Tanaï là sotto 'l freddo cielo,   27

Canto XXXII

With harsh and clacking rhymes that could convey
    the nature of that hole of misery
    on which all other rocks converge and weigh,   3
I would press out the juice more thoroughly
    from my conception. Lacking them, I fall
    to the work at hand with some anxiety.   6
To try to describe the very floor of all
    the universe is nothing to attract
    an idle mind, no task for tongues that call   9
to mama and papa. May my attempts be backed
    by those ladies that inspired Amphion when
    he walled Thebes, that my words may hold the fact.   12
O most misbegotten rabble in that den
    so hard to speak of, better far had you
    been born as sheep or goats instead of men!   15
Down in the dark pit we'd been carried to,
    far beneath the giant's feet, I was standing where
    I had the enormous wall still fixed in view   18
when I heard a voice that said to me: "Take care
    not to step upon the poor heads, as you pass,
    of the weary brothers who are lying there."   21
Then I saw around me, under me, a mass
    of solid water, a lake so frozen over
    that it looked much less like water than like glass.   24
Never in Austria did the Danube river
    or the distant Don, where winter is most bleak,
    provide their currents with so thick a cover   27

com' era quivi; che se Tambernicchi
    vi fosse sù caduto, o Pietrapana,
    non avria pur da l'orlo fatto cricchi.   30
E come a gracidar si sta la rana
    col muso fuor de l'acqua, quando sogna
    di spigolar sovente la villana,   33
livide, insin là dove appar vergogna
    eran l'ombre dolenti ne la ghiaccia,
    mettendo i denti in nota di cicogna.   36
Ognuna in giù tenea volta la faccia;
    da bocca il freddo, e da li occhi il cor tristo
    tra lor testimonianza si procaccia.   39
Quand' io m'ebbi dintorno alquanto visto,
    volsimi a' piedi, e vidi due sì stretti,
    che 'l pel del capo avieno insieme misto.   42
«Ditemi, voi che sì strignete i petti»,
    diss' io, «chi siete?». E quei piegaro i colli;
    e poi ch'ebber li visi a me eretti,   45
li occhi lor, ch'eran pria pur dentro molli,
    gocciar su per le labbra, e 'l gelo strinse
    le lagrime tra essi e riserrolli.   48
Con legno legno spranga mai non cinse
    forte così; ond' ei come due becchi
    cozzaro insieme, tanta ira li vinse.   51
E un ch'avea perduti ambo li orecchi
    per la freddura, pur col viso in giùe,
    disse: «Perché cotanto in noi ti specchi?   54
Se vuoi saper chi son cotesti due,
    la valle onde Bisenzo si dichina
    del padre loro Alberto e di lor fue.   57
D'un corpo usciro; e tutta la Caina
    potrai cercare, e non troverai ombra
    degna più d'esser fitta in gelatina: 60

as there was here, and if the entire peak
    of Tambernic or Pietrapana were
    to fall on it, not even the edge would creak.   30
As when the croaking frogs will barely stir,
    with mouths out of water, while the peasant will
    dream of the gleaning that means so much to her,   33
so the dolorous souls in the ice were livid till
    their heads emerged with faces shame had dyed.
    Their teeth were clicking like the stork's long bill.   36
Each face looked down. Their mouths all testified
    to the bitter cold, and all their eyes were signed
    with the depths of misery that gnawed inside.   39
I looked about, and then glanced down to find
    two who were pressed together so intimately
    that the hair upon their heads was intertwined.   42
"Tell me," I said to them, "who you may be,
    frozen chest to chest." They craned their necks, and when
    they turned their faces up to look at me,   45
their eyes, which had been only moist within,
    now overflowed. Tears trickled down and froze,
    and locked them even tighter than they'd been.   48
Two boards were never clamped as close as those
    two souls. Like goats they butted head to head
    because such anger held them in its throes.   51
Face down nearby was another of the dead,
    whose ears had broken off in the bitter air.
    "Why reflect yourself in us so long?" he said.   54
"If you really want to know about that pair,
    the valley of the Bisenzio was their father's,
    who was called Alberto. Then it was theirs to share.   57
They came from the same womb, and there are no others—
    search all Caïna and you'll see it's true—
    more fit to set in aspic than those brothers.   60

non quelli a cui fu rotto il petto e l'ombra
con esso un colpo per la man d'Artù;
non Focaccia; non questi che m'ingombra   63
col capo sì, ch'i' non veggio oltre più,
e fu nomato Sassol Mascheroni;
se tosco se', ben sai omai chi fu.   66
E perché non mi metti in più sermoni,
sappi ch'i' fu' il Camiscion de' Pazzi;
e aspetto Carlin che mi scagioni».   69
Poscia vid' io mille visi cagnazzi
fatti per freddo; onde mi vien riprezzo,
e verrà sempre, de' gelati guazzi.   72
E mentre ch'andavamo inver' lo mezzo
al quale ogne gravezza si rauna,
e io tremava ne l'etterno rezzo;   75
se voler fu o destino o fortuna,
non so; ma, passeggiando tra le teste,
forte percossi 'l piè nel viso ad una.   78
Piangendo mi sgridò: «Perché mi peste?
se tu non vieni a crescer la vendetta
di Montaperti, perché mi moleste?».   81
E io: «Maestro mio, or qui m'aspetta,
sì ch'io esca d'un dubbio per costui;
poi mi farai, quantunque vorrai, fretta».   84
Lo duca stette, e io dissi a colui
che bestemmiava duramente ancora:
«Qual se' tu che così rampogni altrui?».   87
«Or tu chi se' che vai per l'Antenora,
percotendo», rispuose, «altrui le gote,
sì che, se fossi vivo, troppo fora?».   90
«Vivo son io, e caro esser ti puote»,
fu mia risposta, «se dimandi fama,
ch'io metta il nome tuo tra l'altre note».   93

Not him whose breast and shadow were run through

    by Arthur, not Focaccia certainly,

      and not this one whose head blocks off my view,   63

who was Sassol Mascheroni—which should be,

    if Tuscany is the land from which you came,

      all you have to hear to know his history.   66

So that I need speak no more, know that my name

    was Camiscion de' Pazzi. I'm waiting till

      Carlino comes to mitigate my blame."   69

Then I saw a thousand faces that the chill

    had purpled, and I shudder to this day

      when I cross a frozen stream, and I always will.   72

And I was shivering as we made our way

    through the endless cold to find that central place

      where all gravity collects. I cannot say   75

whether will or fate or pure chance was the case,

    but, passing among the heads, my foot swung out

      and kicked one hard, directly in the face.   78

He wailed at me and then began to shout:

    "What is this? If you're not here to heap on

      revenge for Montaperti, why knock me about?"   81

"Master," I said, "let me linger with this one

    so that I may satisfy a mental craving.

      I will walk as fast as need be when I'm done."   84

Then I turned back to the soul, who was still raving,

    while my leader stopped. "Just who are you," I said,

      "to criticize how others are behaving?"   87

"Stomping through Antenora to kick the head

    of anyone that you please, just who are you?"

      he asked. "It would be too much, if you weren't dead."   90

"I'm not dead," I replied, "and if it's true

    that you crave fame, it's worth your while to know

      that among the others I will name you too."   93

Ed elli a me: «Del contrario ho io brama.

    Lèvati quinci e non mi dar più lagna,

    ché mal sai lusingar per questa lama!».   96

Allor lo presi per la cuticagna

    e dissi: «El converrà che tu ti nomi,

    o che capel qui sù non ti rimagna».   99

Ond' elli a me: «Perché tu mi dischiomi,

    né ti dirò ch'io sia, né mosterrolti,

    se mille fiate in sul capo mi tomi».   102

Io avea già i capelli in mano avvolti,

    e tratti glien' avea più d'una ciocca,

    latrando lui con li occhi in giù raccolti,   105

quando un altro gridò: «Che hai tu, Bocca?

    non ti basta sonar con le mascelle,

    se tu non latri? qual diavol ti tocca?».   108

«Omai», diss' io, «non vo' che più favelle,

    malvagio traditor; ch'a la tua onta

    io porterò di te vere novelle».   111

«Va via», rispuose, «e ciò che tu vuoi conta;

    ma non tacer, se tu di qua entro eschi,

    di quel ch'ebbe or così la lingua pronta.   114

El piange qui l'argento de' Franceschi:

    "Io vidi", potrai dir, "quel da Duera

    là dove i peccatori stanno freschi".   117

Se fossi domandato "Altri chi v'era?",

    tu hai dallato quel di Beccheria

    di cui segò Fiorenza la gorgiera.   120

Gianni de' Soldanier credo che sia

    più là con Ganellone e Tebaldello,

    ch'aprì Faenza quando si dormia».   123

Noi eravam partiti già da ello,

    ch'io vidi due ghiacciati in una buca,

    sì che l'un capo a l'altro era cappello;   126

He said: "I crave the opposite. Now go,
>   get out of here, and leave me to my share,
>   since you don't know how to flatter souls this low."   96
I answered, as I seized him by the hair
>   upon his nape: "Now tell me what you're called,
>   or else you won't have a tuft left anywhere."   99
And he replied: "Go ahead and strip me bald!
>   I won't tell, or show my face, not if you land
>   on my head a thousand times and leave it mauled."   102
I took his hair and wrapped it round my hand
>   as he barked and looked straight down to hide his brow,
>   and I'd already pulled more than one strand   105
when another shouted: "Bocca, what ails you now?
>   Your flapping jaws are hard enough to endure.
>   Now barking? What devil's got you anyhow?"   108
"I don't want to hear another word from your
>   damned traitor's mouth! To your lasting shame," I cried,
>   "I will spread the news of you, you can be sure!"   111
"Tell what you want. Just go away," he replied.
>   "But if you escape this place, take my advice
>   and speak of him who just stretched his mouth so wide.   114
He took French silver. Now he pays the price.
>   'I saw the one from Duera,' you can tell it,
>   'in the bowl where they keep the sinners packed in ice.'   117
And if they ask what others help to fill it,
>   right by your side's a Beccheria, the one
>   the Florentines paid back with a slit gullet.   120
Gianni de' Soldanieri and Ganelon
>   are further along. Tebaldello is another.
>   He opened up Faenza before the dawn."   123
After we left him, I saw two together
>   frozen so close in one hole that the head
>   of the one was like a hood upon the other.   126

e come 'l pan per fame si manduca,
    così 'l sovran li denti a l'altro pose
    là 've 'l cervel s'aggiugne con la nuca: 129
non altrimenti Tidëo si rose
    le tempie a Menalippo per disdegno,
    che quei faceva il teschio e l'altre cose.   132
«O tu che mostri per sì bestial segno
    odio sovra colui che tu ti mangi,
    dimmi 'l perché», diss' io, «per tal convegno,   135
che se tu a ragion di lui ti piangi,
    sappiendo chi voi siete e la sua pecca,
    nel mondo suso ancora io te ne cangi,   138
se quella con ch'io parlo non si secca».

I stood and watched the higher one imbed
    his teeth in the other's nape and brain, and eat
    the way a starving man devours bread.   129
Not even Tydeus in his savage heat
    gnawed Menalippus's head more passionately
    than this one did to the skull and the soft meat.   132
"O you who show such wild hostility,
    attacking him with bestial violence,
    tell me why," I said, "and if it seems to me   135
that you are justified by his offense
    to take such vengeance, then before I die
    in the world above you shall have recompense,   138
unless my tongue should wither and turn dry."

Notes

line 11   The Muses helped Amphion wall Thebes by inspiring him to play so beautifully upon the lyre that the stones came down from Mount Cithaeron to form the walls themselves.

line 29   Mount Pietrapana is in the Apuan Alps; Tambernic is most likely Mount Tambura, in the same range.

lines 55–56   Alessandro and Napoleone were the sons of Count Alberto of Mangona. According to the early commentators, they fought over their inheritance and wound up killing one another sometime in the 1280s.

lines 61–62   King Arthur was killed by Mordred, his treacherous nephew (or son). In their mutually fatal encounter, Arthur pierced him through with his lance, inflicting so gaping a wound that a ray of light passed through Mordred's body.

line 62   Focaccia was the nickname of Vanni de' Cancellieri, who murdered his cousin Detto di Sinibaldo Cancellieri in 1293.

line 64   Sassol Mascheroni murdered one of his relatives over an inheritance. In punishment for the crime, he was rolled through the streets of Florence in a nail-filled cask and then beheaded.

lines 68–69   Of Alberto Camicione de' Pazzi of Val d'Arno, all that is known for certain is that he murdered a relative named Ubertino. In 1302, Carlino de' Pazzi, another kinsman of his, would accept a bribe to betray the castle of Piantravigne to the Black Guelphs. Camicione's guilt will be mitigated because his cousin's treachery will be of a more serious kind than his own and qualify him for the next zone, Antenora (named for Antenor, who in Dante's time was believed to have betrayed Troy to the Greeks).

line 81   At the battle of Montaperti in 1260 (see note to Canto X, line 32), Bocca degli Abati, a Ghibelline infiltrator, cut off the hand of the Guelph standard-bearer, creating a panic that led to a crushing defeat for the Guelphs.

line 116   Buoso da Duera of Cremona, a Ghibelline leader, was allegedly bribed by the French in 1265 to allow the forces of Charles of Anjou to pass unresisted through Lombardy on their way to Naples to attack Manfred (see note to Canto XXVIII, lines 15–16).

line 119   Tesauro de' Beccheria was abbot of Vallombrosa and papal legate of Alexander IV. After the Ghibellines were expelled from Florence in 1258, he was accused of conspiring with them, and was subsequently tortured and beheaded.

line 121   When the Florentines rebelled against their Ghibelline rulers in 1266, Gianni de' Soldanieri deserted his party and joined the Guelphs in an unsuccessful attempt to advance himself politically. For Ganelon, see note to Canto XXXI, line 16.

line 122   Tebaldello belonged to the Zambrasi, a Ghibelline family of Faenza. Because of personal hostility to members of the Lambertazzi, Ghibelline exiles from Bologna who had taken refuge in Faenza, he opened the gates of the city to their Guelph enemies in the predawn hours of November 13, 1280.

lines 130–31   Tydeus, one of the seven kings besieging Thebes (see note to Canto XIV, line 46), exchanged fatal blows with the Theban Menalippus. According to Statius, the dying Tydeus called for the head of Menalippus and proceeded to gnaw it in his rage.

Canto XXXIII

La bocca sollevò dal fiero pasto
  quel peccator, forbendola a' capelli
  del capo ch'elli avea di retro guasto.   3
Poi cominciò: «Tu vuo' ch'io rinovelli
  disperato dolor che 'l cor mi preme
  già pur pensando, pria ch'io ne favelli.   6
Ma se le mie parole esser dien seme
  che frutti infamia al traditor ch'i' rodo,
  parlar e lagrimar vedrai insieme.   9
Io non so chi tu se' né per che modo
  venuto se' qua giù; ma fiorentino
  mi sembri veramente quand' io t'odo.   12
Tu dei saper ch'i' fui conte Ugolino,
  e questi è l'arcivescovo Ruggieri:
  or ti dirò perché i son tal vicino.   15
Che per l'effetto de' suo' mai pensieri,
  fidandomi di lui, io fossi preso
  e poscia morto, dir non è mestieri;   18
però quel che non puoi avere inteso,
  cioè come la morte mia fu cruda,
  udirai, e saprai s'e' m'ha offeso.   21
Breve pertugio dentro da la Muda,
  la qual per me ha 'l titol de la fame,
  e che conviene ancor ch'altrui si chiuda,   24
m'avea mostrato per lo suo forame
  più lune già, quand' io feci 'l mal sonno
  che del futuro mi squarciò 'l velame.   27

Canto XXXIII

He paused in his savage meal and raised his head
    from the one he was destroying in his fit,
    and wiped his mouth upon its hair, and said: 3
"What you ask revives a grief so desperate
    that its recollection tears my heart, even though
    I have yet to tell one single word of it.   6
But if my words are a seed from which will grow
    the fruit of this vile traitor's evil fame,
    then I shall speak, and weep while doing so.   9
I do not know who you are, or how you came
    among us, but from your speech you seem to be
    a Florentine. I should tell you that my name   12
was Count Ugolino, and this one next to me
    is Archbishop Ruggieri. Now I shall explain
    why I am such a neighbor as you see.   15
How I was seized, and executed then,
    having trusted him while he betrayed and lied—
    there is no need to tell that tale again.   18
But of what you cannot know—the way I died,
    the cruelty of it—hear what I have to say.
    Whether he wronged me, you may then decide.   21
A narrow opening in the Mew that they
    call Hunger now in memory of my plight,
    where prisoners are still to be shut away,   24
had shown me more than once the new moon's light
    when the bad dream came to me that tore in two
    the veil that hides the future from our sight.   27

Questi pareva a me maestro e donno,
   cacciando il lupo e ' lupicini al monte
   per che i Pisan veder Lucca non ponno.   30
Con cagne magre, studïose e conte
   Gualandi con Sismondi e con Lanfranchi
   s'avea messi dinanzi da la fronte.   33
In picciol corso mi parieno stanchi
   lo padre e ' figli, e con l'agute scane
   mi parea lor veder fender li fianchi.   36
Quando fui desto innanzi la dimane,
   pianger senti' fra 'l sonno i miei figliuoli
   ch'eran con meco, e dimandar del pane.   39
Ben se' crudel, se tu già non ti duoli
   pensando ciò che 'l mio cor s'annunziava;
   e se non piangi, di che pianger suoli?   42
Già eran desti, e l'ora s'appressava
   che 'l cibo ne solëa essere addotto,
   e per suo sogno ciascun dubitava;   45
e io senti' chiavar l'uscio di sotto
   a l'orribile torre; ond' io guardai
   nel viso a' mie' figliuoi sanza far motto.   48
Io non piangëa, sì dentro impetrai:
   piangevan elli; e Anselmuccio mio
   disse: "Tu guardi sì, padre! che hai?".   51
Perciò non lagrimai né rispuos' io
   tutto quel giorno né la notte appresso,
   infin che l'altro sol nel mondo uscìo.   54
Come un poco di raggio si fu messo
   nel doloroso carcere, e io scorsi
   per quattro visi il mio aspetto stesso,   57
ambo le man per lo dolor mi morsi;
   ed ei, pensando ch'io 'l fessi per voglia
   di manicar, di sùbito levorsi   60

This man was there, as the lord and master who
      pursued the wolf and his young cubs as they sped
      on the mountain that blocks Lucca from the view   30
of the Pisans. Trained hounds, lean and eager, led
      while Gualandi, Sismondi, and that other one,
      Lanfranchi, had been set to run on ahead.   33
The wolves were weary after a short run,
      and then I saw the dogs as their sharp fangs ripped
      into the flesh of the father and every son.   36
It was not yet dawn, but I no longer slept.
      My sons were there with me. Though still asleep,
      they called to me to give them bread, and wept.   39
You are cruel indeed if you can know the deep
      dread that I felt, and not yet shed a tear.
      If not this, what could ever make you weep?   42
The time of our morning meal was drawing near.
      My children were awake. Their dreams had stirred
      in each of them uneasiness and fear.   45
From the base of the horrible tower I now heard
      the door being nailed shut, and I looked into
      the faces of my sons, without a word.   48
I did not weep. I was turned to stone all through.
      They wept. And Anselmuccio spoke up when
      he saw my face, saying: 'Father, what's troubling you?'   51
I shed no tears and I gave no answer then,
      and all that day and night I sat like stone,
      until the sun lit up the world again.   54
As soon as a small ray of sunlight shone
      in the miserable prison, and I could see
      from their four faces the aspect of my own,   57
I bit my hands in grief and agony.
      And they, assuming that I acted thus
      for hunger, quickly rose and said to me: 60

e disser: "Padre, assai ci fia men doglia
    se tu mangi di noi: tu ne vestisti
    queste misere carni, e tu le spoglia".   63
Queta'mi allor per non farli più tristi;
    lo dì e l'altro stemmo tutti muti;
    ahi dura terra, perché non t'apristi?   66
Poscia che fummo al quarto dì venuti,
    Gaddo mi si gittò disteso a' piedi,
    dicendo: "Padre mio, ché non m'aiuti?".   69
Quivi morì; e come tu mi vedi,
    vid' io cascar li tre ad uno ad uno
    tra 'l quinto dì e 'l sesto; ond' io mi diedi,   72
già cieco, a brancolar sovra ciascuno,
    e due dì li chiamai, poi che fur morti.
    Poscia, più che 'l dolor, poté 'l digiuno».   75
Quand' ebbe detto ciò, con li occhi torti
    riprese 'l teschio misero co' denti,
    che furo a l'osso, come d'un can, forti.   78
Ahi Pisa, vituperio de le genti
    del bel paese là dove 'l sì suona,
    poi che i vicini a te punir son lenti,   81
muovasi la Capraia e la Gorgona,
    e faccian siepe ad Arno in su la foce,
    sì ch'elli annieghi in te ogne persona!   84
Che se 'l conte Ugolino aveva voce
    d'aver tradita te de le castella,
    non dovei tu i figliuoi porre a tal croce.   87
Innocenti facea l'età novella,
    novella Tebe, Uguiccione e 'l Brigata
    e li altri due che 'l canto suso appella.   90
Noi passammo oltre, là 've la gelata
    ruvidamente un'altra gente fascia,
    non volta in giù, ma tutta riversata.   93

'Eat of us, Father. It will hurt us less.

 From you we have this wretched flesh we wear.

 Now it is yours to take away from us.'   63

I calmed myself, to stay them from despair.

 Alas, hard earth, you should have opened wide!

 Two more days passed while we sat silent there.   66

And when it was the fourth day, Gaddo cried:

 'Father, why don't you help me!' I watched him fall

 outstretched before my feet. And there he died.   69

Just as you see me now, I saw them all,

 between the fifth and sixth days, one by one,

 drop down and die. Now blindness cast its pall,   72

and for two more days I crawled from son to son,

 calling to them, who were already dead.

 Then fasting did what misery had not done."   75

With eyes asquint, having finished what he'd said,

 as a dog attacks a bone he turned back to

 his gnawing of the other's wretched head.   78

Pisa, disgrace of all the peoples who

 fill the fair land where *sì* is heard, who show

 no readiness to rise and punish you,   81

let Capraia and Gorgona shift, and go

 to dam the Arno's mouth so that it may

 drown all your citizens with its overflow!   84

Even if Count Ugolino did betray

 your castles as was reputed, you did wrong

 to put his sons upon the cross that way.   87

New Thebes, there is no guilt in those so young

 as Uguiccione or Brigata or

 the two already mentioned in my song.   90

We came to another place, where we found more

 who were covered with coarse frost in the bitter chill,

 but these faced up, unlike the ones before.   93

Lo pianto stesso lì pianger non lascia,
e 'l duol che truova in su li occhi rintoppo,
si volge in entro a far crescer l'ambascia;   96
ché le lagrime prime fanno groppo,
e sì come visiere di cristallo,
rïempion sotto 'l ciglio tutto il coppo.   99
E avvegna che, sì come d'un callo,
per la freddura ciascun sentimento
cessato avesse del mio viso stallo,   102
già mi parea sentire alquanto vento;
per ch'io: «Maestro mio, questo chi move?
non è qua giù ogne vapore spento?».   105
Ond' elli a me: «Avaccio sarai dove
di ciò ti farà l'occhio la risposta,
veggendo la cagion che 'l fiato piove».   108
E un de' tristi de la fredda crosta
gridò a noi: «O anime crudeli
tanto che data v'è l'ultima posta,   111
levatemi dal viso i duri veli,
sì ch'ïo sfoghi 'l duol che 'l cor m'impregna,
un poco, pria che 'l pianto si raggeli».   114
Per ch'io a lui: «Se vuo' ch'i' ti sovvegna,
dimmi chi se', e s'io non ti disbrigo,
al fondo de la ghiaccia ir mi convegna».   117
Rispuose adunque: «I' son frate Alberigo;
i' son quel da le frutta del mal orto,
che qui riprendo dattero per figo».   120
«Oh», diss' io lui, «or se' tu ancor morto?».
Ed elli a me: «Come 'l mio corpo stea
nel mondo sù, nulla scïenza porto.   123
Cotal vantaggio ha questa Tolomea,
che spesse volte l'anima ci cade
innanzi ch'Atropòs mossa le dea.   126

Here tears themselves make tears impossible.
    The grief is blocked, turning inward when it tries
      to express itself, making pain more painful still,   96
for knots are formed by the first tears each soul cries,
    resembling a crystal visor as they spread
      to fill the hollows that surround the eyes.   99
Although, as with a callus that is dead
    to all sensation, the cold was so severe
      that all the feeling in my face had fled,   102
I thought I felt a wind come blowing clear.
    "Master," I turned to ask, "what forces drive
      this current? Aren't all vapors dead down here?"   105
He answered: "Very soon you will arrive
    where your own eyes will give you your reply,
      with what rains down to keep this breath alive."   108
One wretch inside the cold crust gave a cry:
    "O you two souls, so cruel that you have been
      assigned to go where the very basest lie,   111
pry the hard veils from my face, so that I can
    vent my heart-soaking pain for a bit before
      my tears begin to turn to ice again."   114
"Tell me who you are," I answered, "who implore.
    If I fail to help you then, may I be made
      to go to the bottom of the icy floor."   117
"I am Fra Alberigo, and I displayed
    the fruits of the evil orchard," he replied.
      "Now, for my figs, with dates I am repaid."   120
And I to him: "Oh, you've already died?"
    "I have no information here," he said,
      "how my body fares up there, on the other side.   123
It often happens that a soul is sped—
    such is Ptolomea's privilege—to this place
      while Atropos has yet to cut its thread.   126

E perché tu più volentier mi rade
 le 'nvetrïate lagrime dal volto,
  sappie che, tosto che l'anima trade   129
come fec' ïo, il corpo suo l'è tolto
 da un demonio, che poscia il governa
  mentre che 'l tempo suo tutto sia vòlto. 132
Ella ruina in sì fatta cisterna;
 e forse pare ancor lo corpo suso
  de l'ombra che di qua dietro mi verna. 135
Tu 'l dei saper, se tu vien pur mo giuso:
 elli è ser Branca Doria, e son più anni
  poscia passati ch'el fu sì racchiuso». 138
«Io credo», diss' io lui, «che tu m'inganni;
 ché Branca Doria non morì unquanche,
  e mangia e bee e dorme e veste panni». 141
«Nel fosso sù», diss' el, «de' Malebranche,
 là dove bolle la tenace pece,
  non era ancora giunto Michel Zanche, 144
che questi lasciò il diavolo in sua vece
 nel corpo suo, ed un suo prossimano
  che 'l tradimento insieme con lui fece. 147
Ma distendi oggimai in qua la mano;
 aprimi li occhi». E io non gliel' apersi;
  e cortesia fu lui esser villano. 150
Ahi Genovesi, uomini diversi
 d'ogne costume e pien d'ogne magagna,
  perché non siete voi del mondo spersi? 153
Ché col peggiore spirto di Romagna
 trovai di voi un tal, che per sua opra
  in anima in Cocito già si bagna, 156
e in corpo par vivo ancor di sopra.

So that you may scrape the glazed tears from my face
    more readily, let me also say to you
    that as soon as the soul betrays, as in my case,   129
its body is taken by a devil who
    will be master over it in everything
    until its allotted time on earth is through.   132
To this cistern then the soul comes plummeting.
    Still walking the earth, perhaps, is the body of
    this one who is here behind me wintering,   135
as you must know if you just came from above.
    He is Ser Branca d'Oria, and I'll attest
    that he has been here many years." "Enough,"   138
I said to him, "I believe you are in jest.
    I know that Branca d'Oria is not dead.
    He eats and drinks, he sleeps, and he gets dressed."   141
"Above, in the ditch of the Evilclaws," he said,
    "where the sea of sticky pitch is boiling hot,
    Michel Zanche was not yet deposited   144
when this one, dropping down here like a shot,
    left a devil to fill his body in his place,
    as did his kinsman who was in the plot.   147
So, now reach out your arm and clear my face
    of the ice around my eyes." But I refused.
    Betrayal was true courtesy in this case.   150
Genoans, strangers to the customs used
    by all good men, and filled with every vice,
    how are you still here on the earth you have abused?   153
For, with Romagna's worst, there in the ice
    was one of you, who for his crimes was hurled
    to Cocytus, where even now he pays the price   156
while his body goes on walking in the world.

Notes

line 13	Ugolino della Gherardesca, Conte di Donoratico (c. 1220–1289) belonged to a noble Ghibelline family of Pisa. He was banished after the failure of his intrigue with the Guelph leader Giovanni Visconti in 1275, but returned to Pisa the following year and quickly reassumed a position of power. He conspired with the archbishop, Ruggieri degli Ubaldini, also a Ghibelline, to rid the city of Nino Visconti, who was a judge, a Guelph, Ugolino's grandson, and a friend of Dante's. After they had driven Visconti out of Pisa in 1288, Ruggieri turned on Ugolino, accusing him of betraying the city because he had, in 1285, ceded castles to Florence and to Lucca. Whether Ugolino's action was intended to betray Pisa or to preserve it by conciliating its powerful foes is open to question. In any event, he was imprisoned in the summer of 1288 with two sons and two grandsons, the youngest of whom was fifteen (not the four young sons that Dante gives him). All five were starved to death early in 1289.
lines 22–23	The Torre della Fame, or "Tower of Hunger," was used as a prison until 1318.
line 30	Monte San Giuliano stands between Pisa and Lucca.
lines 32–33	Gualandi, Sismondi, and Lanfranchi were prominent Ghibelline families of Pisa who supported Ruggieri in his actions against Ugolino.
line 82	Capraia and Gorgona are Mediterranean islands then belonging to Pisa.
line 88	Thebes had a reputation as the worst city of the ancient world for violence and bloodshed.
lines 118–20	Fra Alberigo was a member of the Manfredi family of Faenza and of the Jolly Friars (see note to Canto XXIII, lines 103–8). A close relative of his named Manfred struck him in the course of an argument over the lordship of Faenza. Alberigo pretended to forgive the insult. In 1285, he invited Manfred and one of his sons to dinner. His calling to his servants to bring in the fruit was a signal for assassins to rush into the room and kill Manfred and his son. The comment made by Alberigo (who was still alive in 1300) at line 120 turns on the fact that dates were more expensive than figs.
line 125	Ptolomea is the third of the four zones of Cocytus, named either for Ptolemy XII, king of Egypt, who allowed his guest, Pompey, to be murdered, or for the Ptolemy who killed Simon the Maccabee and two of his sons at a banquet (1 Maccabees 16.11–16).
line 126	The Fates, described by Hesiod as daughters of the night, are represented as spinning women: Clotho winds the yarn on the distaff of Lachesis, and Atropos cuts the thread of life.

line 137   Branca d'Oria, member of a Ghibelline family of Genoa, murdered his father-in-law, Don Michel Zanche (see note to Canto XXII, line 89) at a banquet to which he had invited him. Branca (who lived until at least 1325) was assisted in the murder by one of his relatives, either a cousin or a nephew.

Canto XXXIV

«*Vexilla regis prodeunt inferni*

    verso di noi; però dinanzi mira»,

    disse 'l maestro mio, «se tu 'l discerni».   3

Come quando una grossa nebbia spira,

    o quando l'emisperio nostro annotta,

    par di lungi un molin che 'l vento gira,   6

veder mi parve un tal dificio allotta;

    poi per lo vento mi ristrinsi retro

    al duca mio, ché non lì era altra grotta.   9

Già era, e con paura il metto in metro,

    là dove l'ombre tutte eran coperte,

    e trasparien come festuca in vetro.   12

Altre sono a giacere; altre stanno erte,

    quella col capo e quella con le piante;

    altra, com' arco, il volto a' piè rinverte.   15

Quando noi fummo fatti tanto avante,

    ch'al mio maestro piacque di mostrarmi

    la creatura ch'ebbe il bel sembiante,   18

d'innanzi mi si tolse e fé restarmi,

    «Ecco Dite», dicendo, «ed ecco il loco

    ove convien che di fortezza t'armi».   21

Com' io divenni allor gelato e fioco,

    nol dimandar, lettor, ch'i' non lo scrivo,

    però ch'ogne parlar sarebbe poco.   24

Io non mori' e non rimasi vivo;

    pensa oggimai per te, s'hai fior d'ingegno,

    qual io divenni, d'uno e d'altro privo.   27

Canto XXXIV

"*Vexilla regis prodeunt inferni*
  toward where we are," I heard my master say.
  "Look forward now and see if you discern him."   3
When our hemisphere grows dark at close of day
  or when a thick fog breathes, there still may be
  a turning windmill seen from far away.   6
Just such a structure I now seemed to see.
  Then I walked behind my leader. The wind was raw
  and there was nothing else to shelter me.   9
I tremble to make verse of what I saw.
  The souls were covered over in this place
  in ice like glass-embedded bits of straw.   12
Some are lying flat, some standing in their space,
  some with heads and some with soles in the ascent,
  one like a bow with feet bent toward his face.   15
We continued moving forward. On we went
  till we reached a place at which it pleased my guide
  to show me the creature once so radiant.   18
He moved from before me, bade me stop, and cried:
  "Behold Dis! Here behold the place where you
  must summon courage and be fortified."   21
I cannot, reader—do not ask me to—
  describe the way I felt, for I know that I
  lack words to tell how cold and weak I grew.   24
I did not live and yet I did not die,
  deprived of both states. You may realize
  what I then became, if you have the wit to try.   27

Lo 'mperador del doloroso regno
    da mezzo 'l petto uscia fuor de la ghiaccia;
    e più con un gigante io mi convegno,
che i giganti non fan con le sue braccia:
    vedi oggimai quant' esser dee quel tutto
    ch'a così fatta parte si confaccia.
S'el fu sì bel com' elli è ora brutto,
    e contra 'l suo fattore alzò le ciglia,
    ben dee da lui procedere ogne lutto.
Oh quanto parve a me gran maraviglia
    quand' io vidi tre facce a la sua testa!
    L'una dinanzi, e quella era vermiglia;
l'altr' eran due, che s'aggiugnieno a questa
    sovresso 'l mezzo di ciascuna spalla,
    e sé giugnieno al loco de la cresta:
e la destra parea tra bianca e gialla;
    la sinistra a vedere era tal, quali
    vegnon di là onde 'l Nilo s'avvalla.
Sotto ciascuna uscivan due grand' ali,
    quanto si convenia a tanto uccello:
    vele di mar non vid' io mai cotali.
Non avean penne, ma di vispistrello
    era lor modo; e quelle svolazzava,
    sì che tre venti si movean da ello:
quindi Cocito tutto s'aggelava.
    Con sei occhi piangëa, e per tre menti
    gocciava 'l pianto e sanguinosa bava.
Da ogne bocca dirompea co' denti
    un peccatore, a guisa di maciulla,
    sì che tre ne facea così dolenti.
A quel dinanzi il mordere era nulla
    verso 'l graffiar, che talvolta la schiena
    rimanea de la pelle tutta brulla.

30

33

36

39

42

45

48

51

54

57

60

From midbreast he stood out above the ice,
    the emperor of that realm of misery.
    And I compare more favorably in size   30
with the giants than would any giant be,
    compared with just his arm. With such a limb,
    how monstrous must be his entirety.   33
If he was fair as he is foul and grim,
    and dared defy his maker, it is well said
    that all suffering and sorrow flow from him.   36
I stared to see three faces on his head,
    one of the greatest wonders I had seen yet.
    The middle one faced forward and was red.   39
The other two were joined to it and set
    above each shoulder's midpoint, and they went
    up to his crown, where all three faces met.   42
The right one had a whitish yellow tint.
    The left one had the appearance of the race
    that comes from where the Nile starts its descent.   45
Two enormous wings spread out below each face,
    well scaled to such a bird. Never did I see
    such sails on any ship in any place.   48
His wings were featherless and leathery
    just like the long wings of a bat, and since
    he flapped the six of them incessantly,   51
all Cocytus was congealed by three cold winds.
    Tears from his six eyes, mixing with a flow
    of bloody slobber, dripped down his three chins.   54
Just as a hackle mangles flax, a row
    of teeth in each mouth gripped a soul. He made
    three spirits suffer unremitting woe.   57
The one in the front mouth was far less afraid
    of his biting than the raking of his nails.
    At times the spirit's back was wholly flayed.   60

«Quell' anima là sù c'ha maggior pena»,
    disse 'l maestro, «è Giuda Scarïotto,
    che 'l capo ha dentro e fuor le gambe mena.   63
De li altri due c'hanno il capo di sotto,
    quel che pende dal nero ceffo è Bruto:
    vedi come si storce, e non fa motto!;   66
e l'altro è Cassio, che par sì membruto.
    Ma la notte risurge, e oramai
    è da partir, ché tutto avem veduto».   69
Com' a lui piacque, il collo li avvinghiai;
    ed el prese di tempo e loco poste,
    e quando l'ali fuoro aperte assai,   72
appigliò sé a le vellute coste;
    di vello in vello giù discese poscia
    tra 'l folto pelo e le gelate croste.   75
Quando noi fummo là dove la coscia
    si volge, a punto in sul grosso de l'anche,
    lo duca, con fatica e con angoscia,   78
volse la testa ov' elli avea le zanche,
    e aggrappossi al pel com' om che sale,
    sì che 'n inferno i' credea tornar anche.   81
«Attienti ben, ché per cotali scale»,
    disse 'l maestro, ansando com' uom lasso,
    «conviensi dipartir da tanto male».   84
Poi uscì fuor per lo fóro d'un sasso
    e puose me in su l'orlo a sedere;
    appresso porse a me l'accorto passo.   87
Io levai li occhi e credetti vedere
    Lucifero com' io l'avea lasciato,
    e vidili le gambe in sù tenere;   90
e s'io divenni allora travagliato,
    la gente grossa il pensi, che non vede
    qual è quel punto ch'io avea passato.   93

My master said: "That one whose fate entails
    the greatest pain is Judas Iscariot.
    His head is in the mouth, while his body flails.   63
Of the other two, whose heads are hanging out,
    that is Brutus in the black face, whose control
    keeps his tongue silent as he writhes about,   66
and Cassius is that other, sinewy soul.
    Now the night is rising once again, and we
    must take our leave, for we have seen the whole."   69
I clasped his neck, as he commanded me.
    Then he, when the monstrous wings were opened wide,
    making use of place and time efficiently,   72
took hold of the shaggy fur on the devil's side
    and climbed down clump by clump, conveying us
    between the frozen crust and the matted hide.   75
The moment we came to where the thigh joint was,
    the point at which the haunches spread, was when
    my leader with movements pained and strenuous   78
brought his head round to Satan's shanks and then,
    just like a climber, grappled on the hair.
    I thought we had turned back toward hell again.   81
He spoke like a weary man who gasps for air:
    "Hold tight. We need such stairs to leave this place
    where there is so much evil everywhere."   84
And after that, he came out through the space
    in a rock, upon whose edge he seated me.
    Then he moved toward me with a cautious pace.   87
I raised my eyes, expecting I would see
    Lucifer just as he had last appeared,
    but his legs were tapering upward endlessly.   90
How perplexed I was by this I will let the herd
    of dullards judge for themselves, who do not know
    what point I'd passed and what had just occurred.   93

«Lèvati sù», disse 'l maestro, «in piede:
　　la via è lunga e 'l cammino è malvagio,
　　e già il sole a mezza terza riede».　　　　　　96
Non era camminata di palagio
　　là 'v' eravam, ma natural burella
　　ch'avea mal suolo e di lume disagio.　　　　　99
«Prima ch'io de l'abisso mi divella,
　　maestro mio», diss' io quando fui dritto,
　　«a trarmi d'erro un poco mi favella:　　　　　102
ov' è la ghiaccia? e questi com' è fitto
　　sì sottosopra? e come, in sì poc' ora,
　　da sera a mane ha fatto il sol tragitto?».　　　105
Ed elli a me: «Tu imagini ancora
　　d'esser di là dal centro, ov' io mi presi
　　al pel del vermo reo che 'l mondo fóra.　　　108
Di là fosti cotanto quant' io scesi;
　　quand' io mi volsi, tu passasti 'l punto
　　al qual si traggon d'ogne parte i pesi.　　　　111
E se' or sotto l'emisperio giunto
　　ch'è contraposto a quel che la gran secca
　　coverchia, e sotto 'l cui colmo consunto　　　114
fu l'uom che nacque e visse sanza pecca;
　　tu haï i piedi in su picciola spera
　　che l'altra faccia fa de la Giudecca.　　　　　117
Qui è da man, quando di là è sera;
　　e questi, che ne fé scala col pelo,
　　fitto è ancora sì come prim' era.　　　　　　120
Da questa parte cadde giù dal cielo;
　　e la terra, che pria di qua si sporse,
　　per paura di lui fé del mar velo,　　　　　　123
e venne a l'emisperio nostro; e forse
　　per fuggir lui lasciò qui loco vòto
　　quella ch'appar di qua, e sù ricorse».　　　　126

"The sun returns now to mid-tierce, and so
    you must now stand up again," my master said.
    "The road is hard and we have far to go."   96

It was no palace hall that lay ahead,
    but a natural cellar with a rugged floor
    and little light to show us where it led.   99

"Master," I said when I arose, "before
    I uproot myself from the abyss, I pray
    that you help me understand a little more.   102

Where is the ice? And why is he set this way,
    turned upside down? And how did the sun spin
    so short a transit from the night to day?"   105

And he: "You think we are still where we have been,
    on the other side, where I took hold of the hair
    of the evil worm who gnaws the world from within.   108

As long as I climbed down, you were still there.
    When I turned myself, you were where the halves divide,
    at the center that draws all weights from everywhere.   111

You are under the hemisphere on the opposite side
    from the one that canopies the vast dry land,
    beneath whose zenith he was crucified   114

who was born and lived his life without the brand
    or taint of sinfulness. This little sphere
    is Judecca's other face, where your feet now stand.   117

It is evening there when it is morning here,
    and he whose hair we made a ladder of
    is still secured where you saw him appear.   120

He fell upon this side from the heavens above,
    and the land, in terror as he plummeted,
    used the ocean for a cover as it strove   123

toward our hemisphere. And what was here may have fled,
    rushing upward as he hurtled through the sky
    and leaving this great cavern in its stead."   126

Luogo è là giù da Belzebù remoto
   tanto quanto la tomba si distende,
   che non per vista, ma per suono è noto   129
d'un ruscelletto che quivi discende
   per la buca d'un sasso, ch'elli ha roso,
   col corso ch'elli avvolge, e poco pende.   132
Lo duca e io per quel cammino ascoso
   intrammo a ritornar nel chiaro mondo;
   e sanza cura aver d'alcun riposo,   135
salimmo sù, el primo e io secondo,
   tanto ch'i' vidi de le cose belle
   che porta 'l ciel, per un pertugio tondo.   138
E quindi uscimmo a riveder le stelle.

As far from Beelzebub as it could lie
    within his tomb is a space that no one knows
    by sight, whose presence is detected by   129
the sound of a trickling rivulet that flows
    through a hollow in the rock that it has lined,
    gently wandering and sloping as it goes.   132
We entered on that hidden road to find
    our way once more into the world of light.
    My leader walked ahead and I behind,   135
without a pause to rest, till we were in sight
    of a hole that showed some few particulars
    of those heavenly things that beautify the night.   138
From there we came outside and saw the stars.

Notes

<dl>
<dt>*line 1*</dt>
<dd>"Vexilia regis prodeunt" ("The banners of the King advance") is the first line of a hymn written in 569 by Venantius Fortunatus, bishop of Poitiers.</dd>

<dt>*line 46*</dt>
<dd>Satan, or Lucifer, had belonged to the angelic order of the Seraphim: "In the year that King Uzziah died I saw also the Lord sitting upon a throne, high and lifted up, and his train filled the temple. Above it stood the seraphims: each one had six wings; with twain he covered his face, and with twain he covered his feet, and with twain he did fly" (Isaiah 6.1–2).</dd>

<dt>*line 94*</dt>
<dd>Tierce is the first of four three-hour periods of the day (6:00 to 9:00 A.M.). Virgil had said in line 68 that the moon was rising, but it is now about 7:30 A.M., since he and Dante have crossed the earth's midpoint and are now in the Southern Hemisphere, where it is day when it is night on the other, inhabited side of the world.</dd>

<dt>*lines 124–25*</dt>
<dd>The earth's interior, which rushed upward to avoid the fall of Satan, then formed the Mount of Purgatory. These lines thus create a transition to the *Purgatorio.*</dd>

<dt>*line 127*</dt>
<dd>Although others see them as separate devils, Dante uses the name Beelzebub here to refer to Satan.</dd>
</dl>

line 139   The journey to the surface, encapsulated in the previous two tercets, has taken nearly twenty-four hours. In this concluding line, Virgil and Dante emerge to see the dawn sky. "Stars" (*stelle*) will also be the last word of each of the other two parts of the *Comedy*.

About the Translator

Michael Palma is the recipient of the Italo Calvino Award for his translation of *My Name on the Wind: Selected Poems of Diego Valeri* and of the Raiziss/de Palchi Translation Award from the Academy of American Poets for his translation of *The Man I Pretend to Be: "The Colloquies" and Selected Poems of Guido Gozzano*. The anthology *New Italian Poets*, which he coedited with Dana Gioia, was named one of the ten Outstanding Translations of the Year by the American Literary Translators Association.

Palma has published three collections of verse: *The Egg Shape, Antibodies,* and *A Fortune in Gold,* and his poetry has been anthologized in, among other publications, Penguin's *Unsettling America: An Anthology of Contemporary Multicultural Poetry*.